The Rich Earth between Us

The Rich Earth between Us

The Intimate Grounds of Race and Sexuality in the Atlantic World, 1770–1840

Shelby Johnson

The University of North Carolina Press CHAPEL HILL

© 2024 Shelby Johnson
All rights reserved
Set in Merope Basic by Westchester Publishing Services
Manufactured in the United States of America

Library of Congress Cataloging-in-Publication Data
Names: Johnson, Shelby Lynn, 1988– author.
Title: The rich earth between us : the intimate grounds of race and sexuality
   in the Atlantic world, 1770–1840 / Shelby Johnson.
Other titles: Intimate grounds of race and sexuality in the Atlantic world,
   1770–1840
Description: Chapel Hill : The University of North Carolina Press, [2024] |
   Includes bibliographical references and index.
Identifiers: LCCN 2023045907 | ISBN 9781469677903 (cloth ; alk. paper) |
   ISBN 9781469677910 (pbk. ; alk paper) | ISBN 9781469677927 (ebook) |
   ISBN 9798890887320 (pdf)
Subjects: LCSH: Occom, Samson, 1723–1792—Criticism and interpretation. |
   Prince, Mary—Criticism and interpretation. | Apess, William, 1798–1839—
   Criticism and interpretation. | Wedderburn, R. (Robert)—Criticism and
   interpretation. | Indian authors—United States—Political and social views. |
   Authors, Black—West Indies—Political and social views. | Land tenure—
   Atlantic Ocean Region. | Right of property—Atlantic Ocean Region. | Settler
   colonialism—Social aspects—Atlantic Ocean Region. | BISAC: LITERARY
   CRITICISM / American / African American & Black | SOCIAL SCIENCE /
   Human Sexuality (see also PSYCHOLOGY / Human Sexuality)
Classification: LCC PS153.I52 J64 2024 | DDC 810.9/896—dc23/eng/20231108
LC record available at https://lccn.loc.gov/2023045907

Cover illustration: Topographic map by pixelrobot/stock.adobe.com.

This book will be made open access within three years of publication thanks
to Path to Open, a program developed in partnership between JSTOR, the
American Council of Learned Societies (ACLS), the University of Michigan
Press, and the University of North Carolina Press to bring about equitable
access and impact for the entire scholarly community, including authors,
researchers, libraries, and university presses around the world. Learn more
at https://about.jstor.org/path-to-open/.

. . . return to me, oh Lord of then
and now, my mother's calling,
her young voice humming my name.

—LUCILLE CLIFTON

may we be unafraid to mourn and together and hugely . . .
help us to see the bees yet in the lavender
the spokes of sunlight down through the oaks.

—TEDDY MACKER

Contents

List of Figures ix

Acknowledgments xi

Introduction 1

CHAPTER ONE
Dreaming with Samson Occom 21

CHAPTER TWO
Mary Prince and the Matter of Salt 49

CHAPTER THREE
With William Apess at Forest's Edge 78

CHAPTER FOUR
Robert Wedderburn, Prophet of Unfinished Revolution 109

Coda 141

Notes 145

Index 205

List of Figures

1. Theodor de Bry, "Valboa wirfft etliche Indianer / welche die schreckliche Sünd der Sodomey begangen / den Hunden für sie zuzerreissen" or "Balboa throws some [Indigenous people], who [were perceived to have] committed sodomy, to the dogs to be torn apart" (1580) 13

2. George Cruikshank, "The New Union Club" (1819) 130

Acknowledgments

It does not escape me that this project on collective worldmaking only came into existence through the love extended by colleagues, friends, and family at a moment of global crisis. Much of writing for this book was interrupted by the COVID-19 pandemic and my mother's death in April 2020. Although her passing was ultimately not due to COVID-19, the pandemic certainly shaped my experience of grief, as quarantine prevented family gatherings over that long first year after her death. At the time of her passing, I had been working for the past year on Mohegan writer Samson Occom and proximal intimacies—desire, sensation, touch—in a precarious eighteenth-century world. I know that acute hazards exist in drawing too many parallels between Occom's life and my own, given his experiences of communal vulnerability and racialized violence under settler colonialism. Yet in the years since my mother's death, I have frequently returned to Occom's wrenching testimony of his absence from his daughter Tabitha's funeral in 1785: "Next Morning after Breakfast went on and got home about 9 found my Well three Days ago I heard a heard heavy News, my poor Tabitha is Dead & Buried, the Lord the Sovereign of the Universe Sanctify this Dispensation to me and to all my Family—[.]"

I have often meditated on Occom's inability to record Tabitha's death until three days after he heard the "heavy News" and about the agony archived in his stutter, "I heard a heard"—an echo that lingers with the desperate prayer for sanctification that he cries out for but cannot finish. Occom's words have remained with me in a time defined by delayed services and distant suffering, and I have wondered if his prayer could assemble a recuperative praxis for healing the ruptures of social isolation and communal loss occasioned by the pandemic's longue durée, which encompasses not only the health disparities that have fallen especially hard on communities of color, but also various forms of state-sanctioned violence. "Sanctified," of course, is rooted in the Latin *sanctus*, which means to be "set apart" or "to be made holy," used often in the sense of "to be declared separate" or "to be bound." Put differently, his prayer extends an urgent question: What could it look like to grieve like and with Occom and to bind ourselves in shared commitment to the work of decolonial worldmaking in the days ahead?

I am indebted to Jonathan Lamb, Mark Schoenfield, Hortense Spillers, and Scott J. Juengel at Vanderbilt University, and to Misty G. Anderson at the University of Tennessee, for encouraging the questions this book takes up. I am especially grateful to Scott and Misty for their continuing friendship and mentorship over the years. Early archival work for this project was supported by a Drake Research Fellowship (2015) and a College of Arts and Sciences Summer Research Award (2016) through Vanderbilt University. I also appreciate the assistance extended by the English Department and the College of Arts and Letters at Florida Atlantic University, including the Scholarly and Creative Achievement Fellowship (2019-20), which enabled me to make progress on this book during a difficult year. Eric Berlatsky, Wendy Hinshaw, Regis Fox, Stacey Balkan, Stacy Lettman, Tim Miller, Oliver Buckton, Papatya Bucak, Sika Dagbovie-Mullins, Ash Kini, Tony Stagliano, Andy Furman, Carla Thomas, Ian MacDonald, and Kate Pollack—and while they were at FAU, Adam Bradford, Devin Garofalo, José de la Garza Valenzuela, and R. J. Boutelle—were all generous colleagues, many of whom supported me in ways that I can never repay. I am so grateful for Becka McKay and Clarissa Chenovick, in particular, whose friendship and kindness made all the difference. In addition, I cannot express the fullness of my appreciation to my colleagues at Oklahoma State University, including Jeff Menne, An Cheng, Lisa Hollenbach, Lindsey Wilhelm, Steph Link, Kate Hallemeier, Tim Murphey, Sarah Beth Childers, and Elizabeth Grubgeld, whose hospitality and welcome have sustained me as I have brought this project to completion. My deepest thanks especially to Bill Decker, Alyssa Hunziker, Rafael Hernandez, Cailey Hall, and Chelsea Silva for their friendship during my first year in Oklahoma. I am grateful to the College of Arts and Sciences at Oklahoma State, which provided financial support in preparing the manuscript. And I am indebted to the University of North Carolina Press for supporting this project, especially to Lucas Church, Thomas Bedenbaugh, and Valerie Burton for their attention to the manuscript. I also appreciate David Robertson's assistance with the index.

My scholarship has been fortified by so many dear friends and colleagues. I am grateful for Ana Schwartz, Jessica Taylor, Abby L. Goode, Evelyn Soto, and Blevin Shelnutt for reading portions of this work—their comments enriched my life in unnumerable ways. I thank Ana especially for her unfailing encouragement when I could not find the words during a long year of grief. I deeply appreciate Kerry Sinanan, Mariam Wassif, Ereck Jarvis, Megan Peiser, and Sam Plasencia for modeling their commitments to decolonial praxes in the *Woman of Colour* and Antiracist Pedagogy working group and for thoughtfully engaging with my scholarship—their insights resonate throughout this book. Hannah Manshel, Ben Bascom, Cass Turner, Kate Ozment, Joe Albernaz, and Carrie Shanafelt were also generous readers of parts of this book and incalculably shaped its arc. Conversations with Kimberly Takahata on Samson Occom, Kristina Huang on Mary Prince and Robert Wedderburn, Rebecca Anne Barr on decolonial intimacies, and M. A. Miller on queer ecologies have abundantly influenced my thinking in this work. Caroline Wigginton gave much appreciated guidance on preparing the book proposal and finding a press, and Greta LaFleur and Elizabeth Maddock Dillon offered incisive comments on this project at a vital moment in its development and revision—I cannot thank them enough for their time, labor, and collegiality. Katy Chiles, Emily C. Friedman, Gena Zuroski, Kelly Wisecup, and Ramesh Mallipeddi have been kind friends and mentors over the years. I have been sustained by the boundless support and encouragement Jeremy Chow, Don Rodrigues, and Kirsten Mendoza have shown me—I would not be where I am without their friendship. And finally, my deepest gratitude to my family, especially my sister and brother-in-law, Katie and David Eldridge, and my partner, Sari Carter, for the gift of their abiding love.

The Rich Earth between Us

Introduction

> The earth was given to the children of men, making no difference
> for colour or character, just or unjust; and . . . any person calling a
> piece of land his own private property, was a criminal; and though
> they may sell it, or will it to their children, it is only transferring of
> that which was first obtained by force or fraud.
>
> — ROBERT WEDDERBURN

> It is very clear, that God . . . "has given the earth to the children of
> men," given it to mankind in common. But this being supposed, it
> seems to some a very great difficulty how any one should ever come
> to have a property in any thing.
>
> — JOHN LOCKE

In *The Axe Laid to the Root, or A Fatal Blow to Oppressors, Being an Address to the Planters and Negroes of the Island of Jamaica* (1817), Robert Wedderburn turns to Psalm 115:16 as an origin story for a global commons: "The earth was given to the children of men, making no difference for colour or character, just or unjust."[1] To some extent, his assertion that property is the outcome of "force or fraud" echoes prominent European philosophers, such as Jean-Jacques Rousseau in the *Second Discourse on Inequality* (1755): "You are lost, if you forget that the fruits of the earth belong equally to us all, and the earth itself to nobody."[2] Yet Wedderburn goes much further than Rousseau: he argues that slavery and land enclosure are not separate historical processes but constitutive forms of racial violence.[3] His citation of Psalm 115:16 authorizes a wide-ranging critique of the very foundations of early modern political discourse, an undertaking that becomes clear when read alongside John Locke, whose *Second Treatise of Government* (1689) similarly invokes "an earth given to the children of men," but to a radically different purpose: a gifted earth is a *problem*, for it is "a very great difficulty how any one" should come to make property from what is offered freely.[4] Locke, of course, famously solves the "great difficulty" by portioning the globe through the accumulation of property: he who inherits the earth becomes he who owns it through the improving labor of his hands. Locke's work builds on and extends an entire grammar of civil personhood, endowed with a capacity to amass property and enact contracts.[5] Early modern political theories of propertied individualism index not only global economic systems but also intimate structures of desire — what is yearned for, overt and implicit, when property accumulation is the aim.

Indeed, Black activists like Wedderburn show that practices of racialized extraction organize individual property accumulation and global imperialism: "[The earth] cannot be justly the private property of individuals, because it was never manufactured by man; therefore, whoever first sold it, sold that which was not his own, and of course there cannot be a title deed produced consistent with natural and universal justice."[8] Wedderburn's critique pointedly targets Lockean theories of property, but his insight also challenges canonical texts like Immanuel Kant's *Perpetual Peace* (1795), which speculates on what is necessary to sustain international peace — and thus extends a view of the earth at odds with the Black radical tradition: "Since the earth is a globe, they cannot disperse over an infinite area, but must necessarily tolerate one another's company. And no one originally has any greater right than anyone else to occupy any particular portion of the earth."[9] Although Kant here seems to recognize a "greater right" to shared possession of the earth, perpetual peace can emerge only once global populations adhere to a universal, common law.[10] For Wedderburn, however, to assent to this "common law" leaves no paper trail "consistent with natural and universal justice."[11] In this way, his redefining of significant conceptual terms — *commons*, *property*, *universal law*, *justice* — synthesizes what was for many European philosophers an inherent tension in fictions of a gifted earth: that possibilities for political *plurality* can coexist with global commoning — that international law need not reflect hegemonic European norms.

In *The Rich Earth Between Us: The Intimate Grounds of Race and Sexuality in the Atlantic World*, I argue that early Black and Indigenous writers like Samson Occom (Mohegan Nation), Mary Prince, William Apess (Mashantucket Pequot Nation), and Robert Wedderburn draw from diasporic visions of a gifted earth to challenge forms of propertied individualism governing social life, and, through a defiant witness to enslavement and enclosure, they open new avenues of lived experience for inhabiting the earth, then and now. Broadly, their rehearsals of a gifted earth dissent from the material and imagined configurations of what Cedric Robinson names racial capitalism.[6] For Robinson, while acts of enslavement and enclosure might seem like dramatic breaks with medieval feudal and early modern mercantilist systems, global markets evolved from and were dependent on longstanding racial hierarchies governing African and Indigenous lives, both physically and psychically. And while European and American theorists developed frameworks to challenge proletarian precarity and industrial waste, within diasporic worlds, a separate mode of critique took root: the Black radical tradition.[7]

Guided by Wedderburn, I turn to Black and Indigenous writers as figures who are centrally concerned with colonial expansion and enslavement as systemic expressions of planetary enclosure—and who responded by consistently calling for "all things common," as Wedderburn puts it.[12] Literary scholars and historians have turned to the early modern period as an era animated by conflicts over the commons, where, as Allan Greer argues, colonial governments negotiated a range of legal codes, political institutions, inhabited rituals, and knowledge systems as historically situated social practices of land occupation and resource use—processes he names "property-formation."[13] Drawing from theoretical insights on commons in early American studies, as well as contemporary theories of commoning, I explore how Black and Native writers negotiated property-formation as merely the most *visible* manifestation of diffuse structures of power reorganizing space and time itself.[14] They reveal how property-formation seeped into everyday life in less explicit ways, shaping and reshaping an array of embodied and intimate relations. In what follows in this introduction, I stage a series of encounters with Occom, Prince, Apess, and Wedderburn to consider the affordances of seeing, if only fleetingly, the shape of their *desires* for knowing, being, and belonging to the earth. In this way, I hope to show that their gestures to commons do more than extend frameworks for land use and resource accumulation but (re)assemble worlds. While I cannot always make claims about the *substance* of these desires, which is beyond my purview as a settler scholar, this book marshals methodologies for reading early Indigenous and Black writings *for* and *with* their vibrant worldmaking practices.

Small Plots

In different ways, Black and Indigenous writers responded to emergent property-formation by enacting what I am calling "small plots," or decolonial performances of worlding improvised in everyday intimacies and knowledge systems. For this, I draw from Sylvia Wynter's argument that the novel and the plantation developed as constitutive worldmaking structures within colonial regimes, against which diasporic communities cultivated fugitive lifeways on the plantation's margins—in marronage and provision grounds, in "secretive histories" and spiritualities.[15] Wynter presses on plot's polyphonic meanings, as both a narrative form and a piece of earth, to show how the colonized world was (and is) known, disciplined, and governed. Still, "plot" in this book never quite materializes into anything as discretely recognizable as the novel or the plantation. Instead, each chapter explores orientations to intensely local spatial terrains and fields of sensation: Occom with Mohegan coastal life and Montaukett herbal practices, Prince with Caribbean salt industries and diasporic stories of salt, Apess with Haudenosaunee and Pequot woodland relations, and Wedderburn with material and imagined improvisations of Black commons among Jamaican Maroons and after the Haitian Revolution. To untangle their plots from encounters with colonial power, as far as I can, I turn to seemingly incidental moments or brief texts to consider how they extend fugitive patterns of knowledge production and social reproduction. In this way, my use of "world" builds on what Ariella Aïsha Azoulay calls "worldly sovereignty," or a way of recovering "persisting and repressed forms and formations of being in the world, shaped by and through intimate knowledge of the world and its secrets, of its multiple natural, spiritual, political, and cosmological taxonomies preserved and transmitted over generations."[16] Because these early worldmaking formations would have been largely opaque within colonial records and institutions implicated in erasing Black and Indigenous knowledges, theirs are ways of life archived in hidden sensations and concealed desires—in small plots.

Even so, I acknowledge that a small plot like "the earth was given to the children of men" may not initially appear radical. Sarah Jane Cervenak reminds us that the "givenness" of the earth may not be easily extricated from the conceptions of propertied personhood that underscored Enlightenment philosophies of liberal humanism as exemplified in Locke.[17] Indeed, Locke's fiction of beginnings—of a given and then owned earth—marshalled a critical grammar used to justify Indigenous dispossession, Black slavery, and industrialized agriculture on a massive scale, illustrated in his own involvement in writing the Carolina Constitution and the document's justification of slavery.[18] Near the close of *The History of Mary Prince* (1831), Prince illuminates the ongoing relevance to this violent logic of *gifted* earth and life when she urges that enslaved people "be given free, and slavery done up forevermore."[19] If we recall the intensely mediated nature of her narrative, where English antislavery activists transcribed her testimony, we might wonder how Prince would have enunciated a radically different "freedom dream" under less constrained conditions.[20] Perhaps she approaches something like this critique much earlier in *The History* when she describes the "power which the white people's law had given . . . over me" as the scene of subjection she inhabits on Barbados.[21] The circumstances of her restricted voice show that in the historical arena of an early nineteenth-century Atlantic world, freedom itself is transformed into a gift owned and bestowed only in proximity to settler expansion, a coordination of whiteness and property that theorists of the law, such as Cheryl Harris, Colin Dayan, Joanne Barker (Lenape Nation), and Aileen Moreton-Robinson (Dandrubin Goenpul of the Quandamooka Nation) have argued defines modern organizations of personhood, citizenship, and ownership.[22] Is it possible, then, to read in Wedderburn's announcement of a global commons something like what Cervenak calls a "Black life [that] moves as if flesh and earth were neither givable nor ownable"?[23] Can we, in other words, recover ways that Prince and Wedderburn may have re-signified this script of *given* origins to conceive of *ungiven* life and earth?

To consider these questions, I engage with Occom's early letters from the 1760s to Apess's essays and sermons from the 1830s, an archive assembled within an era engulfed by the extraordinary political upheavals of the age of revolutions and Indigenous removals. This archive includes not only life writing, religious texts, and periodicals but also descriptions of embodied and oral knowledge, as well as cultural artforms and inscribed objects. Occom's life, for instance, was shaped by the danger the American Revolution posed to Indigenous communities.[24] Military incursion and wartime losses framed his painful decision to leave the Mohegan Nation in Connecticut and relocate to Brothertown, New York, in 1783 — a choice staked on the possibility of communal survival elsewhere. Yet sometime after he moved, Occom sent a small carved box to his sister, Lucy Occom Tantaquidgeon, who remained at Mohegan. Metaphorically and materially, the box carries the anguished weight of impossible choices — to stay or to go — that conditioned eighteenth-century Algonquian exigence. Painted with traditional Path of the Sun and Trail of Life designs, the box is also a reminder that the Mohegan who chose to leave were bound in kinship to those who remained in Connecticut. In similar ways, Apess draws on Pequot and Haudenosaunee histories to connect with an Indigenous diaspora in an era when displacement accelerated after the War of 1812 and the Indian Removal Act (1830). Likewise, Prince and Wedderburn's testimonies to enslavement radiate with fugitive practices of survival, as Wedderburn turns to the Haitian Revolution and Prince to Black women's counter-economies to envision radical possibilities for a shared earth out of unimaginably brutal local circumstances, whose violences Wedderburn argues will require a "universal" revolution to fully redress.[25]

While the historical frame of *The Rich Earth Between Us*, 1750–1840, is often bifurcated between the disciplinary emphases of early American studies and eighteenth-century British literature, timely interventions in oceanic and hemispheric methodologies have connected and crossed these fields' geographical borders to explore the production of a global modernity shaped by colonial trade, capitalist accumulation, and imperial expansion.[26] Indeed, British and American imperial policies increasingly pursued continent-spanning acts of Indigenous displacement and Black captivity to construct large plantation empires, exploiting enslaved labor to produce the consumable goods—coffee, sugar, tea—energizing Western appetites.[27] These plantation projects, including the corrosive salt industries where Prince labored for a decade, ruthlessly reformatted bodies and ecologies within global economies that continue to contour the geologic epoch we now inhabit. Recent critical interventions by Jodi Byrd (Chickasaw Nation), Jace Weaver (Cherokee Nation), and Robbie Richardson (Mi'gmaw and Pabineau First Nation) have shown that the discursive and political exercises of transatlantic empires were premised on the conscripted crossings and exploitations of Black and Indigenous peoples. In addition, scholars working at the intersection of Black and Indigenous studies, such as Tiffany Lethabo King, Sharon Holland, Tiya Miles, and Kathryn Walkiewicz (Cherokee Nation), have explored counter-conceptions of nationality, citizenship, and kinship elaborated in the work of writers of color as Western ideologies of race subtended a new global order.[28] Broadly, these critics demonstrate that settler colonial discourses imposed racial designations on people of African and Indigenous descent, eliding their own affiliations with home, territory, community, and family as part of the emerging exigencies of capital extraction.[29] Building on these scholarly pathways, *The Rich Earth Between Us* deploys plot's multiple meanings—a narrative script, a piece of earth, a fugitive conspiracy—to show how late eighteenth- and early nineteenth-century writers of color responded to revolutionary events and removal crossings by reimagining ways of inhabiting their bodies and communities.

As an emergence narrative, "the earth was given to the children of men" illustrates only one way writers like Occom, Prince, Apess, and Wedderburn reconfigured local knowledges to defy imperial property-formations and their shared origins with modes of racial capitalism (extractive enclosure, plantation enslavement) advancing throughout the Atlantic world. Although "the earth was given to the children of men" marks one speculative pathway for tracing worldmaking practices, the citation also interweaves with other expressions of worldly defiance against colonialism, including hemispheric revolts against enslavement, routines of fugitivity and marronage, and Indigenous revitalization movements to restore traditions of care for their homelands.[30] Throughout this book, attending to small plots thus allows me to assemble a methodology that turns to other *scales* of critical investigation—quotidian, local, contingent—and to make visible, so far as is possible, the survivals and revivals of Black and Indigenous worlds. Collectively, then, the worldmaking scripts improvised by Occom, Prince, Apess, and Wedderburn unsettle colonial formations of history by enacting arrangements of sovereignty as large as revolution or as small as a carved box.

Plural Worlds

Throughout, I am invested not only in fictions of what happened to common worlds—or how colonial writers explained the division of the earth into countries and empires, peoples and plots—but also in Black and Indigenous worldmaking alternatives. This commitment arises from a belief that anticolonial archives marshal different organizations of political and material life, of human and nonhuman relation.[31] For this, I draw from scholarship engaged in what some have called an "ontological turn" in the social sciences and humanities, whose major critical strands are challenging philosophical traditions that constructed sharp hierarchies between life and nonlife, subject and object, body and mind, nature and humanity.[32] Yet this body of scholarship seldom extends to the colonial period: while critics in eighteenth-century and early American studies have generatively engaged with ontology through thing theory and animal studies, Black and Indigenous worlds rarely appear in these critical conversations, with analysis instead addressing their strategic adaptations to settler languages and adjustments to property.[33] At the same time, it is clear that settler ontologies were predicated on racialized teleologies—that Indigenous nations were destined to vanish and people of African descent were inherently enslaveable—which marked their land and labor as things whose productive and reproductive potential could be exploited.[34] We know, too, that colonists not only sought to occupy non-European territories and impose a new global order of racialized subjectivity, but they also sought to obliterate Black and Indigenous cosmogonies, or stories of communal origin that enunciate different ways of being in relation with and knowing the world, with John Law calling these settler projects of erasure the imposition of a "one-world world."[35] When Spanish conquistadors destroyed Mayan libraries, for instance, the *Popol Vuh*, a K'iche' emergence cycle, became one of the only codices to survive in an alphabetic translation of its hieroglyphic script.[36] With this history in view, engaging with the ontological turn may help us chart a colonial onto-epistemic regime that "has granted itself the right to assimilate all other worlds and, by presenting itself as exclusive, cancels possibilities for what lies beyond its limits," as Mario Blaser and Marisol de la Cadena argue, circumstances that Occom, Prince, Wedderburn, and Apess all testify to.[37]

But from another perspective, I may not be engaged in the ontological turn at all. Zoe Todd (Métis) reminds us that what we consider "ontology" is nearly always an enunciation of colonial modernity.[38] Walter D. Mignolo and Catherine E. Walsh urge that we must "delink from the traps of Western epistemic ontology" to "open up to epistemic pluriversality"—a task that has become more urgent in an era when neoliberal economic policies and anthropogenic climate change are increasingly placing the possibility of plural worlds or a world at *all* at risk.[39] Because of this, scholars engaged in what we might rename the "pluriversal turn," especially in Black and Indigenous studies, principally take up contemporary literature and activism rather than earlier archives. *The Rich Earth Between Us* engages with this aporia by surveying how late capitalist distributions of exhaustion and ruin are rooted in early modern shifts in property-formations and ecological extraction, which Cass Turner argues rendered the globe "an ontologically flat domain of commerce, in which persons, places, and things were equally available for disposal."[40]

These insights shape my effort to pursue two somewhat counterintuitive aims in this project: to trace how Black and Indigenous cosmogonies are rendered opacities in colonial archives and to improvise methods for recovering alternative worldmaking practices. Because of this, I am less interested in drawing from frameworks tethered to continental philosophy, including thing theory and object oriented ontology.[41] I see so clearly how this critical genealogy *could* unfold—from Martin Heidegger's theorization of animals as "poor in world" and stone as "worldless," to Michel Foucault's and Giorgio Agamben's work on biopolitics, to Jacques Derrida's dialogues on animal life.[42] Instead, by attending to commoning as a point of entry to denser practices of worldmaking, I am inspired by Leanne Betasamosake Simpson (Michi Saagiig) and Robyn Maynard's point that "imperialism and ongoing colonialism have been ending worlds for as long as they have been in existence, and Indigenous and Black peoples have been building worlds and then rebuilding worlds for as long as we have been in existence . . . Building worlds and living in them *anyway*."[43] To extend this critical work, I draw from paradigms in Black and Indigenous environmental studies to argue that stories of an earthly commons emerge as more than biblical citations but also retrieve relational views of the land and nonhuman beings as agential, alive, and kin.[44] This mode of zoetic reading marshals a vital question in much of what follows: What worlds flicker into visibility when our conceptual frameworks are grounded in Occom's oblique citations of Algonquian cosmogonies, in Prince's indirect gestures to salt as a fugitive archive, or in Apess's brief invocations of trees as relatives?

By focusing on pluriversal scripts and vibrant ecologies in this archive, I build on scholarship in Indigenous studies on nonhuman forms of being alive and in Black studies on alternative praxes of being human.[45] Katherine McKittrick, for instance, calls us to look for a Black "livingness," or a "genre of humanness" that is "poised to decode, or is already decoding" colonial (il)logics to render different scenes for knowing African diasporic worlds.[46] Critics such as Joshua Bennett, Zakiyyah Iman Jackson, and Bénédicte Boisseron, among others, have worked to wrest conceptions of Black life from colonial lexicons and generatively unsettle imperial ontologies, while interceding in animal studies, alternative humanisms, and new materialisms to show how Enlightenment epistemologies are rooted in antiblack violence.[47] Although chapters in this book take up questions of the animal and the human, I more often turn to local environmental fields and Black and Indigenous knowledge traditions to show how they offer entry points for engaging with decolonial cosmogonies.[48] Finding these entry points requires reading "along the bias grain," as Marisa Fuentes terms it, for when they appear in early archives, they are nearly always distorted by confrontations with colonial power.[49] Saidiya Hartman contends that while a mode of speculative engagement—what she names "critical fabulation"—may reveal the palimpsestic traces of Black life, colonial archives also configure them as "failure[s], precisely because these accounts have never been able to install themselves as history, but rather are insurgent, disruptive narratives that are marginalized before they ever gain a footing."[50] Building on methods in Black and Indigenous archival studies, I navigate worlds that were (and are still) at risk of distortion, foreclosure, or deferral, often from the very moment of their capture in colonial records. Reading slowly and on a small scale reveals Black and Indigenous pluriverses—including ways of being, belonging, and knowing—as audacious alternatives to colonialism's world-destroying violence.

To offer one example, Wedderburn's *The Axe Laid to the Root* shows how his sister Elizabeth, his mother Rosanna, and his grandmother Amy enact openings for a revolutionary future. Their example prompts Wedderburn to urge those who are *in* but not *of* slavery's worlds of social death to refuse all patriarchal authority, which he furiously voices at his trial for blasphemy and sedition in 1819: "Acknowledge no King—Acknowledge no priest. Acknowledge no Father."[51] While the trial brief's use of the dash illustrates Wedderburn's critique of patriarchal authority, *The Axe Laid to the Root* takes these imperatives even further by improvising a layered narrative practice that mediates Wedderburn's visions through the words of his sister, Elizabeth. The periodical's final issues are structured as a series of letters between Elizabeth and Robert, and in one she reports an enslaver's violent call "to inflict death on the slaves for preaching . . . new doctrines, which are calculated to impress the minds of the slaves with a desire for liberty, which is a direct violation of the laws of England, which authorise us to hold the Africans and their offspring as private property."[52] This polyphonic narration—where Robert writes as Elizabeth, who rehearses an enslaver's (il)logic—lays bare the (ir)rationality of slavery through a sequence of clauses ("which ") that cohere in the commodification of Black flesh enshrined by law ("private property").[53] Wedderburn's writing illustrates what Christina Sharpe calls a Black anagrammatical reordering of capitalist logic, a way of "putting pressure on meaning and that against which meaning is made."[54] Although geographically separated—Elizabeth lives in Jamaica, while Robert is in London—their letters also enact a simultaneity of revolutionary possibility, suggesting that fugitive insurgencies can emerge from within transatlantic networks of Black solidarity. As a revolutionary reconfiguration of colonial grammar and geographical dominion, the fierce eruption of a "*desire* for liberty" overwrites the subjection of Black flesh with a vibrantly sororal world-making, one that interrupts the sequences of fungibility wherein Blackness is a *thing* endlessly owned, commodified, and exploited.[55] In this way, Wedderburn illustrates a point that Kevin Quashie makes when he dares us to "imagine a Black world": "Such a world might not exist in modernity," but radiates in the audacity of Black art and writing—"as an embracing generative quality of indisputable aliveness."[56] By attending to Wedderburn's small grammatical and geographical improvisations in *The Axe Laid to the Root*, I show how he assembles new genres of revolutionary kinship, which enable him to envision the world anew.

Throughout this book, I linger with similar vocabularies of dissent within Indigenous and Black archives. Yet these archives are shadowed by ontological and epistemological debates over the veracity and verifiability of anticolonial testimonies, which circulated within evangelical and abolitionist print networks that extensively regulated authority and affect.[57] By exposing the fantasies of property that organize racial capitalism, writers of color like Occom, Apess, Prince, and Wedderburn unflinchingly attend to how political myths of origin animate colonial expansion and enslavement—animate the very scenes of writing and grammars of possession that shape everyday life. In this way, they plumb the facts of everyday life to unearth the very frameworks of fictionality that sustain colonial onto-epistemic regimes, offering in their stead not history—for their orientations to history are illegible under capital modernity—but counter-sites of history's unwitnessed and disavowed emergences in the world.[58] This is not to say that scholars are precluded from making historical claims about Indigenous or Black experiences based on eighteenth-century records, for dilemmas over worldmaking empirically play out across iterative scenes of inventory, calculation, and removal, but to suggest that Occom, Prince, Apess, and Wedderburn sometimes tell us less about what *happened* than about what *mattered*. Because of this, I contend that writers of color gesture toward counter-cosmogonies at the very moment exercises in hemispheric imperial expansion, and the political theories supporting them, engaged in extended maneuvers of enclosure and erasure, where Locke's "very great difficulty" represents a larger onto-epistemic impulse to enfold mastery over land and life within ostensibly secular accounts of state- and subject-formation. This is another way of saying that for these writers, there is no ground *but* ground.

Improvised Intimacies

In countering the procedures of a "one-world world," Black and Indigenous texts sometimes invoke "an earth given to the children of men" not only to resist geopolitical enclosures and enslavement, but also to challenge how these logics seep into intimate life. Still, the verse's emphasis on patrilineal continuity—"the children of *men*"—fractures its seeming pronouncement of a world held in common, which Wedderburn historically contextualizes as a process of racial disinheritance and kinlessness: "Though they may sell [land], or will it to their children, it is only transferring of that which was first obtained by force or fraud."[59] When Wedderburn conceives the globe as an outcome of Black subjection, he draws attention to what Orlando Patterson would later call regimes of "social death" inherent to slavery as a brutal system of natal alienation from home and kin.[60] In early Black and Indigenous studies, scholars like C. Riley Snorton, Brigitte Fielder, and Elahe Haschemi Yekani, and critics like Deborah Miranda (Chumash and Esselen Nations), Kai Pyle (Mekadebinesikwe), and Leanne Betasamosake Simpson, among others, have sought to recover forms of lived embodiment and relationality ultimately condemned as nonnormative under colonial regimes of power.[61] Because colonial projects constellated people of color within narrow regimes of gender and sexuality, intimacy and genealogy become the grids through which imperial governance becomes embodied.[62] In this way, Lisa Lowe suggests that intimacy can offer "a means to observe the historical divisions of world processes into those that develop modern liberal subjects and modern spheres of social life," a provocation I take up throughout this book.[63]

An early instance of these brutal encounters between colonial empires and Indigenous cultures—and thus something of an origin story for the subjugation of Native lands and intimacies—occurred in 1530 when Vasco Núñez de Balboa encountered a community in Quarequa (now Panama) where, as Pietro Martire d'Anghiera, an Italian historian in the service of Spain, reported: "[Balboa] discovered that the village was stained by the foulest vice. The king's brother and a number of other courtiers were dressed as women."[64] While Balboa interpreted the figures as "sodomites" and subject to massacre (in this case, by imported Spanish dogs), colonial archives are unclear on if they were assigned male at birth and were taking on clothing and roles typically fulfilled by women within the community, or if they were men who were intimate with other men.[65] Belgian artist Théodore de Bry's widely circulated engraving of the genocide reproduces an emergent racial and gendered hierarchy: the Spanish—upright, clothed, bearing the armaments of rule—occupy the image's upper horizon, above the tangled limbs and twisted torsos of Indigenous persons and dogs.[66] Here, we confront the impossibility of fully reconstructing precontact sexualities based on Spanish records, for d'Anghiera locates an insidious desire for execution *with* many of the Native members of Quarequa: "They begged him to exterminate them, for the contagion was confined to the courtiers and had not yet spread to the people."[67] Balboa, moreover, projects these intimacies onto the landscape: "Raising their eyes and their hands to heaven, they have it to be understood that God held this sin in horror, punishing it by sending lightning and thunder, and frequent inundations which destroyed their crops."[68] Here, too, a perilous environmental ontology indexes the dire effects of a seeming Indigenous "degeneration."[69] In the end, Balboa's exercise of what Miranda terms

FIGURE 1 Theodor de Bry, "Valboa wirfft etliche Indianer / welche die schreckliche Sünd der Sodomey begangen / den Hunden für sie zuzerreissen" or "Balboa throws some [Indigenous people], who [were perceived to have] committed sodomy, to the dogs to be torn apart" (1580). Courtesy of the University of Houston Library.

"gendercide" contours early modern race and sexuality as the embodied and ecological scenes through which colonial violences pass into sovereignty and sovereignty, eventually, into law.[70]

While I am influenced by scholars working to recover Indigenous and Black embodiments and intimacies in scholarship on gender and sexuality, this book more often draws from environmental studies to show that when writers of color turn to a shared earth, they rehearse a tremulous reprieve to unbearable realities of stolen life and land. Guided by critics of ecological intimacies, such as Jeremy Chow and Greta LaFleur, I survey Black and Indigenous ecologies as sites of recalcitrance to colonial efforts to master the "wilderness" and contain people of color within attendant projects of civilization, including domesticity, heteronormativity, and patriarchy.[71] By challenging colonial environmental ontologies illustrated by d'Anghiera, scholars in Black and Indigenous ecocriticism, such as Robin Wall Kimmerer (Potawatomi Nation), Melissa K. Nelson (Anishinaabe and Métis), Jessica Hernandez (Maya and Zapotec), Dianne Glave, and Kimberley Ruffin, show that Black and Indigenous worlds precede colonial encounter and exploitation and continue to exist despite histories of removal, slavery, and resource extraction.[72] In this vein, Megan Peiser (Choctaw Nation of Oklahoma) has shaped my methods for recovering Indigenous ecological perspectives by reminding us that Indigenous botanic knowledge can be preserved in the smallest of beings—in seeds: "These seeds hold stories, histories, families and relationships, they hold sacred covenants between people and our more-than-human relatives."[73] I carry these insights to my consideration of other small or seemingly incidental archives and textual moments—Occom's herbal writings on local plants, Apess's fleeting citations of woodland kinship, Prince's evocations of salt's granular formations, and Wedderburn's brief letters to his sister. In these small plots, they dissent to colonial erasures of their worldmaking practices and enunciate alternative ways of belonging to the earth.

Indeed, dissent to the hegemonic colonial violences of "a one-world world" is perhaps nowhere more poignantly voiced than in a 1785 petition Occom composed for the Montaukett Nation. The text surveys an agonizing litany of Montaukett vulnerability to colonial property-formation and details the mundane legal imperatives that foreclose its very existence: the Montaukett "have only two Small necks of Land to plant on" and "are not allowd to Sow Wheate" or practice traditional routines of cultivation and gathering.[74] As a genre, petitions typically extend a fraught premise, then: they mark the existence of a different form of life at the very moment it is most embattled. This petition is likewise conscripted within colonial discourses of appeal—"For God's Sake help us"—that forbid Montaukett sovereignty even as it conceives no place beyond the reach of colonial governance—"For we have no where to go now." Occom lingers with ontological stakes of imposed precarity: "We are undone for this Life. . . . We fare now harder than our Fore Fathers—For all our Hunting, Fowling, and Fishing is now almost gone and our Wild Fruit is gone," where the repetitions of "gone" bear witness to the near total upending of ecological relationships that Montaukett life both depended on and sustained.[75] The text measures a regime of unliveability that contours distributions of survival and loss under colonialism, but also quietly evinces a desire for another world: for wild fruit, for familiar foraging sites, for a communal homeland, for traditions of social life. Montaukett resilience exceeds the conditions through which colonial modernity hails history and its subjects into being, suggesting that other modes of inhabiting the earth are possible. Put more simply, the petition enables us to attend not so much to the discrete events that typically organize literary and historical studies but to the plural forms of life Occom implicitly gestures toward.[76]

Grammars of race index the devaluations that accord Black and Indigenous worldly desires their very illegibility within colonial archives. But if I have so far emphasized the spatial formations of racial capitalism's unlivable history in plantations and removal projects, it is also worth remembering that race and sexuality mark a temporal emplotment into settler domestic and patrilineal time.[77] Writers of color principally understood this emplotment through systemic foreclosures of kinship, genealogy, and futurity. Still, Occom, Prince, Apess, and Wedderburn do not seek a recuperation of intimacy within a linear teleology in service to settler-national progress, a colonial ordering of space and time that they all differently critique. Instead, their writings often dwell with vexed sites of struggle over whose intimacies are granted epistemic legitimacy and political visibility. Prince and Wedderburn's writings elaborate how they are obliged to not only inhabit Blackness in a particular time and space but also come to *desire* its imbrication within colonial spheres of intimate life.[78] Likewise, Occom's and Apess's careers reflect settler-national conscriptions of Indigenous communities within regimes of vanishing as a *telos* toward which colonial domesticity inexorably progresses. Drawing from interventions in queer ecologies and sexuality studies, my aim is not to recover the fullness of Indigenous and Black intimacies but to chart their material conditions of (im)possibility. This archive shows what it was possible to *think* and *feel* about a gifted earth — and its past, present, and future relations — at a moment when these are the very desires disavowed under colonial modernity.

Put more simply, the work of Occom, Prince, Apess, and Wedderburn not only reflects material conditions for recording impressions, but also what it was conceivable to desire at *all*. To that end, their writings index "a struggle to preserve what was desired within what was possible," as Ana Schwartz puts it.[79] Foucault, of course, argued that the real project of modernity centered in persuading people of color to discipline (enclose, bound) the self in accordance with European rubrics of subjectivity and sociability: persons within heteronormative routines, families within individual plots of land, women within the home, nonwhite subjects within American legal and political regimes.[80] These processes were premised on consensual participation in imperial governance and a willed turning away from alternative identities and intimacies, with Black and Indigenous ways of producing and reproducing desire nearly always framed as irreconcilable with settler-national progress. Throughout this project, I trace desires that exceed imperial epistemic projects of enclosure and enslavement by turning to small-scale improvisations of worlds otherwise. For this, I extend Madhavi Menon's point that "desire is that which in every instance hollows out ontology. . . . It keeps moving, which is why it disables ontological fixes."[81] While desire's unruly motions mobilize possibilities for refusing capture within seemingly stable ontological categories, this restlessness registers differently for Black and Indigenous families, who have little choice in their movements—indeed, whose very re/movability coordinates colonial expansion.[82] The writers I explore express desires for grounded attachments to familiar ecologies, but untethered from the intimate norms of settler modernity. Instead, they often render desire in the briefest of inscriptions: as a flare of emotion, a fleeting kinship formation, a tremulous allusion to a different future—a small plot.

To that end, early writers of color characterize the world as an animate sphere of tremulous intimacies, a view expressed by Audre Lorde in a poem from which this book takes its title: "If you come as softly / as the wind between the trees, / you may hear as I hear." For Lorde, this haptic proximity is not a mere accident of occupying the same space and time, but a transhistorical posture that enables impossible, simultaneous intimacies: "But we shall sit here softly / beneath two different years," she promises, while "the rich earth between us" will sustain these encounters.[83] I engage with Lorde's insight to trace improvised praxes of listening *to* and *for* subjugated worlds across time and space, where one way to recover early Black and Indigenous worlds is through attention to their representations of sensation—of plural perceptual worlds.[84] As I show, these worlds reside not only in the psychic transits of differently felt desire but also in the aural textures of dreams and visions, in the haptic impressions of ceremonies and everyday lifeways, and in patterns of embodied resistance to a colonial formatting of earth and life.

Chapter Overview

Chapter one, "Dreaming with Samson Occom," argues that Occom cultivates expressions of mutual embodiment in the face of colonial dispossession. The paradigmatic example of this appears in the *Sermon on the Execution of Moses Paul* (1772), where Occom turns to Moses Paul, a condemned Wampanoag prisoner, and calls him "the bone of my bone and flesh of my flesh."[85] Here, Occom revises Adam's first words to Eve in the book of Genesis to express a kind of queer intimacy. I am calling this proclamation of shared intimacy a "cosubstantial kinship"—it is not a reinscription of autonomous personhood, but an enactment of conjoined being. Drawing from scholarship in Native sexuality studies and queer ecologies, I show how Occom grounds his cosubstantial scripts within a grammar of boundlessness— "Boundless Continent" is a term he uses repeatedly, for instance—which challenges what Scott Lauria Morgensen describes as an "ontology of settler colonialism . . . premised on its own boundlessness: always capable of projecting another horizon over which it might establish and incorporate a newest frontier."[86] Instead, Occom is preoccupied with coextensive forms of existence that exceed boundaries—a mode of being that drifts with flows of water, with echoes of desire, with extended kinship relations, with dream touches. Indeed, I trace how a second life of sleep and dreams, including Adam's loss of consciousness to facilitate his rib's removal, illuminates an Algonquian orientation to the permeable boundaries between body and spirit. Across his oeuvre, Occom's cosubstantial awareness is nearly always *of* and *beyond* embodiment, thus challenging colonial preoccupations with a seemingly "inevitable" Indigenous vanishing.

Building on chapter one's consideration of embodiment, chapter two, "Mary Prince and the Matter of Salt," traces how *The History of Mary Prince* (1831) captures an association between enslaved torment and Black archives as a problem of perception. Prince's text was produced within British antislavery and Moravian imperatives, which often emphasized transparent modes of sympathy—or "feeling with"—one another. Yet *The History* lingers with Prince's labor in the salt industries on Grand Turk, where salt's barely visible granular assemblages provoke great agony. Her portrayal of porous bodies vulnerable to sympathetic voyeurism and salt's corrosion seems a deliberate demand to exercise opacity, as Édouard Glissant terms it.[87] Prince says as much when she claims that although British readers might *know* about slavery, only she can *feel* it: "Few people in England know what slavery is. I have been a slave—I have felt what a slave feels, and I know what a slave knows."[88] Although *The History* offers few sites for recovering Prince beyond British antislavery and Moravian discourses, I consider how her performances of opacity retrieve a Caribbean world that counters not only dominant colonial ways of knowing, but also ways of feeling: "I *feel* something that you cannot understand." By evading forms of sympathetic entrapment, Prince therefore extemporizes what I am calling a *salt line*—a contour, a border, or a profile—for sketching the opaque boundaries of African diasporic worlds, rather than approaching anything like a full account of their substantial presences.

While chapters one and two focus on Native and Black modes of embodiment, chapters three and four turn to commoning practices depicted in Black and Indigenous writings. Chapter three, "With William Apess at Forest's Edge," lingers with a brief passage from *A Son of the Forest* (1829), when Apess describes living with the Mohawk during the winter of 1815–16: "I then turned my eyes to the forest, and it seemed alive with its sons and daughters. . . . And they held all things in common." Yet Apess would ultimately remove "they held all things in common" in the 1831 edition of *A Son of the Forest*.[89] "In common" and its erasure reverberates with tensions that would preoccupy Apess throughout his career: how to tell stories of Indigenous peoples and places when the onto-epistemic structures of modernity are premised on their vanishing. To explore this tension, I turn to Native cultivation practices—specifically to edge ecologies—as an analytic for tracing a counter-history of Indigenous commoning. Algonquian seasonal routines included burning low brush in forests, which produced an ecotone or "edge effect" as a dense habitat for a variety of species. Apess's citation of commoning reflects living memory of an edge ecology as a zone of cultivated extension rather than a discrete boundary. I am using these material spaces to extricate what I am calling an *edge work*—a mode of figuration, a recuperative historiography, an epistemological throughline—to recover a sense of Indigenous place-based knowledges. When Apess contends that "God has given to all men an equal right to possess and occupy the earth," or his version of an "earth given to the children of men," he thus portrays an earth that cannot be divided, implicitly drawing from an edge ecology's blurring of discrete ecosystems to imagine a decolonial praxis of being human and being with history.[90]

Chapter four, "Robert Wedderburn, Prophet of Unfinished Revolution," turns to the Haitian Revolution as an incomplete exemplar for future revolts. In *The Axe Laid to the Root*, for instance, Wedderburn prophetically announces: "Prepare for flight, ye planters, for the fate of St. Domingo awaits you. . . . Recollect the fermentation will be universal. . . . O ye planters, you know this has been done; the cause which produced former bloodshed still remains, —of necessity, similar effects must take place."[91] I contend that Wedderburn's rehearsals of revolution's unfinishedness speculate on un/thinkable histories from below and improvise a critical practice Lisa Lowe names "what could have been" as a perspective that "revisit[s] times of historical contingency and possibility to consider alternatives that may have been *unthought* in those times" but which allow him "to imagine different futures for what lies ahead."[92] In this way, Wedderburn's critical practice embraces a future that may not be salvageable, and yet his is "not a politics of despair brought about by a failure to lament a loss, because it is not rooted in hope of winning," as Jared Sexton puts it.[93] By speculating on what futures become *thinkable* after the Haitian Revolution, Wedderburn instead embodies an irreconcilable ethos of tense expectation, where transforming the future requires, counterintuitively, revising the past itself. This chapter thus presses on the political horizons that open up when we reconsider Wedderburn's revolutionary dream not in its failure to arrive, but as merely—and perhaps forever—unfinished.

Throughout *The Rich Earth Between Us*, I draw from critical methodologies developed by scholars in Black and Native studies, sexuality studies, environmental humanities, and political ontology to consider how Occom, Prince, Apess, and Wedderburn conjure plural worlds that disrupt colonial formations of history by reconceiving the very grounds of their descent and dissent.[94] Archived across diverse textual forms, embodied knowledges, and material objects, their small plots perform alternative arrangements of social assembly and affiliation in the face of world-destroying violence, and ask what it means to remake sustainable life in the ruins of settler colonialism and plantation slavery. In doing so, they persistently challenge imperial enunciations of governance over land and life to coordinate differently desired futures.

Even so, these writers' meditations on the promises that Psalm 115:16 seemingly extends—a gifted earth, a shared inheritance, a planetary commons—shed light on gulfs and impasses within some lines of critical inquiry. Research in political ontology often begins with the proposition that alternative worlds *are* extant and extend affordances that Audra Simpson (Mohawk) and other scholars in Indigenous studies have used to explicate modes of refusal to settler sovereignty and to reimagine political life.[95] From this view, Occom, Prince, Apess, and Wedderburn's rehearsals of reciprocity with the earth mobilize a mode of inquiry that may enable us to think beyond inhuman extractive economies and their persistent undoing of peoples and places, which continue to shape the world we live and work within. Yet a strand of investigation within Black studies has embraced a radical pessimism about these very possibilities, aware that past revolutionary projects are so often denied from the very moment of their enunciation and may only reflect "superseded future[s]" and "our futures past," as David Scott and Stephen Best have explored.[96] By tracing the convergences and divergences in Black and Indigenous worldmaking, I speculate within and across their critiques of enclosure and enslavement as grounds for living otherwise — not as univocal plots, but as provisional praxes of being human, as plural acts of improvised becoming with nonhuman kin, as always unfinished communities in the making.

CHAPTER ONE

Dreaming with Samson Occom

And the Lord caused a deep sleep to fall upon Adam, and he slept: and he took one of his ribs, and closed up the flesh; And the rib, which the Lord had taken from man, made he a woman, and brought her unto the man. And Adam said, "This is now bone of my bone, and flesh of my flesh: she shall be called Woman, for she was taken out of Man."

—GENESIS 2:21–23

As it was your own desire that I should preach to you this last discourse, so I shall speak plainly to you. —You are the bone of my bone, and flesh of my flesh.

—SAMSON OCCOM

Near the midpoint of the *Sermon on the Execution of Moses Paul* (1772), Mohegan preacher Samson Occom echoes Adam's first words to Eve in the book of Genesis and announces to the condemned Wampanoag prisoner Moses Paul: "You are the bone of my bone, and flesh of my flesh."[1] Paul was accused of fatally striking Moses Cook, a white miller, with a flat iron during an altercation outside a tavern in New Haven, Connecticut in December 1771. However, in his appeal before the Connecticut General Assembly, Paul testified that he reacted in self-defense when Cook drove him from the tavern with a whip, all while calling Paul "a Drunken Dogg"—a legal defense that ultimately failed.[2] As a genre, the eighteenth-century execution sermon often imbricates Christian beliefs on "the frailty of corrupt nature" with emergent racial discourses that portray Indigenous people as unable to manage their desires.[3] Occom's words to Paul thus appear in a text constrained by colonial investments in the inevitability of Indigenous death-bound desires— in this case, of Paul's apparently ungovernable surrender to drunkenness.[4] Occom early suggests that alcohol is one catalyst for Paul's fall: "When we are intoxicated with strong drink, we drown our rational powers, by which we are distinguished from the brutal creation; we unman ourselves, and bring ourselves not only level with the beasts of the field, but seven degrees beneath them."[5] Yet Occom's pronoun usage—"we"—renders this diagnosis a collective reckoning. Indeed, his fear that Paul is at risk of becoming something less than human brings into relief his own intense desire—that Paul *cannot* be a member of "the brutal creation" because he shares his existence with Occom's very flesh and bone.

Broadly, Occom's *Sermon* grapples with whether Paul could have sustained his "rational powers" even in circumstances where a loss of sobriety is, in its own way, a reasonable response to colonial precarity—he ponders what it means to desire at *all* under settler occupation.[6] Kelly Wisecup likewise argues that Occom tries to recuperate Indigenous agency by depicting encounters with alcohol as a "series of decisions" and not the result of "inherent desires or weakness."[7] Even so, his effort uneasily coexists with models of colonial masculinity that required disciplined and unaffected mastery of one's reason, a nearly impossible standard when settlers assumed the utter captivity of Indigenous impulses.[8] Colonial ministers like Eleazar Wheelock, for instance, believed that Native students required "constant care," a paternalistic oversight that questioned their capacity to manage desire.[9] Occom, in other words, seems to be probing whether reasoned masculinity can serve as an attainable model for safeguarding desire, both for individuals and within communities.

In this way, the two instances of naming—"Drunken Dogg" and "bone of my bone"—that index the *Sermon*'s historical circumstances expose irreconcilable perspectives on how desire conceptually animates different views on human being.[10] Outside the tavern, Cook's words reduce Paul to creaturely abjection, but Occom's citation from Genesis enlarges Paul's humanity toward coextensive life. By denying an attenuation of existence encompassed by Cook's sneer that Moses is a "Drunken Dogg," Occom shows that Paul matters because his bodily matter is also, somehow, Occom's own. Occom recognizes that colonialism seeks to divest Indigenous people not only of lands and lifeways but also of their very selves and relations to each other, as he laments to Paul, "You have lost your substance."[11] I want to suggest that shadowing the *Sermon*'s conflicted assent to self-willed sobriety and mastered desire as palliatives to settler violence is a form of life that could be spoken another way: "You have lost your substance. You have lost *yourself*. But here, receive mine, for you are the bone of my bone, and flesh of my flesh." Reimagined in this way, Occom's words embrace what I am calling a "cosubstantial kinship," a script of worldmaking rooted in a recognition of mutually embodied life.[12] His is not a discourse of autarchic selfhood but "an embodied practice of sovereign belonging," as Daniel Heath Justice

(Cherokee Nation) puts it.[13] As such, Occom, with haunting precision, anticipates a praxis of kinship that Elizabeth Povinelli calls a "socially cosubstantial corporeality" in Indigenous Australia.[14] To delineate this mode of being, Povinelli tells of a young Belyuen man suffering from the dire effects of congestive heart failure and addiction, but he maintains he can do what he wishes with his body, even if those desires lead to his death. Yet the boy's aunt refuses not only "the location of his risk but also . . . the underlying logic of his social imaginary," and responds, "No, that is not your body; that is my body. When you die, my body will suffer and die."[15] Instead of reproducing a bounded self so central to colonial personhood, this kinswoman, like Occom, believes that any one life is jointly lived.[16]

This chapter lingers with moments where Occom yearns for cosubstantial relations because they constitute scenes where something *otherwise* to colonialism's presumptive governance over Native desire flickers into visibility. Desire is a difficult thing to trace, perhaps nowhere more so than in the *Sermon*, but even here, it is Paul's "own desire" for his friend to "preach . . . this last discourse" that occasions Occom's longing for another life for Paul.[17] Moreover, this scene traces another itinerary for desire at the very moment Occom names a relationship to Paul through *Eve*. Genesis, of course, offers more than an origin story for man and woman—one that subordinates Eve's creation, formed from and after Adam—but for marriage too: "Therefore shall a man . . . cleave unto his wife: and they shall be one flesh" (Gen. 2:24). Despite this, Occom revises a heteronormative script into an elegiac declaration of such tenderness, avowing a relation that is, unusually for the period, for neither a spouse nor a child, but for another Indigenous man, one condemned to execution.[18] Although the *Sermon* might not initially register as a queer text, Occom's words to Paul recognize that if their world is one of shared flesh, then it exceeds the demands of self-willed masculinity.[19] And Occom embraces this intimacy with such intensity that it transgresses colonial subjectivity and the generic limits of the execution sermon.

By reading the *Sermon* as a confession of mutually obligated life, I wish to trace what it was possible to desire in a colonized world, where yearning can mark a counter-structure of feeling.[20] As scholars in Native studies have long explored, Algonquian writers who dissented from colonialism often had to do so from within settler languages, which made it increasingly difficult to express alternatives to possessive personhood and propertied improvement as both political ambitions and private aspirations.[21] To an extent, Occom's public life was defined by strategic accommodations to Anglo-American culture, perhaps nowhere clearer than his assistance in leading a multitribal migration to Eeyawquittoowauconuck, or Brothertown, whose residents staked their shared survival on timely adjustments to Christianity, property, and literacy—priorities much discussed in scholarship on Occom.[22] Still, we often encounter moments where Occom refuses settler imperatives by calling on Indigenous cosmologies of shared embodiment. In a 1764 petition, for instance, he turns to generational land-based relations as a bulwark against colonial expansion: "[They] want to render us as Cyphers in our own land—they want to root us out of our land root & Branch."[23] Here, Occom pulls from arboreal metaphors to depict a symbiotic world intimately united "root & Branch" in the face of English desires to evacuate these very entanglements of meaning.[24] Firm and nonporous, bone and branch might seem strange signs for unbounded life, but across his writings, Occom cites Adam's rib and Algonquian botanic genealogies to summon an interwoven existence, where limbs, human and otherwise, touch and uphold each other.[25]

Indeed, Occom's return to Genesis in a later 1785 sermon, composed thirteen years after the *Sermon on the Execution of Moses Paul*, indicates his awareness that Native worldmaking relations are inherently intertribal and profoundly somatic: "To all the Indians in this Boundless Continent, —I am an Indian also, your Brother and you are my Brethren the Bone of my Bone and Flesh of my Flesh." In this sermon, coextensive lives and desires endure within dense sensory intimacies—touch, sight, sound—as Occom indicates when he tells his audience that he has "a great Desire to Write to you a long While . . . [So] listen with great attention, and let nothing Croud into your Ears."[26] Here, Occom may also be echoing elements of the Haudenosaunee condolence ceremony, which he would have witnessed when visiting the Oneida in 1761.[27] His Mohican contemporary Hendrick Aupaumut describes the condolence rite as a restoration of senses occluded by deep grief: "I now put my hand on your face and wipe your tears, so that you may see things clear. . . . I now stretch my hand and take away all the dust from your ears, that you may hear."[28] Occom's synesthetic speech similarly initiates a curative ritual by calling for his "Brethren" who live in a "Boundless Continent" to cultivate clear senses, a perspective likely shaped by his own training in Montaukett medicinal practices.[29] If a physical altercation—a fatal strike with hands and iron implements—indexes Paul's fall from grace, then Occom's voice and hands extend a different somatic field for reconstituting the "flesh and bone" of Indigenous shared relations.

In this chapter, I track "bone of my bone" and "Boundless Continent" as phrases that extend a queer ground for boundless life. For this, I draw from Chickasaw scholar Jodi Byrd's staging of the material and semiotic significance of *ground* to Indigenous and queer studies: "[Queerness as] lack of fixity is . . . still and importantly grounded through the ongoing dispossession of Indigenous lands," even while "ground—as land, as base, as territory, as wellness, and as center—persists as a guiding principle for decolonization."[30] Read this way, "Boundless Continent" and "bone of my bone" index a mode of *rooting*, without *capturing*, unbounded life in ongoing praxes of sovereignty, which manifest in Occom's writings in acts of love fractured at scenes of execution, in dreams for personal and communal healing, and in scripts that surpass the missionary genres he wrote within and, to a certain extent, adapted to. Put more simply, these terms embrace a resonant small plot—as interruptions to a juridical regime premised on Indigenous vanishing, whether enacted through displacement or execution.

The methodology I have been unfolding here—reading for expressions of cosubstantial life as nonnormative acts of Indigenous worldmaking— opens new avenues for investigation into early Native environmental and sexuality studies.[31] Occom's tenacious grounding of sovereignty in a "Boundless Continent" informs a politics of personhood and place incongruent with colonial self-possession and propertied land tenure, maneuvers of enclosure that depended on and elided "imaginative and real encounters with Native people," as Robbie Richardson (Mi'gmaw and Pabineau First Nation) argues.[32] As such, the imbrication of place and people within settler domains of sexuality, race, and ecology suggests why *boundless* is such an important critical grammar for Occom. In what follows, I situate Occom's delineation of cosubstantial kinship as a sensation-based epistemology that coordinates generational relations to lands and bodies without borders.[33] As I show, his early writings, such as "A Short Narrative of My Life" and "Herbs & Roots," ground generational knowledge of local landscapes in vivid sense impressions and medicinal routines. Moreover, his petitions trace Indigenous expertise in navigating coastlines and waterways, whose aquatic images render a "Boundless Continent" with no borders within and only fenced by the ocean's waters without—thus troubling colonial protocols of property-formation. Above all, Occom's awareness of the cosubstantial is nearly always *of* and *beyond* embodiment—assembling modes of sensing Mohegan histories, of knowing flourishing plants, of moving with flows of water, and of dreaming across time and space.

In August 1676, several decades before Occom was born, Mohegan leaders struggled to alleviate a persistent drought and save their beleaguered crops. A few men went to James Fitch, the local Congregational minister in Norwich, for his help in "Seek[ing] to God for rain."[34] The minister consented, but only if the Mohegan would declare any acts of rain a work not of their own shamans or spirits but of a Christian God. The Mohegan agreed, desperate for rain during a moment of acute crisis. English settlers had just emerged victorious in the conflict now known as King Philip's War, with the execution of Wampanoag sachem Metacom, or Philip, occurring that summer. Uncas knew of Metacom's capture and went so far as to promise Fitch: "If God should then send rain, it could not be ascribed to their Pawawing, but must be acknowledged to be an Answer of [English] prayers."[35] In Mohegan, *pauwau* signifies one who has "the power to dream dreams and make them come true," as Mohegan medicine woman Gladys Tantaquidgeon argues.[36] Notoriously resistant to missionary endeavors, Uncas's oath to forswear *pauwau* thus constituted a grave choice. Satisfied by his pledge, Fitch asked his congregation to fast and pray, and after three days, the rains came. The Pequot River ran high with water, rising over two feet.[37]

Yet Fitch records a fantasy of transformed desire only unevenly reflected in Occom's writings composed several decades later, including "A Short Narrative of My Life," which he drafted in 1765 and revised in 1768. "Short Narrative" is a difficult text, where Occom seems to narrate his early life as a surprising encounter with English literacy, settled agriculture, and spiritual conversion as a young adult, even though the Mohegan certainly practiced farming and were familiar with missionary projects. But Occom's account is also "Constrained," as he puts it, by its rhetorical exigence, by rumors circulating among his sponsors that Occom was "bro't up Regularly and a Christian all my Days."[38] Colonial readers were disinclined, in other words, to credit Occom's testimony of conversion, just as others were skeptical of Uncas's sincerity.

In this section, I read clashes over the weather and land as a mode of untangling settler ecological and racial discourses from Occom's (often ironic) portrayal of his adjustments to colonial norms in early texts. "Short Narrative" reflects these accommodations in its emphasis on "heathenism," a discursive regime that renders Mohegan corporeal rituals and relations unintelligible to English readers. On the edges of these maneuvers, Occom offers a subtle portrayal of Mohegan sense impressions as a vehicle for local territorial knowledge. By turning to weather and sensation, I draw from Mary Favret's point that early meteorological discourses provide a "felt sensation of history."[39] Weather is both material condition and metaphor, a collection of atmospheric settings that frame everyday controversies over inhabiting the land.[40] In its representations of perception and ecological relations, "Short Narrative" reflects what Osage scholar Robert Warrior calls "embodied discourses," the transfer of Native knowledges through social routines, in its portrayal of sensation-based epistemologies.[41] Surveying sense impressions, however, means that I spend less time on more famous incidents in Occom's life, such as his 1765–1768 preaching tour in England to raise funds for an Indigenous college at the behest of Eleazar Wheelock.[42] Although scholars have extensively addressed Wheelock's theft of the £12,000 Occom raised to instead found Dartmouth College, it is also worth pointing out that even this incident reflects the colonial sensation regimes that Occom navigated.[43] Occom's pastoral labor, as he was always acutely aware, was interpellated within an English gaze — on the painful experience of being perceived as pitiable.[44] Occom believed Indigenous education was worth enduring this, as he tells Wheelock: "I was quite Willing to become a Gazing Stock, Yea Even a Laughing Stock, in Strange Countries to Promote your Cause."[45]

Occom was born into a world in conflict over how land should be inhabited and perceived. From the seventeenth century on, Connecticut claimed authority to grant Mohegan lands to settlers, and over the following decades, the colony circumscribed Mohegan hunting and farming grounds. The Mohegan brought a land case against Connecticut, *Mohegan Indians v. Connecticut* (1705–1773), which spanned nearly a century.[46] In 1723, the year Occom was born, Connecticut supported one claimant, Ben Uncas, to the sachemship against the heir much of the nation supported, splitting the community into factions. In the years that followed, wage and debt economies forced land sales and drove many Mohegan away to work as itinerant sailors, agricultural laborers, and domestic servants.[47] As a community advisor during this period, Occom sought to halt land sales and revive a consensus-sachemship. In one 1764 petition sent to William Johnson, English agent to the Haudenosaunee Confederacy, for instance, he argued that Connecticut had "Proceeded with arbitrary Power over us, — and we want to know from whence they got that Power."[48] In March 1765, however, the Connecticut Board of Correspondents compelled him to answer charges of misconduct for his work on the land case and make a public apology.[49] Although Occom never published "Short Narrative," he wrote it that same year for members of Boston's Society for Propagating the Gospel. The "Short Narrative" is directed to readers skeptical of Occom's history and invested in exercising "arbitrary Power" over Native lands.

While Fitch's account strives to entangle Mohegan bodies with Christian ecologies, Occom's writings from nearly a century later show how a host of ideas about race were distributed across contested cultural and geographical coordinates. Occom reflects these conflicts in the opening to "A Short Narrative": "I was Born a Heathen. . . . my Parents were altogether Heathens, and I Was Educated by them in their Heathenish Notions."[50] While the first draft indigenizes Occom's home by giving its Mohegan name, Mmoyanheeunnuck, he erases this in the second draft, where he repeats the qualifier "new" to intensify the territory's inscription as a colonial settlement: "I was Born . . . at a Place Calld Mohegan in New London Connecticut, in New England."[51] Occom's efforts to map his adolescence seem to emphasize his alienation from all things English, even while English nomenclature renders Indigenous placemaking invisible. "My Parents Livd a wandering life," he recalls of Joshua and Sarah Tomacham, and "they Chiefly Depended upon Hunting Fishing & Fowling for their Living and had no Connections with the English . . . and they Strictly maintain'd and follow'd their Heathenish Ways, Customs & Religion."[52] The text initially appears to replicate the racial values settlers assigned to Native pursuits, where Occom draws a distinction between Mohegan and English subsistence practices, such as hunting instead of farming, and living in roundhouses instead of English-style homes: "Neither did we Cultivate our Land, nor kept any Sort of Creatures except Dogs, Which We Used in Hunting; and Dwelt in Wigwams."[53] Although the Mohegan certainly practiced agriculture (they were, after all, troubled by drought when they turned to Fitch for aid), British tropes of heathenism hinged on Indigenous itinerancy—on persons, animals, and homes always in transit.

Even so, Occom's portrayal of communal routines—the social, rather than the solitary, pursuits of a "wandering life" that unite "all the Indians at Mohegan"—denies colonial efforts to fully contain Indigenous bodies within English settlements.[54] Indeed, "Short Narrative" flickers with sensations as a shared ground for communal life. Mohegan orientations to space, as Occom delineates, relied on dogs' sense of smell, which aided in locating humans in the environment through their dogs' sounding of alarms, assistance in tracking game, or, more spectrally, howling when someone was close to death.[55] In this way, Occom's attention to human and nonhuman partnerships corresponds with what Elizabeth Freeman calls a "queer sense method," a nonnormative "sociability felt and manifested along axes and wavelengths beyond the discursive and the visual" but embodied in "a simultaneity of movement in which the several become one."[56] Occom's parents "Strictly maintain'd and follow'd" seasonal choreographies, enabling routines where "the several become one" in the face of settler constraints—or *bounds*—on Indigenous worlds. Occom's account thus reflects what Mark Rifkin names a "generational inheritance of sensations" that operates as "a means for (re)imagining and (re)connecting to place."[57]

Read with frameworks in queer studies and Indigenous somatic practices, the "Short Narrative" pulses with Indigenous sense-worlds that also, perhaps obliquely, vex Occom's encounters with colonial Christianity. "Short Narrative" culminates in Occom's condemnation of missionary societies who fail to support Indigenous teachers with adequate pay and resources, even though ministers like Occom are often the "Ear, Eye & Hand, as Well Mouth" for Algonquian communities, mediating their relations to colonial authorities and their adjustments to English settlement practices. Occom concludes with a painful parable about a young Indigenous boy "Who [is] Bound out" or indentured "to an English Family." While Occom gives no indication on whether the boy can sustain relations with his own kin and community—another way in which the boy is "bound" by English customs— he does linger with his mistreatment by the English family, who frequently "[find] fault with him." When asked why, the boy responds, "he Beats for the most of the Time, because I am an Indian."[58] For Occom, Indigenous interpellations within colonial economies of labor are contoured by punishing atmospheres of racial violence and ongoing ruptures to landed belonging.

Occom's deep sensitivity to sensation extends not only to labor economies but also to the Great Awakening in the Native Northeast, beginning with "a Strange Rumor . . . that there were extraordinary Ministers Preaching from Place to Place."[59] After attending services delivered by itinerant preachers "who began to visit us and Preach the Word of god," Occom and his mother became members of David Jewett's North Church in Montville, Connecticut.[60] New Light preachers were notable for expressing an emotive sensibility—"a sweet burning in my heart," as Jonathan Edwards puts it—which could include fainting or "falling out," wailing and shouting, crying and moaning.[61] Occom rarely seems to share the somatic sensitivity so central to revivalist practice, although he may have seen these responses at Jewett's church. Instead, his conversion evinces one of his most painful accounts of feeling uprooted: "I don't know but I am Looking for a Spot of Ground where my Bones must be Buried, and never to See my Poor Family again, but I verely believe I am Calld of god by Strange Providence and that is Enough. . . . I want nothing but the Will of God, to be Wholly Swallowed up in it."[62] Misty G. Anderson contends that "the Pauline, kenotic, self-emptying Christian 'I'" invited a believer to suspend self-possession through a "sensuously immediate" encounter with the divine.[63] Occom's idiom is similarly one of kenotic negation—"don't know," "nothing but," "want nothing"—and emphasizes an epistemic drift in self-knowledge. While such confessions of doubt are common in devotional literature, what *is* unusual is Occom's representation that his desires to be "Wholly Swallowed" in the "Will of God" are in tension with his rootedness in Mohegan life.

The minimal ground of Occom's "verely" grasped belief appears less as a spiritual exercise of unmoored possibility and more as a terrifying physical and existential distance from his family, which comes into visibility if we compare Occom to other conversion accounts. Edwards's "Personal Narrative" (1740) limns kenotic detachment with a sensory language of "sweetness" (at once a taste, a smell, a feeling) to express the pleasure of being "swallowed" up in God, calling it "an inward sweetness, that used, as it were, to carry me away in my contemplations."[64] He further describes his conversion as "a calm, sweet abstraction of soul from all the concerns of this world" and "a kind of vision . . . of being alone in the mountains, or some solitary wilderness, far from all mankind, sweetly conversing with Christ, and wrapt and swallowed up in God."[65] Here, he locates conversion within an unspecific "wilderness," where he can evade local belonging (a "sweet abstraction"). Yet Edwards's non-space elides historical Indigenous existence, for his "wilderness" is empty of all other human presence, which is very different from Occom's pain of not being able to conceive worldly relations for he "know[s] not Where [he is] going."[66] Moreover, Occom dreads finding no proper resting place for his bodily remains: "I dont know but I am Looking for a Spot of Ground where my Bones must be Buried."[67] Here, he seems to be alluding to the story of Joseph when he pleads with his family to "carry up my bones" when they leave Egypt (Gen. 50:25). And indeed, when the Israelites flee slavery, Joseph's descendants keep their word and carry his remains to the land of Canaan (Ex. 13:19). Occom likewise contemplates the specter of interrupted burial—of finding no final resting place until the well-being of his people is secure.[68] He yearns for a Mohegan sovereignty rooted in generational attachments to familiar lands, and yet his conviction does not figure as a kenotic abstraction from place, a wholesale "swallowing" of sense into the divine, but rather as a "boundless" soul that nonetheless maintains a tangible connection to Mohegan territories.

In all these ways, "Short Narrative" clarifies that part of the attraction of conversion was access to the literacy tools needed to defend the Mohegan in their ongoing land case. If "Short Narrative" seemingly portrays Occom's adaptation to the imperatives of colonial modernity, he elsewhere expresses the stakes of these adjustments as colonial projects of desire, acutely aware that colonial projects facilitated enormous brutality towards Indigenous and Black communities: "When I Come to . . . See the Conduct of the Most Learned, Polite, and Rich Nations of the World, I find them to be the Most Tryanacal, Cruel, and inhuman oppressors of their Fellow Creatures in the World."[69] The relations between peoples and places that Occom so intricately narrates oppose colonial efforts to displace Indigenous nations through the disciplining of desire along with the slow creep of land loss, which Jean M. O'Brien (White Earth Ojibwe) aptly calls "dispossession by degrees."[70] Occom's early writings thus strive to gather Mohegan sense-worlds as coordinated practices that sustain embattled Indigenous communities across a "Boundless Continent."

"We Shall Look upon One Another as One Family . . ."

In some ways, Occom's "Short Narrative" and *Sermon on the Execution of Moses Paul* are the most difficult texts for tracing nonnormative sensory work. Given their historical exigencies, both texts stress his Christian commitment and seeming accommodations to settler domesticity. In this, Occom's writings reflect how colonial modernity imbricated people of color into a narrowly uniform regime of gender and sexuality, where compulsive conjugal coupledom and the patriarchal household constituted the only legible postures of relation.[71] To align with European culture required repudiating the particularities of local Indigenous customs, notably the routines that colonial observers perceived as nonnormative and queer, including practices of itinerant residency, matrilineal relational practices, and stories of kinship with non-human relatives.[72] In Occom's early writings, we can trace how the politics of place and intimacy, including cultural conflicts over maintaining traditional Mohegan lifeways, animates a critical practice of survival and resurgence. Moreover, I am interested in how Occom's meditations about local environments and ecologies—his yearning for a Mohegan world—animates what Sharon Holland calls a "queer place": "To think about desire is to arrive at a queer place."[73] Yet as with "A Short Narrative," recovering the queerness of Occom's orientations to space in these early texts requires a careful reading praxis attuned to the exigencies of their writing, circulation, and audience.[74]

By turning to Occom within these conflicts, I consider methods for conceiving his botanic and land-based knowledge as instances of Indigenous relational forms of embodied coexistence. For this, I draw on Métis and Anishinaabe ecologist Melissa K. Nelson's work at the intersection of Indigenous science studies and theories of gender and sexuality.[75] Nelson argues that Indigenous storytelling traditions, especially emergence narratives, offer elaborations not only on Native intimate *practices* but also on traditional knowledge about natural *processes*—oral stories, in other words, often archive Indigenous insights on everything from gravitational systems to plant cycles. In particular, she contends that the central intervention of many Indigenous original instructions and first teachings is that all life is mutually constitutive and interconnected, which she names a "pansexual" worldmaking predicated on interspecies and multispecies relations.[76] In this vein, Occom's sensation-based modes of knowing illustrate what Nelson calls "getting dirty," a "messy, visceral, eco-erotic boundary-crossing entanglement" with the world that can engender . . . a lived environmental ethic."[77] Occom's catalogue of Montaukett plant lore, "Herbs & Roots" (1754), and his short report on Montaukett cultural practices, "Account of the Montauk Indians, on Long Island" (1761), illustrate a "lived environmental ethic" by archiving varied forms of dissent to English property-formation and land-use practices.[78] When living with the Montaukett, for instance, he trained in medicinal routines with a local healer named Ocus, and utilized this knowledge in his pedagogical and pastoral care. Put more simply, I draw on studies in Indigenous networks of intimacy—queerly embodied, vibrantly ecological, densely cross-communal—to argue that Occom's portrayals of relational knowledge index a differently desired form of life to colonial expansion.[79]

Occom's pastoral practice was both rooted in Native ecological knowledges and counter to emergent European scientific discourses. In "Herbs & Roots," for instance, his medicinal catalogue lists various plants and the physical ailment each heals, such as in "A Long Notched Leaf" that is "good" for healing a "Boil."[80] In these lists, Occom establishes Indigenous knowledges in their local environments, rather than rendering plants' appearances, uses, and habitats within colonial taxonomies, as European scientists like Carolus Linnaeus were beginning to do.[81] Instead, Occom's booklet works as a mnemonic, requiring preexisting familiarity with Algonquian pharmacology in order to parse individual treatments, such as *which* plant is the "Long Notched Leaf" that can heal a "Boil."[82] His mnemonic knowledge resists what Greta LaFleur describes as emergent Western scientific discourses that sought to explain racial and sexual variety "through an environmental logic in which the climatic, humoral, physical, and social milieu of the body was understood to be a determining force."[83] For Occom, the environment does not subtend racial determinism or hierarchy but rather grounds acts of gathering, curing, and applying remedies as dynamic, shifting processes of care.[84] In particular, "Herbs & Roots" is keenly concerned with preserving Native reproductive agency, reflected in recipes like "a wead good to Restrain women from bearing Children," a "flax Sead" mixture "good for to Ease Women that are in Traval," and a "Pitch Pine Budes and Small Wiled Cherry Tree" tincture "good for young Women whose Flowers [menstrual cycles] are Stopt."[85] In these remedies, Occom implicitly evades Christian discourses that portray reproduction as a form of dominion over the earth—"Be fruitful and multiply and fill the earth and subdue it"—to portray healing as a way of living in interdependence with local communities and ecologies.[86]

Indeed, eighteenth-century legal codes were implicated in suppressing Algonquian family structures, especially intimacies between different Indigenous communities. Occom's marriage to Mary Fowler, a member of the Montaukett Nation, in 1751 is illustrative of this. Their relationship repudiated colonial regulations forbidding Montaukett exogamous marriages. These "laws [were] designed," Joanna Brooks observes, "by the colony of New York to hasten Indigenous population decline."[87] In 1712, East Hampton trustees forced Montaukett representatives to promise not to "take any strange Indians in nor suffer any to be on Montauk to use or improve any part of said land directly or indirectly by taking of a [squ—] or [squ—s]"—a code intended to weaken Native land title as much as regulate intimacy.[88] In 1754, only three years after Occom's marriage, New York officials further enlarged this decree by requiring that any Montaukett person who married a "Stranger" would forfeit "all rights to land and membership at Montauk."[89] While Occom's marriage would seem like an exemplary instance of conjugal coupledom at first glance, its very illegality reveals how colonial laws racialize and render nonnormative Indigenous enactments of desire, domesticity, and kinship.[90]

In this way, Occom's early writings index a colonial logic of *carnality*, or what Povinelli terms a "socially built space between flesh and environment" that becomes a "physical mattering forth" of "juridical and political maneuver," which renders Indigenous relations to land and kin undesirable.[91] To that end, settler legal codes in Occom's New England evince contests over the accepted contours of kinship, with Algonquian practices sometimes traceable only at the moment of their denial or foreclosure, as in the New York decrees against the Montaukett. However, Occom's oeuvre shows that the Mohegan formally dissented from these and similar laws, resolving in 1778 to pursue an entirely different kinship reckoning: "We Shall look upon one another as one Family, and Will Call or look upon no one as a Stranger, but Will take one another as pure and True Mohegans."[92] As a practical matter, the Mohegan connect this shared embodiment to their reciprocal stakes in the community: "We unanimously agreed that the Money [taxes] does belong to the Whole Tribe, and it shall be dispos'd of accordingly for the Benefit of the Whole."[93] And by denying laws that produce "strangers," the Mohegan perform what Abenaki scholar Lisa Brooks calls "an Algonquian practice of familial inclusiveness."[94]

Occom's "Account of the Montauk Indians" similarly traces how Montaukett marital customs could encompass more than one conjugal norm, a perspective shaped by his position as both a Native Christian observer and a kinsman participant in Montaukett life. A brief text, "Account of the Montauk Indians" spans only five or six pages in modern editions and portrays "some of the ancient customs and ways of the Montauk Indians"—where "ancient" emphasizes the *ongoingness* of Montaukett traditions.[95] In particular, Occom describes the different methods for assembling marital relations, practices that would have resonated as nonnormative to colonial observers. In the first two, parents arrange marriages for their children and exchange dowries, while in the other two, the couple chooses a partner. If the proposal is acceptable to the child's parents, the two families will "deliver their child to the man and his wife, and they receive their daughter in law with all imaginable joy." The betrothal is then solemnized by sharing food, which, depending on the age of the children, includes "the mother [suckling] the young couple," or "if the children are weaned, they must eat out of one dish."[96] Partaking of one dish was a widely shared ceremony across the Native Northeast, a way of extending diplomatic and kinship bonds.[97] Although diverse conjugal practices also existed in early modern Europe, Ann Marie Plane reminds us that church authorities nevertheless "tried to depict alternative practices as deviant."[98] In "Account of the Montauk Indians," however, Occom depicts marriage as less important than the ceremonies that forge extended clan relations. Broadly, then, when Occom names Moses Paul "bone of my bone and flesh of my flesh," when his medicinal vocation purposely centers Native reproductive well-being, and when he expands conjugal partnerships, he seeks to enlarge Indigenous intimacies to include generational traditions and land-based knowledge.

Everyday incidents in Occom's "wandring Life" similarly reverberate with representations of extended kinships as acts of mutual embodiment.[99] Early in his journals, Occom tenderly refers to his brother-in-law David Fowler as "our David" in a passage where he confesses that David's exposure to disease deeply worries him: "Found Mr Wheelocks Family very Poorly with the Measels Especially our David."[100] His term of endearment may appear incidental, but as Lisa Brooks explains: "Algonquin languages express kinship through pronouns like 'my,' 'our', and 'his.' Yet these terms do not denote possession, but rather evoke responsibilities and shared histories that bind people to each other and the land."[101] Occom's claim of shared intimacy in David's body connects extended kinships to a "Boundless Continent" even across the spaces of diaspora. When Occom and his family came to Brothertown in 1785, they arrived in time for two ceremonies: the first marriage service and the Green Corn festival, a harvest rite celebrated across the Native Northeast.[102] Now called the Wigwam Festival (which the Mohegan translate as "come into my home"), the celebration reaffirms Mohegan relations to each other and the land.[103] Although the Green Corn celebration fell out of practice in the middle of the nineteenth century, the Mohegan reestablished the festival in the early twentieth century after elders dreamed of its continuance. Thereafter, the Green Corn rite constituted a time, as Gladys Tantaquidgeon puts it, when the Mohegan "[learn] to be Muhukiniuk, or 'One with the spirit of all Mohegans.'"[104] For Occom, the celebration of the Green Corn and marriage ceremonies at Brothertown sustain connections with the Mohegan who decided to remain in Connecticut.

Near the end of his journals, Occom portrays becoming "one with the spirit of all Mohegans" when he joins David and their families in the autumn reaping: "David gatherd his Corn [and] he had a number of Hands tho it was Cloudy in the morning and little Rain, and in the after noon he husked his Corn, and the Huskers Sung Hymns Psalms and Spiritual Songs the bigest part of the Time."[105] Here, Occom's journal represents a conjoining of the Mohegan green corn festival and Christian song in a plural performance that integrates touch, sound, movement, and weather—a shared consciousness of communal and ecological work. At the same time, the passage reflects painful histories of adjustment to English farming and the community's estrangement from regional relationships with familiar plants and animals.[106] Yet we might imagine the community reaping their corn while singing a song from Occom's hymnal, "O Happy Souls How Fast You Go": "There all together we Shall be, / Together we will Sing."[107] Accompanied by endurance, obligation, and hope, this hymn portrays a curative vision of shared communal well-being, one that resonates with Occom's representations of cosubstantial relations with the land and human relatives.

Thus far, I have been exploring how Occom's early writings archive embodied knowledges as modes of desiring otherwise, and in this section, I turn to his petitions as texts that challenge what Marisol de la Cadena and Mario Blaser name a "colonial ontological occupation"—or epistemic protocols that attempt to erase Indigenous place-based knowledge.[108] When Occom argues that English settlers "want to render us as Cyphers in our own land," he shares in lineages of resistance to past and ongoing settler occupations, as recent scholarship in Indigenous studies has surveyed.[109] Many Algonquian communities told stories of Manit or Manitou, sometimes translated as "spiritual power," but which represents a living personhood that manifests within an animal, plant, or landmark.[110] Because Manitou consensually gave themselves as food and medicine, relations with the natural world were rooted in mutuality and reciprocity rather than dominion.[111] Although Occom never overtly invokes Manitou, he reflects their palimpsestic presences in his valuation of animal life and in his allusions to Algonquian emergence stories, which told of the continent's creation by animals out of what had been a global ocean.

By articulating pluriversal forms of sustainable desire, Occom's petitions orient to Mohegan shore life as challenges to what he understands as a colonial excess of desire—as settler overconsumption of lands and animals. Here, I explore how Occom's petitions turn to aqueous entities to think through nonhierarchical, unbounded flows in animate relation, which mark not only sensations of intimacy but also a politics of living well with neighbors, human and otherwise. Mohegan aquatic knowledge inflects a political praxis of boundlessness, given that fluids flow to fit the shape of their containers and possess no intrinsic boundaries.[112] In this way, Occom's riverine sensibility emulates what Glen Coulthard (Yellowknives Dene) calls "grounded normativity," an epistemological framework embedded *within* and inseparable *from* Indigenous spaces and stories.[113] With Occom, normativity derives from living memories of a coastal commons, what Astrida Neimanis calls a "more-than-human hydrocommons," in which "the flow and flush of waters . . . connect [us] to other bodies, to other worlds beyond our human selves."[114] To that end, Occom's perspective is at odds with the militant dominance of European navies, as well as the rise of extractive fishing and transatlantic shipping.[115] His visions of aqueous sovereignty show that the cosubstantial manifests not only in shared fleshly and botanic relations but also in fluid intimacies that illustrate how "a human is alive water," as Linda Hogan (Chickasaw Nation) puts it.[116] The petitions do more than relate colonial events that affected his community; they make visible possibilities for boundless life.

Before turning to the petitions in more detail, first I want to consider how Occom depicts humans and nonhumans as agents in shaping landscapes. Traditionally, the Mohegan moved between seasonal settlements along the Connecticut (Kwenitekw) River and the Atlantic coast, where bodies of water—"our Seas, Rivers, Brooks, and Ponds every where"—shaped daily activities.[117] Salt marshes and river coastlines were key to subsistence patterns because grasses that grew along the edges prevented soil erosion and preserved micro-environments for a variety of species.[118] Beavers also contributed to biodiversity by building extensive dams on rivers, enabling the sedimentation of organic matter in marginal soils and creating habitats for species that required slow-moving waters to thrive.[119] Beavers felled trees along forest edges, which in conjunction with periodic burns created woodland clearings that fostered foraging and hunting. The Mohegan benefited from these micro-ecosystems and planted fields of mixed maize, squash, and beans on rich alluvial soils, while also gathering wild plants along verdant shorelines. However, English settlers encountered the intricate wetlands of the Connecticut River Valley as an unhealthily damp environment, requiring extensive draining and adapted tillage practices.[120] In the case of the beaver, commercial fur economies caused populations to plummet by the seventeenth century's end. This decline had a dramatic effect throughout the Connecticut River Valley, as wetland habitats receded, imperiling regional biodiversity and causing more frequent floods.[121] These transformations informed Algonquian story traditions of colonial occupation: Ktsi Amiskw, the Great Beaver, causes untold pain when he constructs a dam to hoard resources. Lisa Brooks and Cheryl Savageau (Abenaki) argue that this narrative of hoarding mediates an Indigenous critique of colonial overhunting, especially of beavers, as Savageau writes: "In this world out of balance, Ktsi Amiskw dreams a hard dream: a world without beavers."[122] Occom's petitions maintain that immoderate consumption of coastal and riverine life invites lasting chaos.

For Occom, all the beings who inhabit a "Boundless Continent"—dogs, beavers, fish, fowl—feel what Gerald Horne calls "the apocalypse of settler colonialism" as an existential threat to shared survival.[123] And his petitions further identify this as an apocalypse of settler governance over *desire*. Pleasure and privation, of course, are central to the genre's formal idioms of supplication, but Occom draws on Algonquian stories to contest

Anglo-American definitions of what it is proper to desire at all. Colonial records, by contrast, continually linger with a seeming degeneration of Indigenous desire, as Native communities seem to yearn for all the wrong things. For instance, Cadwallader Colden, an early lieutenant governor for New York, believes Indigenous peoples possess an insatiable craving for alcohol: "It is strange, how all the *Indian* Nations . . . are infatuated with the Love of strong Drink; they know no Bounds to their Desire, while they can swallow it down."[124] John Locke, moreover, disparages Indigenous cultures as "rich in land, poor in all the Comforts of Life," which William Wood diagnoses as a refusal to adapt to "settled" labor unless "sweetened with more pleasures and profit than pains or care."[125] British writers thus fancy themselves models of sobriety and moderation, as they encourage each other to pursue only those lands "he should reasonably desire."[126] Occom, however, believes that settlers cultivate a psychically unbearable excess of desire that leaves lands and waters nearly unrecognizable, while taking no thought for the needs of nonhuman beings, in contrast to Algonquian conceptions of mutually obligated, cosubstantial bodies.

Occom's sense of this crisis of desire accrued additional urgency during the dangerous years of the American Revolution. In 1773, just prior to the outbreak of war, the Mohegan lost their land claim against Connecticut and had to decide whether to make a future elsewhere, an agonizing prospect that involved retreat from longstanding relations to neighbors and to familiar plant and animal life. Some who contemplated migrating to Brothertown worried "that they would suffer and come to poverty if they should move as a body into this part of the world, where there were no oysters and Clams."[127] In 1774, Occom's son-in-law Joseph Johnson (who married Occom's daughter Tabitha) traveled to New York to engage in diplomatic negotiations with the Oneida.[128] When Johnson received word that the Oneida had agreed to cede land to the immigrants, he joyfully responded: "We thank you that ye have received us into your Body, so that now we may say we have one head, one heart, and one Blood, and may God keep us united together in very deed untill we Both grow white headed."[129] Here, Johnson's cosubstantial profession of shared blood reflects Haudenosaunee diplomatic rituals, where "one head, one heart, and one Blood" serves as a mutual adoption script in which the Brothertowners are incorporated as younger siblings into the Haudenosaunee Confederacy.[130]

Yet the onset of the American Revolution, a civil war between the colonies and Britain, caused ruptures in relations throughout Indigenous country, as the Tuscarora and Oneida were enticed to the American cause, while the Mohawk tended to support the British. Yet the war was so ruinous to Native nations that it accentuated a need for Brothertown and halted its planning, as military enlistment and wartime upheaval killed nearly half of Mohegan young men, including Johnson, who died sometime between 1776 and 1777, while General John Sullivan's 1779 genocidal incursions in western New York, near the proposed site of Brothertown, devastated Haudenosaunee villages.[131] On a practical level, Occom's petitions center multitribal solidarities with a recognition that they constitute mutually obligated bodies.[132] In 1778, for instance, the Mohegan and their Niantic neighbors protested constraints on their "Natural Priviledges," including fishing rights on the Thames River.[133] Indeed, they challenged the bewildering shifts in colonial diplomacy: "Alas, where are we? If we were slaves under tyrants, we must submit; if we were captives, we must be silent, and if we were strangers, we must be contented; or if we had forfeited our priviledges at your hands by any of our agreements we should have nothing to say."[134] The anguished "where are we?" indicates not only a geopolitical but also an ontological dislocation, which Occom attempts to assuage by including all who inhabit "this boundless continent" within the protest's scope: "What will the various tribes of Indians, of this boundless continent say, when they hear of this restraint of fishing upon us? Will they not all cry out, mmauk, mmauk, these are the good that the Mohegans ever gloried and boasted of."[135] The interjection of "mmauk"—the Mohegan word *piyamáq* ("fish") or the possessive *nimauk* ("our fish")—performs an "intertribal rhetoric," which Kimberly Roppolo Wieser (Muscogee and Choctaw Nations) maintains "carries messages intended for Indians and other messages intended for both those outside the culture and within it."[136] The text thus evinces what Scott Lyons (Leech Lake Ojibwe and Mdewakanton Dakota) calls "rhetorical sovereignty," or the "inherent right and ability of peoples to determine their own communicative needs and desires."[137]

Throughout the war, moreover, Occom had pleaded for neutrality, and in a 1783 letter, he grieves the losses reverberating across Indigenous country: "This war has been the most Distructive to poor Indians of any wars that ever happened in my Day."[138] The Brothertown initiative thus illuminates how Occom's community was constrained, to some extent, to acculturate to English property ownership, farming methods, and commodity circulations as a mode of survival in an uncertain postwar world, as evident in planning documents:

We proceeded to form into a Body Politick—We Named our Town by the Name of Brotherton, in Indian Eeyawquittoowauconnuck . . . Andrew Acorrocomb and Thomas Putchauker were chosen to be Fence Viewers to Continue a year. . . . Concluded to live in Peace, and in Friendship and to go on in all their Public Concerns in Harmony.[139]

Drew Lopenzina observes that the plan is "a palimpsestic reimagining of space that privileged European style 'improvements'" in "the election of 'fence viewers' to maintain and enforce the integrity of apportioned property lines."[140] While the plan embraces some elements of fixed property lines, it also safeguards Indigenous jurisdiction over the town, with Occom working to ensure the settlement received a state charter in 1787 and evicting white settlers in 1792.[141] Given these efforts, in a late letter he recognizes that if Indigenous peoples "have very great . . . Prejudice against the White People," then "they have a too much good reason for it."[142]

Occom returns to an idiom of fluid sovereignty in a petition he sent on behalf of Brothertown in 1785. There, he foregrounds Brothertown's adaptation to European settlement practices by requesting "a grist mill and a Saw Mill," as well as "Husbandry Tools" for their fields.[143] After the American Revolution, many Indigenous nations also lost financial support from British missionary societies, obliging the Brothertowners to request "a little Liberary" for their children.[144] While Occom highlights the town's accommodations to colonial lifeways, the text also retains Algonquian political praxes by framing communal need as an obligation to be met by human or more-than-human powers.[145] Indeed, Occom demands epistemological space for two origin stories, one of the continent's aquatic beginnings and one of the onset of settler conquest:

The Supream Spirit above Saw fit to Creat This World, and all Creatures and all things therein; and the Children of man to Inhabit the Earth and to enjoy, and to overrule all the rest of the Creatures in this World—and the good, and the Great govr of the Worlds, —Saw fit in his good pleasure, to Divide this World by the Great Waters, and he fenced this great Continent by the Mighty Waters, all around, and it pleased him, to Plant our fore Fathers here first, and he gave them this Boundless Continent. . . . This World was full of all manner of four footed Wild Creatures great & small both on the Land and in the Waters, and Fowls Without Number. . . . Our Fathers knew not the Value of Lands . . . [but] have Sold all their Country, along the Sea Shore, and all our Hunting, Fishing and Fowling is now gone.[146]

Here, Occom's language elusively references both Christian and Algonquian emergence narratives. While his appeal to the "Supream Spirit" may allude to the Christian God, I want to suggest that the earth diver origin story, a narrative with variations across Haudenosaunee and Anishinaabe communities, also informs the petition. This story relates that all living creatures—otters, turtles, muskrats, fish, fowl—once inhabited a global ocean. When these creatures see a woman falling from a hole in the sky, they work together to form a soft place for her to land. Each dives below the waters to bring a piece of earth to the surface, but only the last and smallest—in some versions a muskrat, in others a water beetle or an otter—succeeds, grasping a handful of loam that expands to form the continent.[147] Given that his first act is to "Divide this World by the Great Waters," could the "Great govr" be the creature who emerges with a little mud clasped in his paw? If so, then Occom may be leaving the "Supream Spirit" deliberately unnamed, which leaves open the possibility that he is not citing the Biblical creator, but the ocean's creatures, as well as their praxes of consensus and care. In its affirmation of boundlessness, the petition therefore retreats from a colonial exercise of enclosure ("This is mine") to voice a cooperative response to another's survival ("This is ours").

And yet on first reading, the petition also seems to echo Genesis when God commands Adam to "have dominion . . . over every living thing that moveth upon the earth" (Gen. 1:28). Occom, too, renders "the Children of man" the inheritors of a rich earth and suggests that humans reflect the "good pleasure" with which the "Supream Spirit" divided the world when they "Inhabit the Earth . . . to enjoy."[148] Here, the text apparently reflects early modern political theories which insisted that the earth exists to sustain human flourishing. In *Second Treatise on Government* (1689), for instance, Locke offers his own origin story for civil society and turns to the "wild Indian" as an exemplary instance of a consumption that, once joined to labor and agricultural improvement, creates property. "The fruit, or venison, which nourishes the wild Indian," he writes, "who knows no enclosure, and is still a tenant in common, must be his, or so his, *i.e.* a part of him, that another can no longer have any right to it."[149] The fruit of the earth and the beasts of the field become his through consumption, by becoming so much "a part of"—or cosubstantial with—him that no one else can own them. Much has been made of Locke's equation between labor and property, but it is also worth exploring its implications for conceiving desire and pleasure: "The same law of nature, that does by this means give us property, does also bound that property too. 'God has given us all things richly' . . . . But how far has he given it us? To enjoy."[150] For Locke, acquisitiveness requires limits, for too much pleasure can only end in pain. However, Hannah Arendt argues that Locke's is ultimately a ruinous vision because accumulation can only truly end when resources are exhausted: "Property by itself . . . is subject to use and consumption and therefore diminishes constantly. The most radical and the only secure form of possession is destruction, for only what we have destroyed is safely and forever ours."[151] Read this way, Occom's Indigenous reworking of Genesis locates pleasure in *one another's* pleasure, rather than in Locke's Protestant ontology of consumption.[152] I am arguing that although the petition might initially view sovereignty as fully expressed in a sensuous gratification, an "enjoy[ment]" from "overrul[ing] all the rest of the Creatures in this World," the text ultimately dissents from an emergent colonial structure of feeling grounded in dominance over all life.[153]

Occom's emphasis on governance's affective dimensions, where a posture of dominion yields a desiring subject, comes to question an aspect of colonial subjectivity that Jeremy Chow has explored as a troubled relationship between settler violence and waterways.[154] By tethering a grammar of boundlessness to aquatic life, however, Occom shows that settlers bring not pleasure but ruin by pursuing economies where enjoyment for some denies possibilities for survival to others, leaving no epistemic space for nonhuman desires.[155] I am not suggesting that Occom's is an argument against consuming animals at all, for he certainly enjoyed fishing, but his knowledge of Algonquian subsistence practices nevertheless recognizes that shared survivance depends on valuing animal habits and habitats—on valuing, in a real sense, nonhuman pleasures and desires.[156] In his retelling of colonialism's origins in the 1785 petition, Occom shows that only continental geologies circumscribed Indigenous relations before English conquest, but now settlers are transforming a "Boundless" earth into lands and waters to be profitably used and consumed, threatening *all* forms of life with ruin.

As an alternative to colonial borders, Occom's 1785 petition and its narrative(s) of creation turn to a "Boundless Continent" as an onto-epistemic space for flourishing life.[157] Indeed, his pluriversal gestures to fluid life may reflect something his friend Phillis Wheatley Peters maintains in her poem "On Imagination," which urges that writers of color must conjure "new worlds" that "amaze the unbounded soul."[158] To remake a "new world" is to evade a colonial episteme that Isabelle Stengers contends is not a world, for it "recognizes no world" but thrives as a "machine" that "destroy[s] both politics and ontologies."[159] Perhaps the worlding praxis the petition gestures toward is this: to inhabit a "Boundless Continent" is to take no pleasure in dominion but rather to conceive a world that, as José Esteban Muñoz suggests, prompts us "to desire differently, to desire more, to desire better."[160] Put somewhat differently, Occom's recapitulation of these origin stories asks what a desiring subject's enjoyment of the earth can embrace not only in his present, but also in a future of colonialism's apocalyptic unfolding. In a 1785 sermon, he takes up this question again when he identifies the fall in Eden as a loss of "all this World, and the fullness thereof."[161] Caroline Wigginton argues that Occom's sermon "simulates a different Genesis story" to show that "the only way to survive and flourish [is] to build . . . a new future."[162]

Above all, Occom yearns for a future that fulfills the promise of an "earth given to the children of men," as is clear in one of his final letters from 1792: "I think the Time must come, when they shall beg to Jesus Christ for his Inheritance and the uttermost parts of the Earth his Posistion."[163] Here, he dreams of a prophetic return to a shared world in a letter that is otherwise bleak in its sense of Brothertown's embattled existence: that white settlers are encroaching and vowing to "Kill kill . . . Damn em kill."[164] Later, under immense pressure with the passage of the Indian Removal Act (1830), Brothertown residents, together with members of the Stockbridge-Munsee and Oneida Nations, moved to Wisconsin in the 1830s, walking most of the way.[165] Many of the Brothertowners live there still but have been unsuccessful in gaining federal recognition of their sovereignty. Brothertown's unsettled history testifies, with grim precision, to all the ways colonial expansion *bounds* a continent that ought to remain *boundless*.

"I Awoke, and Behold It Was a Dream"

In the world of matter what is valuable lives, in much the same way as in dreams, beneath the ground, just outside of human sight, sometimes just a bit beyond reach.

— LINDA HOGAN

I have been arguing that Occom's cosubstantial plots oppose colonial ontologies of bounded spaces and selves, even while colonial archives systemically erase plural worlds.[166] To consider these aporias, I close this chapter by turning to three scenes of dreaming with Occom. These dreams offer a complex, and even counterintuitive, horizon for tracing Indigenous worlds because they surface with such variety and tangibility in Occom's writings. And they suggest three pathways for conceiving Indigenous sovereignty as an elaboration of cosubstantial relations across space and time and with nonhuman and human kin. For Occom, Algonquian knowledges, as elaborated in his geographical familiarity with waterways and landscapes, fundamentally conflict with Enlightenment frameworks premised on universal knowledge: that information can be abstracted from discrete cultural settings. That dreams, as flashes of differently felt desire, have appeared across this chapter as a way of knowing otherwise is thus no coincidence. Dreams have surfaced to testify to Mohegan *pauwau* rituals and as signs to Mohegan elders to reconstitute the Green Corn festival. In their manifestations in Indigenous ceremony, these visions transfer historical memories across time and space, as in Algonquian stories about beavers. Across Occom's writings, a second life of sleep and dreams extends possibilities for recovering Indigenous interventions of existence, for dreams pulse with haptic sensations that manifest and assemble "attachment sites for world making," as Donna Haraway puts it, where "touch, regard, looking back, becoming with—all these make us responsible in unpredictable ways for which worlds take shape."[167]

"Account of the Montauk Indians," for one, gives an extended treatment of Montaukett dream *soma* as a reconstitution of haptic relations between human and nonhuman existences. According to Occom, the Montaukett believe dreams manifest as aural and visual impressions, appearing "sometimes in the shape of one creatures, sometimes in another, sometimes by a voice."[168] Occom also locates dream interpretation at the intersection of medicinal and spiritual knowledge, as shamans respond to unseen powers who penetrate the body's threshold: "At other times they feel no manner of pain, but feel strangely by degrees, till they are senseless."[169] In this way, he portrays healers as permeable to supernatural influences, as they cultivate an embodied openness that gives dreams their interventions in a boundless world. Indeed, healers "say they get their art from dreams," but instead of belittling such practices as English settlers might, Occom adds: "I don't see for my part, why it is not as true, as the English or other nation's witchcraft, but is a great mystery of darkness."[170] Above all, Occom's "great mystery of darkness" positions these tactile epistemologies as a hidden matter—as a small plot that exceeds a settler epistemology of evidential visibility and capture.

Likewise, as a material conduit for dreams, perhaps no object has taken up more critical interest in Occom studies than a small carved box.[171] In 1995, members of the Mohegan Cultural Resources Department discovered an elm carved *manu'da* at the Peabody and Essex Museum in Salem, Massachusetts. Gladys Tantaquidgeon recognized the box as one Occom sent to his sister, Lucy Occom Tantaquidgeon, after his move to Brothertown. Tantaquidgeon, along with Mohegan historian Melissa Tantaquidgeon Zobel, both descendants of Lucy, relate that elders touched the box to dream with it. Their touch interrupted settler models of verifiability, for "dreams were the best way to uncover" the box's provenance and history.[172] The elders' visions followed the routes depicted in the box's painted iconography, which included the Path of the Sun and Trail of Life designs as images that signal patterns of life and seasonal cycles. Indeed, Tantaquidgeon interpreted the patterns as a reminder of "a circular link between past, present, and future" and the relations of the "seven tribes [who] joined" together "in unity" in Brothertown.[173] During the winter months, women often worked together to make baskets and boxes while telling stories, meaning that Mohegan elders may have been dreaming not only with Occom but also with Mary, whose hands may have shaped its curve. Created from trees, the box would have also carried the living memory of arboreal relations to all the Mohegan, at home and in diaspora.[174] In this way, while the box inscribes the weight of multiple desires—to stay or to go—for those contemplating the move to Brothertown, the box carries the community's human and more-than-human relations into the future, as Cree scholar Stephanie Fitzgerald suggests.[175] By dreaming with a small box, the Mohegan thus extend the vessel's history into a mutually *desired* future.

In April 1786, around the time he made a small *manu'da*, Occom recorded a dream where he is visited by the famous evangelical British preacher, George Whitefield, who died fifteen years before in 1770.[176] As with other dreams explored in this chapter, Occom's sleeping encounter with Whitefield radiates with layered impressions of touch and sound:

> Last Night I had a remarkable Dream about Mr Whitefield, I thought he was preaching as he use to, when he was alive . . . and I had been Preaching, and he came to me, and took hold of my wright Hand and he put his face to my face, and rub'd his face to mine and Said, —I am glad that you preach the Excellency of Jesus Christ yet, and Said, go on and the Lord be with thee, we Shall now Soon done. and then he Stretchd himself upon the ground flat on his face and reachd his hands forward, and mad a mark with his Hand, and Said I will out doe and over reach all Sinners, and I thought he Barked like a Dog, with a Thundering Voice. . . . [And then] I awoke, and behold it was a Dream.[177]

Here, Occom's representation of this "remarkable Dream" extends as many questions about its contexts as it answers—if Occom dreamed in Mohegan-Pequot and translated the vision into English, and if he draws on

Mohegan beliefs that the spirits of the elders sometimes visit the living to help them prepare for death, which he alludes to at the end of the passage, "This Dream has put me much upon thinking of the End of my Journey."[178] As an elder, Whitefield does not linger in the realm of the spectral but appears with warm greetings and soothing touch, encouraging him that "we Shall now Soon done." As such, Whitefield's presence extends a promise: that Occom may *feel* that his efforts toward Mohegan survivance will be fulfilled.

These promises also elusively frame Whitefield's dreamscape presence, notably in the moment when he barks "like a Dog."[179] On the one hand, Whitefield's canine similarity reflects an ongoing preoccupation in diaspora studies, as scholars explore the material and metonymic deracination of Black and Indigenous persons *as* dogs, as well as the imperial weaponization *of* dogs, as in Vasco Núñez de Balboa's massacre of what contemporary scholars have named Two-Spirit persons in Quarequa.[180] In this context, Occom invokes dogs to critique a racial hierarchy encoded in epithets flung at Paul— and at himself. On one occasion, Occom was not able to fulfill a preaching engagement in New Haven, but at least one attendee mistook a white minister for Occom and grumbled, "See how the black dog lays it down."[181] At the same time, while some Indigenous cultures believed dogs were always subordinate to humans, the Mohegan belonged to the Lenape Wolf Clan and tended to perceive dogs and wolves as mediators of spiritual power, perhaps most emblematic in the figure of a "great dog" who guards the realm of the dead in Algonquian cosmogonies, a resonant context for Occom's dream of his deceased friend.[182] Dogs, as Colin Dayan puts it, always "bear the burden of revelation," as an interruption of colonial presumptions of sovereignty over Indigenous and animal life.[183]

Indeed, dogs hover at the center of fraught conflicts over the very terms of Indigenous survival. In 1712, the colony of New York passed a law restricting the Montaukett to only three dogs, and in 1727 and 1742 colonial trustees "sent agents to kill all dogs at Montauk except the permitted three" when settlers accused the dogs of killing their sheep.[184] As I earlier considered in the introduction, Occom penned an agonized petition over these laws: "We are undone for this Life. . . . For God's Sake help us; For we have no where to go now."[185] Against a form of colonial biopower, where settler livelihood matters more than Native life does, the dog within Whitefield blurs the borders between human and nonhuman existence, summoning a recuperative reality where canine similitude no longer signals an embattled Montaukett Nation becoming "undone for this Life."[186] Read in this context, Occom's vision concatenates a thick refraction of touch and proximity along the edges of what

Jodi Byrd terms the "ungrievable spaces" of colonial governance, which render Native cosmogonies a matter of "suspicion and unintelligibility."[187] While Whitefield's extravagant profession of sin embraces an intense spiritual self-regard, perhaps his touch and barking radiate outward to acknowledge another form of life—perhaps his presence returns Occom to something like the haptic intimacies that suffuse Algonquian and interspecies relations, entanglements nearly "undone" through settler policies designed to bound Indigenous survivance. If so, then Occom's sleeping consciousness evades a brutal trajectory of colonial appellation—of epithets like "the black dog" and "Drunken Dogg"—to urge a different reckoning of Native worldmaking, powerfully encompassed by his turn toward curative self-recognition in the *Sermon*: "If we don't regard ourselves, who will regard us?"[188]

As these three dreams suggest, for Occom, sovereignty does not reside in a state of war that erupts when life is "solitary, poore, nasty, brutish, and short," nor in a propertied citizenship, nor in an exceptional decision made in a moment of crisis, as European philosophers from Thomas Hobbes to John Locke to Carl Schmitt have differently theorized.[189] Rather, sovereignty marks a worldmaking capacity within Indigenous peoples to sustain cosubstantial postures of pleasure and obligation with every being who dwells in a "Boundless Continent." His is a vision of sovereignty that Amanda Cobb (Chickasaw Nation) maintains has "existed before colonization and [will] . . . exist after colonization. Sovereignty is *the going on of life*—the living."[190] For Occom, this living sovereignty endures in hidden knowledges in origin stories of a global ocean and herbal remedies, in basket carving and dream interpretation, in kinship relations and connections to nonhuman relatives.

In the end, the *Sermon* differentiates between two forms of sovereignty: the mandate to take life through execution (which the settler state has seized) and the power to restore life through grace (which only God can bestow).[191] Occom's citation of "bone of my bone" subverts not only this legal structure but also settler stories of their providential arrival in New England, which pulled from biblical idioms of desiccation, such as the valley of dry bones animated by God's breath in Ezekiel 37, to represent a New World in need of Christian conversion.[192] By opposing grace to settler sovereignty, Occom turns to an authority beyond the court and its presumptions of Indigenous unsurvival to reworld grace within an Algonquian relational cosmogony, where grace does not signal a bounded conversion event but an ongoing process of growth, imperatives echoed in his call for Paul to receive salvation as "an active principle" and "a living principle in the soul."[193] By the *Sermon*'s end, he urges Paul to "[breathe] towards God" and inhale "a living breath," reconceiving grace as a respiration and not an expiration.[194] Above all, Occom's perspective describes a view also expressed by Deborah Miranda (Chumash and Esselen), where grace is not "the achievement of a sublime mystical state," but an act of mutual embodiment—an "indigenous erotic."[195] In this way, the *Sermon* revises a notion of Paul's afflicted soul—"dry bones"—to carry an evanescent impression of his beloved body—"bone of my bone." Across his waking life and in his dreams, Occom's small prayers for breath rupture the scale of colonial expansion, which unfolds in both quotidian exercises of occupation and pervasive projects of disciplined desire. And he continually strives to summon new scenes—far beyond a Connecticut scaffold—for facing one another and saying, "You are the bone of my bone, and flesh of my flesh."

CHAPTER TWO

Mary Prince and the Matter of Salt

> Oh, the trials! the trials! they make the salt water come into my eyes
> when I think of the days in which I was afflicted—the times that are
> gone; when I mourned and grieved with a young heart for those
> whom I loved!
>
> —MARY PRINCE

> Every man jack of us as we got off the slave ships, the white god's
> priests used sea water to make the magic cross on our foreheads
> and bind us with salt to this land.
>
> —NALO HOPKINSON

The History of Mary Prince, a West Indian Slave, Related by Herself (1831) early offers an extended account of Mary Prince's labor on the salt ponds of Turk's Island. In 1802, Prince was separated from her family and sold to Robert Darrell, who owned salt industries on Grand Turk.[1] She recalls that the toil to convert saltwater to consumer salt was unfamiliar and brutal: "I was given a half barrel and a shovel, and had to stand up to my knees in the water, from four o'clock in the morning till nine, when we were given some Indian corn boiled in water, which we were obliged to swallow as fast as we could for fear the rain should come on and melt the salt."[2] As Prince describes struggling to harvest the salt before it dissolves in the rain, her testimony indexes an entire onto-epistemic regime of racialized subjugation and environmental hostility: "Our feet and legs, from standing in the salt water for so many hours, soon became full of dreadful boils, which eat down in some cases to the very bone, afflicting the sufferers with great torment."[3] Through her witness to these scenes of embodied vulnerability, Prince's gestures to salt underscore a conflict at the heart of *The History*: a limitation of language, including Prince's inability to convey the "great torment" of this coastal industry's routine horrors. As a substance and semiotic site of excess meaning throughout *The History*, salt continually emerges at material and figurative intersections that at first sight might appear incompatible.[4] Salt is at once an essential food preservative within transatlantic economies and an ingredient in plantation anti-curative practices, for when ill "the only medicine given to [the enslaved] was a great bowl of hot salt water, with salt mixed with it, which made us very sick."[5] Salt is both a material rubbed into an enslaved person's wounds, extending their agony, and a resonant symbol for spiritual sustenance in the liturgical imagery memorializing Christ's death in the Moravian church, which Prince joined in 1822, with one hymn inviting believers to taste his injuries: "I've lick'd this Rock's salt round and round. / Where can such relish else be found!"[6] Put more simply, salt can enrich the soul, corrode the flesh, and keep biological tissues suspended in time.

Because of this, scholars have turned to salt as a multivalent index of bodily exploitation and environmental extraction, with Matthew Rowney arguing that the salt industries marshalled "the conditions of the modern" in their brutal commodification of Black flesh, and Michele Speitz that while there Prince "retrieves and salvages stories amassed from the very realms that contorted her subjectivity."[7] In its material and semiotic properties, salt also implicates British evangelical and antislavery discourses of sympathy, which often depend on scenes of embodied exposure and the visibility of Black suffering.[8] British religious and political cultures shared an imperative to foster sensitivity to instances of bodily precarity as a ground for sentimental subjectivity and, ultimately, human being.[9] Anglo-American antislavery literature emphasized spectacles of Black abjection that, as Saidiya Hartman explains, required a spectator to "[project himself] into another in order to better understand the other."[10] The Moravians similarly cultivated practices centered on ecstatically becoming coextensive with Christ's injuries, or "like as [his] wounds," as one hymn professes.[11] In this chapter, I bring an environmental lens to these conversations to trace how Prince counters British discourses of sympathy emerging at the very moment the plantation exposes Black bodies to the corrosive salt industries. I argue that Prince takes the communalist ethos of "an earth given to the children of men" to improvise new relations to human and nonhuman life when plantations depend on "a geologic axiom of the inhuman," as Kathryn Yusoff puts it, or on economies premised on a conjoined extraction of value from Black life and from the land.[12] In this way, Prince's sense of embodied and ecological precarity rehearses what Tiffany Lethabo King names "an unstable ecozone and nervous landscape where boundaries between the human and Black and Indigenous bodies continually shift."[13]

When Prince recalls her time on Turk's Island, for instance, she cries, "Oh, the trials! the trials! they make the salt water come into my eyes when I think of the days in which I was afflicted—the times that are gone; when I mourned and grieved with a young heart for those whom I loved!"[14] In the passage's grimmest irony, Prince's grief-stricken body is compelled to produce the very substance that is the instrument of her "great torment"—as soon as she asserts her humanity as a suffering subject, her body materializes her sorrow as salt. Her tears mark plantation economies that violently conscript enslaved persons within regimes of fungibility, processes that both tear at her body and rouse her tears at the limits of endurance. For Prince, moreover, these systems rupture her orientation to time itself: the "times that are gone" are foreclosed by enslavers' avidity, and the times that remain are preserved in salt. *The History* thus presses on what it means to formally represent these experiences, for (to paraphrase Roland Barthes) who can compose a history of these tears?[15] In this sense, Prince's tears *are* history. Manifesting what Christina Sharpe names "residence time," they are a reminder that modernity's chronologies are inextricably ensnared with the very matter of slavery: "They, like us, are alive in hydrogen, in oxygen; in carbon, in phosphorous, and iron; in sodium and chlorine. This is what we know about those Africans thrown, jumped, dumped overboard in the Middle Passage; they are with us still."[16] And we could add: this is what we know of those who survived the Middle Passage and arrived at the saltwater shoals, whose labor in plantation regimes ended in their skin being "[eaten] down . . . to the very bone." They are with us still, too.

These material histories further shape *The History*'s print circumstances as a mediated text: Prince's voice is framed by her editor, Thomas Pringle, and amanuensis, Susannah Strickland.[17] If *The History* offers few sites for recovering Prince beyond British antislavery and evangelical discourses, then we might instead approach the text as a critical intervention in theorizing the operations of environmental exposure under plantation capitalism.[18] Read this way, Prince keeps vernacular environmental knowledge and practices of resistance invisible, deliberately exercising her "right to practice opacity," as Édouard Glissant terms it.[19] Prince says as much when she claims that although British readers might *know* about slavery, only enslaved persons can *feel* it: "Few people in England know what slavery is. I have been a slave—I have felt what a slave feels, and I know what a slave knows."[20] *The History* illustrates Hazel Carby's point that Black place-based knowledge is furtive—is fugitive—and manifests in "paths that led to and from their provision grounds; tracks trodden quietly at night to attack the Spanish and British settlers; trails between estates used to visit kin, or gather at secret meeting places; routes of escape on which to run."[21]

Building on Carby's point, I argue that Prince indicts white antislavery and evangelical discourses as forms of sympathetic entrapment, which collaborate in rendering Black bodies as vulnerable to sentimental voyeurism as to the corrosive conditions of the salt industries.[22] Across salt's temporal and se-miotic emergences, Prince thus extemporizes what I am calling a salt line—a contour, a border, a profile—for sketching the opaque formations of African diasporic life, rather than approaching anything like a full account of its substantial presences. Put somewhat differently, I am suggesting that because slavery's affective unshareability flickers only briefly in salt's material transformations, Prince gathers a critical practice only glimpsed in retreat—in tears falling, in salt melting, in sea currents.

In what follows, I explore how *The History* presses on the two discursive regimes that mediated Prince's voice to British readers—antislavery activism and Moravianism—which often stressed sentimental, and even over-wrought, responses to enslaved suffering.[23] In navigating this terrain, I consider how Prince implicates the processes by which antislavery discourses on sympathy, inextricable from an imperial biopolitics and evidential visibility, projected white affect onto Black bodies. I then turn to Moravian congregational exercises, such as *das sprachen* ("speakings" or confessional meetings) and *lebensläufe* ("life courses" or eulogies), to untangle *The History*'s cultivation of opacity from an evangelical background that emphasized penetrable bodies. In scenes that vex antislavery and evangelical imperatives, Prince often lingers with alternative registers of Black sensation: with unhealable injuries, with barely visible durations of endurance, with intimacies largely unheard within British political and spiritual networks.

Drawing from scholarship on Black ecologies and new materialisms, I examine how Prince's delivery of opacity, while constrained by some of the imperatives of British antislavery activism, coordinates another archive, a view echoed in Alexis Pauline Gumbs's recent meditation that salt "is an ancestor. Older than ocean, old as stars. Salt flows through your saltwater body even now like blood, as blood. . . . Salt is first and lasting."[24] In a similar way, *The History* charts the exploitations that inflect the production of imperial history, where salt contours the discursive apparatus of plantation regimes, and, as substance and symbol, appears throughout nineteenth-century records, from plantation ledgers to Moravian hymnody. Salt yields revelations about colonial records "as the fruit of power," in Michel-Rolph Trouillot's words, where enslavers, as Prince recognizes, evade diasporic testimony: "They put a cloak about the truth."[25] To read against the contortions of Moravian and antislavery discourses, which elide Black embodied and ecological knowledge, I cultivate what Hartman calls a method of "critical fabulation," or a way of tracing material and spiritual worldmaking only faintly visible in *The History*.[26] For Hartman, this mode of speculative engagement "mimes the figurative dimensions of history . . . to tell an impossible story and to amplify the impossibility of its telling"—a caution that critical fabulation cannot fully mend aporia constitutive with colonial archives and their print circulations.[27] I navigate these aporia by forging a transhistorical methodology rooted in diasporic stories about salt as alternative sites of resistance to slavery, a sensibility evoked by Nalo Hopkinson, whose words open this chapter.[28] By reading Prince with Black artists like Hopkinson and Gumbs, I consider how her salt lines contour small plots across time and space—how they assemble archives of secret knowledge, performances of refusal against dominant British imperatives of embodied porosity, and orientations to hidden worlds beyond the confines of the plantation.

"I Have Felt What a Slave Feels"

The History details how Prince's life necessitated navigating saltwater flows from the moment of her birth in 1788 in Brackish Pond, Bermuda—a geographical name that brings into relief her lived proximity to briny and salt-suffused water. Prince's parents were enslaved on different plantations, but she recalls her ability to live near them in her early life. In 1800, however, Prince was separated from her family and sold to John and Mary Ingham in Spanish Port, who severely abused her.[29] Prince often fled to her parents for relief, and after one abusive incident, her mother conceals her in "a hole in the rocks," while her father assists from where he lives across a "salt-water channel."[30] What might appear to be incidental details of Prince's proximity to saltwater landscapes in The History instead highlight how her relatives use fugitive geographical knowledge to hide from plantation surveillance. These contingent knowledges in turn animate her father's response to Ingham's brutality: "The treatment she has received is enough to break her heart. The sight of her wounds has nearly broke mine."[31]

Sympathy, a way of sharing a "broken heart," preoccupied a British conceptual terrain rooted in visuality, sensation, and proximity, with Adam Smith's Theory of Moral Sentiments (1759) invoking these terms in an infamous speculation on what we would feel on seeing torture:

> Though our brother is upon the rack, as long as we ourselves are at our ease, our senses will never inform us of what he suffers. They never did, and never can, carry us beyond our own person, and it is by imagination only that we can form any conception of what are his

sensations . . . By the imagination we place ourselves in his situation . . . [and] we enter as it were into his body, and become in some measure the same person with him.[32]

Here, Smith posits a critical gap between perception and imagination: merely seeing someone else's pain may not discomfort a spectator's "ease." Instead, intersubjectivity is only initiated when the spectator surrenders to what they *believe* the tormented feels. Jean-Jacques Rousseau similarly calls this affective surrender a mode of feeling "in common": "How do we let ourselves be moved to pity? By transporting ourselves outside ourselves. . . . How could I suffer when I see another suffer if I do not even know that he suffers, if I do not know what he and I have in common?"[33] For Rousseau, feeling "in common" requires *a priori* knowledge: spectators must recognize what another feels before they can feel it too. Yet from the perspective of histories of slavery, how is one to feel in common across experiential domains, when the embodied regimes "entered into," to use Smith's phrase, include everyday routines of physical and sexual violence?

In one disquieting passage in *The History of the Rise, Progress, and Accomplishment of the Abolition of the African Slave-Trade* (1808), Thomas Clarkson approaches this question by bearing out Smith's point that proximity does not guarantee sympathy, when sailors on slave ships, those closest to scenes of torment, become hardened: "It was impossible for them to be accustomed to carry away men and women by force, to keep them in chains, to see their tears, to hear their mournful lamentations, to behold the dead and dying. . . . [In] short, it was impossible for them to be witnesses."[34] His conclusion that nearness leads only to affective distance is denied in antislavery prints, such as the widely circulated image of the slave ship *Brookes*, which ostensibly made discursively and epistemologically visible enslaved suffering. Yet an account of suffering remediated in an engraving like the *Brookes*—or in meditations on suffering in eighteenth-century political theory—cannot fully bridge these distances, as Avery Gordon reminds us: "The invisibility and the insignificance of the men, women, and children" who inhabited the dark spaces "allotted to them is an offense that cannot be avowed in the representation itself."[35] In short, when Clarkson depicts persons for whom "it was impossible . . . to be witnesses," he creates a speculative allegory, a fabrication of the imagination that emphasizes the spectator's response rather than the experiences of the one who suffers.[36]

If sympathy emerges only through imagination, then Smith contends that these affects cohere during its most emblematic act, reading: "Our joy for the deliverance of those heroes of tragedy or romance who interest us, is as sincere as our grief for their distress."[37] Confidence in the authenticity of a reader's "fellow-feeling" is perhaps what led William Wilberforce to arrogantly assert that "few feel" the horrors of slavery "so strongly as myself," given his own extensive research into the slave trade.[38] Pringle similarly portrays reading as a spur to action, alluding to the aid he hopes will result from The History's publication (whose proceeds would support Prince in her declining health): "Whatever be the subsequent lot that Providence may have in reserve for her, the seasonable sympathy thus manifested on her behalf, will neither be fruitlessly expended nor unthankfully received."[39] Even so, Pringle's gesture to "seasonable sympathy" troublingly replicates some of the vulnerabilities Prince bears witness to throughout The History. By qualifying sympathy with "seasonable," he calls to mind the Black labor expended in cultivating "seasonings" (such as salt and sugar) and the time frame during which the newly enslaved are "seasoned" to the epidemiological and environmental conditions of monocultural industries.[40] Put simply, "seasonable sympathy" indexes a mode of Black abjection continually reproduced in antislavery discourses writ large and in antislavery texts about Prince's body.

Given this, Prince's words often contest the visual and textual regimes on which much eighteenth-century ethical theory depended. Whatever Smith's reservations on the possibilities that proximity afforded, for many ethicists sympathy demanded visuality.[41] David Hume, for instance, insisted that "pity depends, in a great measure, on the contiguity, and even the sight of the object," which required British antislavery activists to construct discourses capable of connecting Black suffering in the Caribbean to metropolitan readers.[42] Yet bridging these distances obligated Black disclosure, which for Prince meant an unwilling exposure of her scars, as Kerry Sinanan has explored.[43] Samantha Pinto contends that Prince's unsentimental descriptions of her wounded body wrest affective and epistemological authority from British frameworks "not to tell white people how to feel about Blackness but to claim the primacy of Black ways of knowing and feeling, or Black feeling as knowing."[44] To this point, I add that when Prince describes her separation from her mother, she presses on antislavery pretensions to sympathy at one of slavery's most paradigmatic scenes of subjection—the auction block: "I cannot bear to think of that day, —it is too much. —It recalls the great grief that filled my heart, and the woeful thoughts that passed to and fro through my mind, whilst listening to the pitiful words of my poor mother, weeping for the loss of her children. I wish I could find words to tell you all I then felt and suffered. The great God above alone knows the thoughts of the poor slave's heart."[45] Here, Prince's lament recurs to an unexpected scriptural cadence: her mother's "weeping for the loss of her children" evokes Jeremiah 31:15: "A voice is heard in Ramah . . . Rachel weeping for her children and refusing to be comforted, because they are no more." As evidence of Pringle's editorial hand or Prince's own familiarity with Biblical text, the passage ponders how one mother's sorrow could encompass collective pain—in this case, the desolation of Hebrews carried into captivity by the Babylonians and the heartbreak of those who remain. After giving birth to Benjamin (originally named Benoni, or "son of my sorrow"), Rachel was buried between Ramah and Bethlehem centuries before Jeremiah's prophetic career (Gen. 35:16–19). Jeremiah thus turns to Rachel as a ghostly analogue for the wholesale devastation wrought by war. Drawing from Orlando Patterson, we can say that slavery places Prince's mother in a spectral "condition of liminality" where she "forever mourns [her] own" and her children's "social death."[46] This brief allusion in *The History* opposes an ongoing disembodiment of enslaved grief, what Prince castigates as the colonial conviction that people of African descent are "without natural affection."[47] At the same time, Prince also refuses to recite her mother's "pitiful words," instead shrouding her mother's suffering as much as she can from readers. While she gestures toward her own turbulent grief—"the woeful thoughts that passed to and fro through my mind"—she makes a radical distinction between an English reader's ability to inhabit her experiences and God's capacity to dwell in this scene of suffering.[48] This scene, burdened by a theology of suffering and an agony that exceeds language, indexes an experiential knowledge Jennifer L. Morgan calls a "critical comprehension among captive Africans about the relationship between the disruption of family and the production of children for a marketplace."[49]

By eluding embodied openness, Prince confronts the impetus to make pain *visible* as the key affective movement in antislavery provocations of sympathy and instead makes her assault on its ocular logic a crucial part of the narrative's exigence: "Oh the horrors of slavery!—How the thought of it pains my heart! But the truth ought to be told of it; and what my eyes have seen I think it is my duty to relate; for few people in England know what slavery is. I have been a slave—I have felt what a slave feels, and I know what a slave knows."[50] Later, Prince reiterates, "I have been a slave myself—I know what slaves feel—I can tell by myself what other slaves feel, and by what they have told me."[51] Inhabiting every register of sensation, including sight, sound, and touch, she reclaims enslaved impressions from colonial biopolitical regimes that abstract enslaved bodies as capital, while also doubting that British readers can access those experiences through sympathetic imagination. In this way, she grounds her authority in shared affect — "what other slaves feel" — and in collective witnessing — "what they have told me."

By pressing on sympathy's speculative fictions in eighteenth-century theory through Prince's evocation of Black sensation, I build on Ramesh Mallipeddi's point that acute etymological and epistemological imperatives are implicated in the term *specular*: slavery's speculative financial maneuvers and antislavery discourses that emphasized spectacles of violence are constitutive. Enslaved captives responded to exploitative financial abstractions by creating a "counter-knowledge of slavery" that served as "an affective response to the forces of abstraction" that "commodified their bodies."[52] However, their counter-knowledges show the "incremental and quotidian sufferings that beleaguer a slave's daily existence," which are different emphases from the "spectacular suffering" so frequently depicted in British antislavery tracts.[53] For this point, Mallipeddi extends Rob Nixon's claim that environmental injustice often unfolds as a "slow violence" — "a violence that occurs gradually and out of sight, a violence of delayed destruction that is dispersed across time and space, an attritional violence that is typically not viewed as violence at all" — to argue that Prince portrays plantation violence as similarly slow and quotidian.[54] From this, we can begin to apprehend the global environmental impacts that the plantation contributed to, and trace how Prince turns to multiple sense repertoires to improvise a mode of witness to these extractive processes.[55] While I suggest that she extends a *collective* archive of enslaved sensations, I also recognize that hers is so often an opaque archive because enslaved chronologies of pain are illegible within British discourses of sympathy.

By "telling the truth" about slavery, Prince documents the everyday mutilations of the salt industries, an embodied reality only shareable with those who feel "what other slaves feel," because no wound is representative or fungible, as is so often the case with British antislavery print culture. Prince tells of a young captive named Ben, impaled in the foot with a bayonet by Darrell's son, "Master Dickey": "I was not by when he [was stabbed], but I saw the wound when I came home, and heard Ben tell the manner in which it was done."[56] She also speaks of Sarah, an old woman thrown "among the prickly-pear bushes" for being unable to work fast enough to suit Darrell; she finally died of the "venomous prickles."[57] And she remembers Daniel, who is disabled and whipped because he cannot endure the grueling labor in the salt ponds: "Poor Daniel was lame in the hip, and could not keep up with the rest of the slaves; and our master would order him to be stripped and laid down on the ground, and have him beaten with a rod of rough briar till his skin was quite red and raw. He would then call for a bucket of salt, and fling upon the raw flesh till the man writhed on the ground like a worm, and screamed aloud with agony. This poor man's wounds were never healed."[58]

Daniel's "raw . . . agony" limns the limits of representation. His wounds will not heal and extend in perpetuity a form of agony—"writh[ing] on the ground like a worm"—that subjects him to non(human)life under plantation biopolitics. His body forecloses British readers' potential for intersubjective encounter because salt tears at his flesh until he can do nothing but feel, even as *The History* fleetingly captures forms of grief made visible by "salt water" tears. Moreover, the ongoing duration of Daniel's suffering has theological stakes given evangelical perspectives on pain—that contemplative practices focused on suffering can lead to spiritual renewal and even ecstasy. Contra this theology, Prince exemplifies the difference between what Sue Tait categorizes as "bearing witness" and "eye-witnessing," where the latter subtends the routine ocular-centrism of plantation surveillance; "bearing witness," however, "exceeds seeing, and this excess lies in what it means to *perform responsibility*."[59] In the end, Prince performs responsibility through collective testimony: "In telling my own sorrows, I cannot pass by those of my fellow-slaves—for when I think of my own griefs, I remember theirs."[60]

"I've Lick'd This Rock's Salt Round and Round"

As with eighteenth-century discourses on sympathy, moravianism offers a spiritual imaginary rich and strange for contextualizing salt's affective resonances in *The History*. Within Christian discourses broadly, salt often emblematizes spiritual purity and enrichment, an image deployed in the Sermon on the Mount when Christ urges his listeners, "You are the salt of the earth" (Matt. 5:13). At the same time, salt also occasionally charts willfully destructive desire, perhaps most memorably in the story of Lot's wife, who is transformed into a pillar of salt when she yearns for Sodom and cannot help but look back (Gen. 19). Within Moravian liturgy, more particularly, salt often coordinates the sect's habits of intense meditation on Christ's death, what their detractors disparagingly called a "blood and wounds" theology.[61] A Moravian hymn from the 1754 *Collection of Hymns*, for instance, urges the singer: "Smell to and kiss each Corpse's wound," while recognizing that "at the *Pleura's* smart, / There pants and throbs my Heart."[62] The hymn's sensations escalate from contemplating to smelling to kissing Christ's wounds, a somatic encounter that the singer euphorically announces: "I see still, how the soldier fierce / Did thy most lovely *Pleura* pierce, / That dearest Side-hole!"[63]

Although I will turn later to the erotic implications of venerating the "dearest Side-hole," for now, I am interested in how the hymn implicates woundedness in service to spiritual growth, a devotional theology that clashes with scenes where the ruination of enslaved bodies continually shadows Prince's narrative throughout *The History*. The hymn's adoration of Christ's injuries crescendos in a scene of material transformation—a proclamation that his body has become a mineral that offers spiritual and physical sustenance: "I've lick'd this Rock's salt round and round / Where can such relish else be found!"[64] Where Prince's toil in the salt ponds testifies to a captive's bodily vulnerability, here Christ's transfiguration from bloody corpse to "relish[ed]" mineral propels the singer on a very different transhistorical trajectory. Indeed, Misty G. Anderson argues that "the intensity" of a Moravian hymn like this "pivots on the implication of the singer in the event of crucifixion, a position that dislocates singers from historical time and launches congregations into an imaginatively tactile relationship that breaks down the boundaries of Christ's body and, by extension, a believer's subjective autonomy."[65] Put somewhat differently, the hymn relies on and seeks to elaborate a powerful form of somatic ecstasy—of losing sense of where Christ's body ends and the believer's begins in both space and time.

Prince, however, can never lose sight of where she is in space and time in the corrosive sites that Stephanie Smallwood identifies as "saltwater slavery," or a "social geography of Black life in the Atlantic . . . demarcate[ed] by the blurred and bloodied boundaries of captivity, commodification, and diaspora."[66] In 1815, Prince was sold to John Adams Wood, who took her to Antigua, where a thriving Moravian congregation existed. Organized in 1722 on the estate of Nikolaus Ludwig, count von Zinzendorf, the Moravians became a major missionary presence in the Caribbean, founding their first church in the Danish colony of St. Thomas in 1732. Moravian missionaries founded a congregation in 1756 on Antigua. In 1822, Prince joined the local church at St. John, and while it boasted the largest congregation of African converts on the island, a majority of the diasporic community belonged to other denominations.[67] By 1824, over six thousand captives had joined Methodist congregations and over eleven thousand were attending Moravian services, or more than half of the enslaved population on Antigua. In addition, by the 1770s many were gathering at small confessional gatherings, *das sprachen* or "speakings," which were often led by "helpers" (called "godmothers" or "godfathers") drawn from members of African descent in the congregations.[68] Along with local services, Moravian missionaries organized a school that Prince attended for instruction in reading, writing, and religious doctrine.[69] Once Prince joined the Spring Gardens congregation—what she describes as "[having] my name put down in the Missionaries' book"—she would have been able to attend services and classes.[70] Natasha Lightfoot has extensively explored the gendered dimensions of Black ties to the Moravian church, where church disciplinary proceedings, or exclusion hearings, reveal how officials used religious doctrine to police Black communicants' nonmonogamous romantic partnerships.[71] While the popularity of the Moravian mission seems to have stemmed from a perception among Caribbean planters and members of the proslavery lobby that the Moravians encouraged sexual purity, as well as obedience and submission to enslavers, Prince's rehearsals of the conversion narrative's conventional rhythms of penitence and joy suggestively contour her spiritual yearning with a subtle desire to contravene the will of her enslavers. "I followed the church earnestly every opportunity," she confesses; "I did not then tell my mistress about it; for I knew that she would not give me leave to go. But I felt I *must* go."[72]

The History's representation of Moravian piety is fraught—and here, I trace how the text suggests that certain features of Methodist and Moravian practices appealed to Prince because they provided material resources for challenging her enslavers beyond a strategic investment in literacy, even while congregational practices conscripted Prince within systems of surveillance over Black women's affects, bodies, and intimacies.[73] Prince, for instance, hints that she used Moravian infrastructures to enable some freedom of movement in Antigua and Britain, which reflects a dominant thread in *The History* related to autonomous negotiations of space. Ifeoma Nwankwo argues that through "her emphasis on spatial language, Prince powerfully asserts her own agency, her own right to determine where and why she moves."[74] When accompanying her final enslavers, John Adams and Margaret Wood, to London in 1828, Prince was aided by the ship's steward, who attended the same Moravian class as her husband.[75] "I was thankful that he was so friendly," Prince recalls, "for my mistress was not kind to me on the passage; and she told me, when she was angry, that she did not intend to treat me any better in England than in the West Indies—that I need not expect it. And she was as good as her word."[76] When the Woods were true to their word and continued to abuse her in London, Prince used her Moravian connections to leave the Woods's household: "And so I came out, and went and carried my trunk to the Moravians."[77] In these moments, Prince perhaps exemplifies Katharine Gerbner's call to complicate an understanding of conversion as more than an expression of "accommodation" or "resistance" to European spiritual mores, for Christian conversion may not always reflect an exchange "of one set of ideas for another" but rather "a process in which Protestantism itself evolved as a lived practice," especially in Prince's own difficult navigations of London.[78]

Along with practical matters of education, financial support, and shelter, Prince rearticulates Moravian lived practices in order to pursue individual and communal remedies for a peculiarly paralyzing intersubjective nexus: shame.[79] Shame, as Gershen Kaufman observes, "is a wound felt from the inside, dividing us both from ourselves and from one another."[80] Shame corrodes social worlds by distancing a person from kinship bonds, already violently under pressure from slavery, while its recognition offers possibilities for communal cohesion. Caribbean captivity, supported by proslavery Christian rhetoric, shaped the conditions through which Prince and others grieved and understood spiritual affects like guilt and shame. To that end, Prince addresses expressions of personal and collective shame when she attends a Methodist speaking in her earliest extended account of evangelical penitential practices.[81] Methodist speakings frequently included an emphasis on hymn singing, prayer, and public confession as communal traditions that facilitated intense self-reflection, appearing in *The History* as fraught practices for captives. "I never knew rightly that I had much sin till I went there," remembers Prince.[82] The service begins with a prayer led by one of the women: "They were the first prayers I ever understood. One woman prayed; and then they all sung a hymn . . . and then they all spoke by turns of their own griefs as sinners."[83] She listens as another captive named Henry speaks before the gathering: "He confessed that he had treated the slaves very cruelly; but said that he was compelled to obey the orders of his master. He prayed them all to forgive him, and he prayed that God would forgive him. He said it was a horrid thing for a ranger to have sometimes to beat his own wife or sister; but he must do so if ordered by his master."[84] Prince pauses with this devastating ethical aporia, where Henry is "compelled to obey" the enslaver, a dilemma with few options for redress: "a horrid thing." Henry testifies to the emotional toll his forced punishment of "his own wife and sister" elicits and seeks solace from the community. As a lived practice, the speakings also may have provided space for uttering ethical denouncements: here, Henry can publicly name the "horrid thing[s]" rendered legal under the auspices of slavery. Late in *The History*, for instance, Prince applies a similar logic to repudiate colonial behavior in the Caribbean: "Since I have been here I have often wondered how English people can go out into the West Indies and act in such a beastly manner. But when they go to the West Indies, they forget God and all feeling of shame, I think, since they can see and do such things."[85]

After hearing Henry's condemnation of his enslaver, Prince then speaks of her own initiation into evangelical penitential exercises: "I felt sorry for my sins also. I cried the whole night, but I was too much ashamed to speak. I prayed God to forgive me. This meeting had a great impression on my mind, and led my spirit to the Moravian church."[86] Unlike Henry, Prince does not (or cannot) name the sins she seeks forgiveness for, only that she is too "ashamed to speak" of them. Prince's emphasis on shame seemingly initiates her into Moravian penitential practices that linked a sinner's contrition to the affective burden Christ bore during the crucifixion, where, through his willing surrender to suffering, he "hast to shame submitted," as one hymn put it.[87] This scene of prayer, however, covertly connects to other moments in the narrative that hint at the sexual oppressions that shape everyday life for Black women. Early in *The History*, for instance, Prince recalls how Darrell would compel her to bathe him: "He had an ugly fashion of stripping himself quite naked and ordering me then to wash him in a tub of water. This was worse to me than all the licks. Sometimes when he called me to wash him I would not come, my eyes were so full of shame. He would then come to beat me."[88] Lindon Barrett argues that in *The History*, "the master's body enters the narrative not as an emblem of physical danger or distress but, it seems, as the embodiment of a mental state not to be endured. . . . [The] act of washing this body rehearses with patent symbolism the extremes of subjugation and degradation implicit to New World slavery."[89] To Barrett, I add that *The History*'s oblique portrayals of sexual violence reflect exploitations of not only gender but also kinship—above all, the pain "not to be endured" indexes communal losses to family separations and denials of kin, as in Henry's experiences.

On multiple registers, Prince's experiences with "the torments of slavery" were indexed in *The History*'s publication and legal contexts—institutions implicated in negotiating what forms of enslaved suffering are legible and under what circumstances.[90] *The History* went through three editions after its publication in 1831, and came under intense public scrutiny when James Macqueen, a fervent supporter of British West Indian interests, published a virulent diatribe against Prince in *Blackwood's* in late 1831.[91] Although Thomas Pringle successfully sued Macqueen for libel through the London-based distributor of *Blackwood's*, he was awarded damages of only £5.[92] John Adams Wood then counter-sued Pringle for libel—he won and was awarded £25 in damages.[93] Prince testified in both cases, and during the trials Wood questioned her reliability as a witness, calling her "an abandoned and worthless woman, ungrateful towards him, and undeserving of sympathy from others."[94] Pringle, of course, assured readers of Prince's authority, promising that *The History* "was written out fully, with all the narrator's repetitions and prolixities, and afterwards pruned into its present shape. . . . [Not] a single circumstance or sentiment has been added," suggesting that Prince's sentiments were more than enough to appeal to readers.[95] Despite this, his editorial imprint certainly constrained Prince's witness to sexual violence, underscoring Nicole N. Aljoe's point that "every single West Indian slave narrative is explicitly mediated in some way—by a white transcriber, editor or translator."[96] Because British paradigms of whiteness and witness shaped *The History*'s historical circumstances, reading Prince requires listening for Black vernacular life that evaded Pringle's "pruning."[97]

Read in this historical context, the March 1, 1833, transcript for *Wood v. Pringle* refracts Prince's reformatting of Moravian theology to redress regimes of sexual exploitation and details her recourse to an unnamed "Moravian black leader" in the face of everyday violence:

> One night she found another woman in bed with the Captain in her house. This woman had pretended to be a friend of witness. (Laughter). Witness licked her, and she was obliged to get out of bed. (A laugh). The captain laughed, and the woman said she done it to plague witness. Witness took her next day to the Moravian black leader, when she denied it, and witness licked her again. (A laugh). . . . She had been a member of the Moravian Society, and discharged herself in consequence of her connection with Captain Abbot.[98]

Here, the court record presupposes an unflinching colonial hermeneutic with repeated parenthetical breaks of "(Laughter)" and "(A laugh)," which overdetermine Prince's presumed guilt. Indeed, the cross examination purportedly exposes Prince's own unreliability as a witness, including her supposed sexual promiscuity and her reaction to Abbot's infidelity, which falls on the unnamed woman, perhaps also enslaved. "The Moravians," Lightfoot argues, "focused their makeover of Antigua's black community on marriage and public comportment, but they accepted abuse in the private relations" among Black communicants "as routine," a reproduction of white sexual predation and violence within diasporic interpersonal relations exemplified in the conflict between Prince and this unnamed woman. These court reactions are premised on a brutal conviction that sexual consent can ever be meaningful under slavery, even while much of the passage's tone of smug amusement rests on the linguistic instability of "licked," which functions as both an erotic gesture (one even deployed in Moravian hymns, as

I earlier explored) and an expression of violence. The emphasis, in other words, is clearly on the unregulated reactions of these two women, rather than on the systems of exploitation that shape their daily lives.

Yet Prince's recourse to an unnamed "Moravian black leader" may also imply something more ambivalent: that Moravian spaces can offer redress *and* coercively silence Black women. Outside of anti-Moravian literature that suggested otherwise, Moravian doctrine stressed the importance of sexual purity, especially for women, and confessional gatherings routinely regulated Black sexuality by having communicants give public accounts of private relations.[99] Even so, Prince seems to have perceived something in Moravian lived practices that challenged her exploitation, although it remains difficult to fully access those possibilities in these archives. If the transcripts seemingly outline Prince's intense conviction in the church's reparative affordances—visible even through the palpable hostility of court witnesses— they nevertheless end by stating that she "discharged herself" (or more likely was forced to discharge herself in disciplinary proceedings) from the congregation "in consequence of her connection with Captain Abbot," suggesting that whatever transgressive potential she may have believed Moravian theology possessed had real limits.[100]

"Till the Water Burst from Her Body . . ."

By the time Prince began attending Moravian services in 1822, she had been with the Woods for at least seven years and was seeking remedy for grave bodily harm. Her health, never stable after over ten years of labor in the salt ponds, continued to decline, and she campaigned to purchase her own freedom.[101] Prince took in laundry and traveled to the docks to buy and sell goods, such as coffee, yams, or livestock.[102] When Prince became so ill with rheumatism that she became "very lame," she worked to negotiate her own manumission, negotiating with Adam White, a cooper and free Black man, and Mr. Burchell, a white colonist, to barter her service for freedom.[103] None of these offers moved the Woods, who refused to allow Prince to purchase her freedom or sell her to someone who would. After describing her efforts, Prince admits, "A gentleman also lent me some [money] to help to buy my freedom—but when I could not get free he got it back again. His name was Captain Abbot."[104] The only overt reference to Abbot in *The History*, the passage locates him within Prince's bid for freedom, before her health— chronically afflicted by rheumatism and erysipelas, an inflammatory disorder of the skin—failed.[105]

While the evasion of Abbot is unsurprising, that Prince invokes him in a passage detailing her declining health does make her appeal to the Moravian church more revealing. He clearly took advantage of Prince's deteriorating well-being, and when this coercive arrangement unraveled through her enslavers' recalcitrance, she turned to the unnamed "Moravian black leader" for redress, which also failed, revealing how the Moravian church circumscribed Black communal support, both in Antigua and elsewhere. When Prince attempted to rejoin the Moravian church while in London, rumors of Abbot's exploitation hampered her efforts, and her membership was denied.[106] While this church record is the last archival trace of Prince, it is also worth pointing out that Moravian disciplinary proceedings retain traces of her husband, Daniel James, who was excluded from the Moravian church for living with a woman named Mary Ann Williams in 1834.[107] By this point, Prince had been gone from Antigua since 1828, and James may not have known where she was or if she still lived. Still, the church condemned James as an adulterer, indexing how church doctrine constrained Black desires and intimate lives by linking these practices to a conjugal sanctity out of reach for most Black men and women.[108]

Even so, The History suggests that Prince continued to view the Moravian church as a shelter against her declining health. By the time Prince married James, her ailments centrally figure in her account of the Woods' harsh treatment, as they escalated their cruelty: "[Mrs. Wood] could not forgive me for getting married, but stirred up Mr. Wood to flog me dreadfully with his horsewhip. . . . Mrs. Wood was always abusing me about him. She did not lick me herself, but she got her husband to do it for her, whilst she fretted the flesh off my bones."[109] In this passage, Prince traces a harrowing image of her body "fretted" by punishment until only bones remain to testify that skin had once been present. Perhaps the redress Prince seeks is to see her wounds transformed from a secular marker of punishment to a spiritual sign of sacrifice endured. At the same time, she is enclosed within systems of intimate subjugation that Marisa Fuentes argues transformed captives "into sexual repositories, objects of commerce, and relentless, destructive desire," a violent transformation that persists in the archive as a "mutilated historicity."[110] Above all, the passage records a disquieting devastation of her body at odds with devotional contemplations of Christ's wounds: not even at his most abject is he portrayed without skin.

In this section, then, I want to trace how Prince's gestures to woundedness further implicate the ecstatic dimensions of Moravian theology, where communicants often encounter Christ through haptic protocols that viscerally expose his wounds to touch.[111] Scenes of touch appear throughout the Gospels, of course, where as Elaine Scarry observes: "Belief comes not, as so often in the Old Testament, by being oneself wounded but by having the wound become the object of *touch*."[112] Christ, for instance, rebukes Thomas's doubt over the reality of his resurrected body by having him touch the wounds still visible on Christ's hands and feet: "Put out your hand, and place it in my side. Do not doubt, but believe" (John 20:27). Moravian liturgy similarly imagined Christ's passion as a materially *seen* and *felt* resource, as one hymn suggests: "Powerful wounds of Jesus / So moist, so gory, bleed on my heart / So that I may remain brave and like as the wounds."[113] Here, the liturgical scene of touch is entirely, and even paradoxically, present—Christ's injuries "bleed" on the believer's heart (an organ not typically open to the sight of others) as an aqueous encounter of blood, iron, and sodium. Powerfully turning this imagery on the enslaver, Prince likewise argues that Darrell's heart cannot be "touched": "Nothing could touch his hard heart—neither sighs, nor tears, nor prayers, nor streaming blood."[114]

Reading Prince in the context of Moravian theology's ecstatic (and to their critics gratuitous) propensity to venerate Christ's injuries summons a queerly transgressive liturgical project, enabling an erotic encounter Carolyn Dinshaw might call a "queer touch across time."[115] Patristic theology, above all in Augustine's works, often portrays Christ's body as pliable in its gender alignment, while he was also rendered as penetrable in early modern metaphysical poetry.[116] And Christ's gender mutability could extend to believers, with Derrick R. Miller pointing out that in Moravian theology "all souls were female since all souls were similarly situated in marriage to Christ."[117] Moravian practices often unfold scenes where Christ's wounds are radically unfixed in gender: he appears as a conduit into spiritual marriage or an image of wounded motherhood.[118] Zinzendorf, for instance, once read Christ's pierced side as a uterus: "His side is the womb in which my spirit was conceived and carried."[119] Moravians even codified atonement as a mystical marriage in the *Wundenlitanei* or *Litany of Wounds of the Husband* (1744): "Come as his body, / And his sinful spouse, / Redeemed and reconciled."[120] Although a socially disruptive "time of sifting" (1743–50) moved the Moravians away from some of its theologically erotic excesses, such language remained part of congregational exercises well into the nineteenth century when Prince encountered them.[121] Within these evangelical histories, Christ's body becomes a field of semiotic surplus—human and god, man and woman, wounded mother and son—that intersects, in fraught ways, with Anglo-American political efforts to interpret Black pain.

Although figurations of Christ as a wounded woman or mother may have been the source for Prince's turn to the Moravian chapel when her own life was ruptured by sexual violence, her effort at redress was systemically and structurally denied. Slavery, as Hortense Spillers reminds us, "ungendered" Black women by "[severing] the captive body from its motive will, its active desire," and these coercive pressures hyper-eroticized Black women's bodies.[122] Black women's bodies index the libidinal economies of fungibility, vulnerability, and violence that accompany slavery, impeding the improvisation of alternatives for queer and feminist intimacies, as Caribbean studies scholars have explored.[123] Black women, barred from the status of mother, cannot attain the category of the human, as Sylvia Wynter has argued.[124] Unlike Christ, who can be both husband and son, mother and woman (and who thus possesses hyper-subjectivity, an excess of human being), Black women are confined as liminal figures, rendering their experiences of suffering illegible.

Read in this context, *The History*'s account of Hetty's death plumbs the limits of a Moravian liturgy that venerated the maternal wounds/womb of Christ. Chronologically, this scene appears early in *The History*, before Prince's conversion and when she calls God the one "whom then I knew not."[125] By contrast, Prince *knows* Hetty—"Aunt Hetty"—because she offers a substitute kinship. Hetty's devastating death indexes a violent colonial ontology, one that wholly denies the irreducible kinship between them. Ingham's brutal treatment of Hetty forces her into premature labor, and after delivering a stillborn child, she suffers an agonizing death: "Ere long her body and limbs swelled to a great size; and she lay on a mat in the kitchen, till the water burst out of her body and she died. . . . The manner of it filled me with horror."[126] Prince's portrayal of Hetty's bodily transfiguration into water may recall Psalm 22, understood by nineteenth-century evangelical readers as a messianic typology of Christ's passion. The psalm begins with the haunting question, "My God, my God, why has thou forsaken me," and continues with a litany of injuries suffered: "I am poured out like water, and all my bones are out of joint: my heart is like wax; it is melted in the midst of my bowels" (Ps. 22:14). Early modern hermeneutic traditions argue that the passage prophetically anticipates Christ's agony, whose side was pierced by a soldier's spear "and forthwith came out blood and water" (John 19:34). In John's gospel, "blood and water" are empirical evidence that Christ died, for this fluid mixture occurs only after the heart ceases beating, allowing blood to pool in lower cavities of the body. This seemingly incidental detail has enormous theological stakes as evidence of Christ's physical (and not merely spiritual) resurrection. For Prince, however, Hetty's "shamed body" evinces no recuperative meaning.[127] In an inversion of Moravian penitential practice, she apprehends Hetty's death as a horrifying event that compels rather than invites meditation, mourning, "I could not bear to think about it; yet it was always present to my mind for many a day."[128] Offering no parallel to communing in and with Christ's wounds, Hetty's death ultimately intrudes on Prince's psyche and is "always present" to her—a wrenching affective counterpoint to Daniel's unhealable wounds.

"The End of All Things near at Hand . . ."

Throughout this chapter, I have been exploring whether we can trace the brief outlines of Prince's opaque affects, even while I acknowledge that this critical task may only illuminate British political and spiritual requirements to align with religious ecstasy and sentimental domesticity. Prince's voice is perpetually circumscribed within regimes of sexual predation and economic fungibility, which ignored or outright denied Black intimacies. Indeed, the simultaneous impositions *on* and refusals *of* Black relationalities signal the difficulties inherent to any methodology that seeks to extricate the substance of African diasporic life.

Even so, if the material conditions of Black women's witness are approached from a Caribbean sensorium—not the visual logics of antislavery discourses, the aural eruptions of laughter evinced in court documents, or the haptic stress on shame in Moravian penitential protocols—then Prince's account perhaps indexes what we could call a queerly Black orientation to porous bodies and environments inassimilable to an onto-epistemic plantation regime. While Prince's stories of permeable embodiment occasionally reflect Moravian depictions of Christ, *The History* implicitly calls Moravian practices to account for searing scenes of trauma where the body's secretions—blood, tears, sweat, edemic fluid, screams—are dispersed as fragments into the water, soil, and air, "a forced [merging of] labor, body, and landscape" that is "a horrific *condition of being*," as Speitz observes.[129] Instead, I suggest that Prince's ecological orientations to salt lines and sea water echo Omise'eke Natasha Tinsley's point that African diasporic intimacies can manifest in a queer refusal "to accept [that] the liquidation of their social selves—the colonization of oceanic and bodily waters—meant the liquidation of their sentient selves."[130]

In this section, I explore Prince's evocations of corrosive climates and extreme weather events because they are frequently unintelligible within British providentialist discourses, which seek to disperse evangelical incentives into the very ground, water, and air.[131] Instead, I interpret Prince with Christina Sharpe's notion of "weather," a term she uses to denote the psychosocial mattering of antiblackness as central to the geographies people of African descent navigate and seek to circumvent: "In what I am calling the weather, antiblackness is pervasive *as* climate. . . . [It] is the atmospheric condition of time and place."[132] Reading the weather may open up *The History*'s subversion of intersubjective voyeurism desired by metropolitan readers, which leaves the body's felt interiors open to colonial plotting, much like environmental events are understood as meaningful within providentialist rhetoric. However, in her descriptions of meteorological and geophysical events — including earthquakes, hurricanes, and floods — Prince often conjures unexpected sites of human and nonhuman resistance and solidarity, which turn tightly surveilled plantations into disordered worlds recalcitrant to colonial aspirations of managed lands and bodies.[133] For Prince, the weather leaves its impression on skin just as skin leaves its impression on the weather, together forming "mutual constitution[s] of entangled agencies," in Karen Barad's words.[134] As such, moments of climate catastrophe in *The History* extend vital opportunities for tracing diasporic cosmogonies as counter-explanatory frameworks.

Prince's fleshly precarity, vulnerable to the weather, functions like a "para-human archive," Monique Allewaert's term for stories of bodies permeated by tropical ecologies that nevertheless conjure diasporic modes of survival — and of human/nonhuman solidarity — beyond the reality of their fragmentation.[135] To that end, in a few key passages Prince seems to express ambivalence about missionary models for interpreting the weather.[136] In one instance, she recounts a cycle of human punishment and weather cataclysm that presses on questions of human and nonhuman agency — for who causes events to occur and toward what ends? While Prince empties an old jar, "a heavy squall of wind and rain came on suddenly" and the jar shatters in her hands, to which Ingham responds with brutal anger.[137] Then, in the midst of Ingham's punishment, further calamity strikes: "There was a dreadful earthquake. Part of the roof fell down, and everything in the house went — clatter, clatter, clatter. Oh I thought the end of all things near at hand . . . The earth was groaning and shaking."[138] Here, Prince interweaves impressions of injury and damage between persons and objects: the jar breaks, the earth groans, all "were shrieking and crying out."[139] These chaotic proximities assemble a fluid circulation of reciprocal damage between ruined objects (broken jar, collapsed roof) and wasted bodies (punished Black flesh).

Although the storm and earthquake seemingly appear by chance, Prince deliberately implies that culpability for this devastation lies not only with Ingham, but with the entire system of racialized violence that leaves Black communities vulnerable to their enslavers' cruelty and to climate disaster. In this sense, she retrieves a Black theology that ruptures colonial providentialist discourses, which operate to coerce submission from those subjugated under slavery: "But the hand of that God whom then I knew not, was stretched over me; and I was mercifully preserved for better things."[140] Prince seems to ask: what could mercy mean in the context of Caribbean slavery? Read this way, the passage registers a profound irony, illuminating the pretense of British—or the Christian God's—"mercy." And perhaps Prince echoes the submerged irony of Phillis Wheatley Peters's poem "On Being Brought from Africa to America," which begins, "Twas mercy brought me from my *Pagan* land," but which Honorée Fanonne Jeffers calls "the story" of "how we've lied to each other."[141]

Elsewhere in *The History*, Prince confronts a similar scene of wreckage that unexpectedly inundates her community. A story reaches her that a few captives have built a separate worship site on Turk's Island, suggesting the presence of what Paul Gilroy terms a "partially hidden public sphere" of improvised social spaces.[142] Prince relates that they "had built up a place with boughs and leaves, where they might meet for prayers, but the white people pulled it down twice, and would not allow them even a shed for prayers."[143] While "prayers" might register to British readers within Christian practices, the gathering place likely provided protection for Creole spiritualities.[144] Prince then describes a flood overtaking the area, and when she lingers with this scene of environmental interpenetration, where sand and salt marshes conjoin, she elusively reads the flood in service to an avenging ethical order: "A flood came down soon after and washed away many houses, filled the place with sand, and overflowed the ponds: and I do think that this was for their wickedness; for the Buckra men there were very wicked. I saw and heard much that was very very bad at that place."[145] As she reconstructs events, the flood appears only a few passages after her portrayal of the suffering she and others experience from the salt marshes: "We made trusses for our legs and feet to rest upon, for they were so full of the salt boils that we could get no rest lying upon the bare boards."[146] I contend that these passages' proximity to each other illustrate how Prince's community is forced to "live in the ruins" of the plantation and climate precarity, to paraphrase Anna Lowenhaupt Tsing.[147] *The History* thus presses us to ask: who sent the flood—the Christian God or someone else? Could Prince be gesturing to spiritual entities who remain unnamed in a text directed at primarily white British readers? One possibility would be that Yemanjá, a Yorubá orisha associated with the Ogun River in Nigeria and with the sea across the African diaspora, commands the storm in vengeance against "the Buckra men" of Turk's Island. If Prince is alluding to Yemanjá, then this moment could embrace an alternative Black cosmology—both an orientation to the movements of the weather and a resistant ethics responsive to captives' prayers. Reading with Black cosmologies may enable us to see that while Prince's voice is constrained within the explanatory grip of providentialism, *The History* still gestures to Caribbean circulations of rumor and resistance, which challenge colonial efforts to bend Black bodies and ecologies to plantation extraction.

Understood this way, Prince's witness reminds me of Elizabeth Povinelli's descriptions of Indigenous Australian cosmogonies, including a moment when as a young woman she encountered fossil remains at *karrabing* (low tide). Betty Bilawa and Grace Binbin, two Belyuen elders, watched Povinelli's progress along the saltwater pools and wondered if the fossil would "manifest" to her in a revelation that "was usually described in creole as 'show himself' and in Emiyengal as *awa-gami-mari-ntheni*—an intentional emergence."[148] For Povinelli, these diffuse emergences—rock formations, fossils, creeks, weather events—habituate patterns of endurance, anticipation, and obligation between human and nonhuman worlds. "The fundamental task of human thought," she recalls, "was to learn how to discern a manifestation from an appearance; how to assess what these manifestations were indicating about the current arrangement of existence; and how to act properly given the sudden understanding that what is is not what you thought it was."[149] Povinelli, of course, writes from a very different cultural and geographical site from Prince's Antigua. It is not easy to extricate *The History*'s fugitive worldmaking from the missionary ecologies that mediated the text, but we must try, for as Katherine McKittrick contends, "black matters are spatial matters."[150] In *The History*, such environmental signs and wonders are not imperceptible—merely aporia in the incomplete archives of slavery—but tremulously throb within a sensorium of Black human and nonhuman coexistence.[151] *The History* reflects the somatic traces of Caribbean counter-ecologies, maintained by enslaved communities against the extractive violences of the plantation, which willfully distort Black humanity.[152] While new materialist scholarship has been tracing the possibilities that arise when nonhuman personhood and agencies are foregrounded, research in Black studies cautions that many ecocritical discourses developed concurrently with slavery. Their epistemological and ethical affordances for illuminating what Camille Dungy calls "Black nature" are historically contingent and unstable, illustrated by Prince's descriptions of chaotic weather patterns and embodied permeability.[153] Put another way, *The History*'s salt lines provoke questions about what, precisely, the text's environmental ethos reveals *about* Black humanity and nonhuman relations, given their collective imbrication within systems of plantation capitalism.

In this chapter's close, I trace another speculative pathway through questions of embodiment and ecology by tarrying with contemporary Caribbean stories about salt. In this way, I show that Prince's gestures to environmental intimacies often work as a shoal—Tiffany Lethabo King's term for improvisational enactments of Black and Indigenous knowledge. Saltwater shoals shift and drift over time, elaborating physical geographies that are never fully knowable or mappable. Instead, they exist as "an interstitial and emerging space of becoming" for human and nonhuman beings alike.[154] Likewise, in African diasporic oral stories and fugitive traditions, salt can facilitate surprising shifts and drifts, enabling human mobility—or impeding movement. At the same time, I recognize that while Caribbean stories about salt may allow us to survey prospects for Black survivance through space and time—knowledges incommensurate with colonial discourses— Prince's commitment to opacity also means that this effort is always incomplete or gestural. In the end, salt "manifests" *The History*'s intercessions to witness within precarious ecologies and weather events that exceed any full reckoning—with storms, earthquakes, and floods.

". . . Under the Vessel's Bottom"

> Stories of Africans flying home to Africa or walking home on the ocean floor abound in continental America and the archipelago. . . . If when they arrived in the Americas, one legend has it, they did not eat salt, they could fly back home. Salt would weigh them down or turn their blood.
>
> —DIONNE BRAND

> Such was the stuff from which legends were made among the Africans. Where to deny one's self the eating of salt . . . was a guarantee of the retention of the power to fly, really fly, home.
>
> —CEDRIC ROBINSON

If Prince's narrative of Hetty's harrowing death evades legibility within a Moravian blood and wounds theology, and if her representations of climate catastrophe exceed the imperatives of missionary ecologies, we must still reckon with what it means to read *The History* alongside evangelical genres adapted to cope with human finitude. Sue Thomas argues, for instance, that *The History* exemplifies aspects of the Moravian *lebensläufe* or eulogy, and she situates it within a growing canon of *lebensläufe* by people of African descent, including *The Memoirs of Salone Cuthbert* (1781/1829) and *The Narrative of Archibald Monteith, a Jamaican Slave* (1864).[155] Often performed at a congregant's funeral, lebensläufe were composed by ministers in consultation with the narrator. Jon Sensbach observes that the genre "combine[s] the subject's own oral testimony and the writer's idealized interpretation" of a person's "spiritual odyssey from bondage to sin to freedom in Christ."[156] Prince's witness to the salt industries suggests, however, that *The History* is an anti-eulogy because she maintains an ambivalent relationship to evangelical itineraries that interpret life experiences as signs of divine intervention. This is perhaps nowhere clearer than when Prince depicts her mother for the final time, when she arrives on Turk's Island. While it is possible to read the passage as a eulogy of Prince's mother—and in an extended footnote Pringle gives all that is known about her mother's life—the scene also evokes enslaved histories that cannot conform to the lebensläufe's generic norms and its presumptions of disclosure. Instead, Prince's narrative of her mother exceeds the eulogy's focus on a single life to reckon with collective histories. As Hartman would put it, she tells an "impossible story" that traces the opaque outlines of lacunae constitutive of colonial archives.[157]

Prince begins by recounting one of her starkest evocations of saltwater capital: her witness to other enslaved captives transported to Grand Turk's salt industries. She uses this opportunity to seek word on family members who, as far as she knows, remain on Bermuda: "When I came upon the deck I asked the black people, 'Is there any one here for me?' 'Yes,' they said, 'your mother.'"[158] What should be a reunion between kin, however, is transformed into an experience of suffering so deep it becomes an acute torment for Prince: "They had been overtaken by a violent storm at sea. My poor mother had never been on the sea before, and she was so ill, that she lost her senses, and it was long before she came quite to herself again."[159] As Prince grieves, she links the extractive violences of plantation capitalism with generational memories of the Middle Passage, which grimly collaborate to rupture her mother's memories of her daughter: "She did not know me." In anguish, her mother can only repeat that "she had been under the vessel's bottom"—can only attest to a vestibular knowledge of being "in the wake," as Christina Sharpe calls it.[160] Dionne Brand's diasporic thanatography suggests that rather than "flying home to Africa," her mother's spirit has been weighed down by seawater—by salt.[161]

What does it mean to encounter Prince's mother and her testimony that she has been carried beneath "the vessel's bottom" as a kind of anti-eulogy? Pascale-Anne Brault and Michael Naas suggest that in eulogies "the singular death is pluralized, opening up a space and time that can be *read* and so reckoned with other times and other deaths."[162] Still, *The History* seems to indicate something quite different: the site of the collective is what *cannot* be reckoned with. By showing how her mother's psychic dislocation is premised on the circulations of slavery, Prince's testimony indexes the very conditions of (un)witnessing by which financial speculation denies the routinized violences of capital modernity.[163] Put simply, to be carried "under the vessel's bottom" rehearses a collective and experiential history of the slave trade— and, perhaps more particularly, the 133 captives thrown overboard the slave ship *Zong* in September 1781, only fifty years before *The History* was published.[164] In this sense, *The History* confronts a limit that M. NourbeSe Philip, in her lyric engagement with the *Zong* massacre, names an obligation to "chart the outline of the wound," even while recognizing that in doing so we can only reckon with these lives at the moment of their loss.[165] "Chart[ing] the outline of the wound," Philip maintains, "is a work of haunting, a wake of sorts, where the spectres of the undead make themselves present. And only in not-telling can the story be told."[166] For Philip, the eulogistic boundary, or the "wake of sorts," for that space of not-telling is delimited by a lexical gap: a term exists for disinterring bodies from the earth— exhumation—but not "for bringing bodies back from the water," to which she offers one: "exaqua."[167] And in a way, Prince's mother *has* been "brought back from the water" in a psychic exaqua, a counterpart to the lone captive during the *Zong* massacre "who, thrown overboard, managed to climb back onto the ship."[168] Prince's mother has survived the passage—or, put differently, she has come back from the dead, returning, in accordance with Zora Neale Hurston's research on Haitian Vodou practices, not quite whole but as a kind of zombie, one who "can never speak again, unless [she] is given salt."[169]

Prince's mother, in other words, invokes a salt archive that exceeds any generic effort to contain, organize, or otherwise structure its evocations of Caribbean slavery.[170] As a reservoir of Caribbean histories, Prince's (anti)lebensläufe throbs as a saltwater wound, a fragment at odds with the order Pringle and Strickland seek to impose on her testimony. While *The History* makes the case for framing the woundedness of Prince's mother as an expression of mourning, it does so without bringing all colonial readers into anything like Rousseau's feeling "in common," for those who follow as *The History*'s (white) readers cannot fully retrace her metaphorical journey beneath the ship's hull. Prince's mother's agonized descent/descant dwells within that space of "not-telling," thereby charting a tension also at the heart of the eulogy. Her mother has psychically survived what for many captives thrown overboard or overworked on the plantations was a very different "spiritual odyssey" than that offered in conventional conversion narratives. Rather than framing this one life as an ascent from "bondage to sin to freedom in Christ," Prince rehearses a reality where for many captives lost during the Middle Passage, in death their bodies "sank without tombs" and their spirits returned to West Africa.[171] Prince stops far short of providing closure on her mother, tarrying instead in the affective limbo of her harrowing journey at sea, echoing a meditation on incomplete witnessing that Giorgio Agamben grapples with in *Remnants of Auschwitz: The Witness and the Archive* (2002). There, he cites Holocaust survivor Primo Levi, who muses that the "'true' witnesses, the 'complete witnesses,'" of atrocity "are those who did not bear witness and could not bear witness. They are . . . the drowned."[172] Prince likewise summons an incomplete history, where her mother's words not only echo the cries of the drowned but also assemble a form of testimony resolutely denied by procedures of capital accumulation. In the end, Prince's last word on her mother only lingers with her return to Bermuda: "My mother worked for some years on the island, but was taken back to Bermuda some time before my master carried me thither."[173] "It was long before she came quite to herself again" is Prince's weary summation of her mother's experiences, which makes no effort to offer precision or closure—"some years," "some time."[174]

Prince's knowledge of her mother—perhaps a deliberately kept secret from British readers but also evidence of how slave systems disrupt kinship networks—exists as a fragment that colonial archives can only assemble and reassemble in incomplete narrative forms (and their elegiac subgenres).[175] Her mother's words, of course, are mediated at multiple removes: retold by Prince, then rendered indirect speech by Strickland, and finally edited by Pringle. Yet in contrast to the multivalent temporalities elicited by her mother's refrain—which cite histories of the Middle Passage, atrocities like the *Zong* massacre, and the quotidian realities of her own slow return to health—Pringle's paratextual notation summons a sense of closure and resolution, editorially rendered in an extended footnote that reflects Prince's own testimony: "Of the subsequent lot of her relatives she can tell but little.

She says, her father died while she and her mother were at Turk's Island. . . . Her mother died after Mary went to Antigua. Of the fate of the rest of her kindred, seven brothers and three sisters, she knows nothing further than this—that the elder sister, who had several children to her master, was taken by him to Trinidad; and that the youngest, Rebecca, is still . . . in Bermuda."[176] Pringle's footnote inverts a dynamic Jacques Derrida explores in "This is Not an Oral Footnote," where he argues that "if one considers that a text . . . is a divine speech act or divine writing, then the hierarchical relationship between the main text and the annotations . . . reproduces a theologico-political model."[177] If for Derrida paratextual annotations remain spatially—and thus politically—subordinated on the page, then Pringle's editorial position functions as its own "divine speech act." His footnote gives the fate of some of Prince's family and plumbs the limits of what Prince herself knows. She relates that her mother and father are long dead, but Rebecca is still enslaved in Bermuda—a pointed reminder to *The History*'s readers of abolition's unfinished work. Yet by subordinating the lives of Prince's kin to the political demands of antislavery activism, Pringle's editorial intrusion aligns with the exigence of Moravian lebensläufe, which unfolds a tight biographical *telos* of a "spiritual odyssey."

By engaging with *The History*'s counter-circulations of diasporic knowledge throughout this chapter, I have tried to heed Simon Gikandi's call to resist "the hold of historicism" as a critical practice that continues to structure academic research: "If I seem to prefer working with emaciated temporal frames rather than epistemological frameworks, it is because I believe that working with a weak sense of history or with porous boundaries is one way of liberating the slave not from history but from the hold of historicism."[178] Documents like the libel case records actively distort Prince's testimonial position, and, while fashioned under less overtly hostile circumstances, even *The History* must negotiate antislavery routines of verifiability and visibility that produce modernity and its historical subjects—routines onerous for Black witnesses required to elicit sympathy. This is not to say that historical claims about Black experiences cannot be made from *The History*, but that Prince's testimony conceptualizes a plot at odds with Pringle's imperatives: she gestures toward lived experiences that may not register *as* history. Instead, *The History* summons opaque affect to underscore a captive's ability to "[perform] without end . . . in body/bodies we are finally never permitted to see," as Rachel Banner argues.[179] Reading Prince with transhistorical methods reveals how she elusively offers more than voyeuristic propaganda predicated on the spectacular violences of Black suffering, more than a spiritual narrative premised on a *telos* of atonement, more than colonial records of racial subjectivities brutally enforced by Caribbean economies.

Above all, *The History*'s geographical itinerary grounds history in extra-textual ecological conditions that encompass the massive—floods, earth-quakes, sea currents—and the granular—salt. Salt contours *The History*'s conscription within British antislavery discourses of sympathy and liberal humanism, a reminder of all the ways the enslaved were required to express their longing for freedom from within British evangelical genres. In its attention to the Turk's Island industries, moreover, *The History* charts the circulations of plantation systems encompassed by salt's fraught status as both a commodity and a symbol throughout the Atlantic world. Nevertheless, *The History*'s gestures to salt—this small plot—quietly outline glimmers of African diasporic practices of repair and redress, practices archived in impossible stories and unspoken histories. In this way, salt's barely perceptual mineral assemblages interweave to create massive geontological forms, much like Prince layers speech and silence, openness and opacity to summon a collective witness to slavery. Because of this, hers is not an easy vision of a "world given to the children of men": the earth she inhabits is not the utopic ground for civil society, as with John Locke's "in the beginning all the world was America," but rather a reminder that the material histories of African enslavement and Indigenous land theft are present within the future we inherited—within a globe warped by the *longue durée* of plantation systems. To read *The History* is to be confronted by Prince's conjuring of precarious scenes of environmental ruin and vulnerable bodies: brine harvests melting in the rain, saltwater tears, shamed bodies distended by edema, fugitive spaces devastated by flood, heavy squalls at sea—all to summon forms of life that are exceeded by and yet endure within the matter of salt.

CHAPTER THREE

With William Apess at Forest's Edge

> I then turned my eyes to the forest, and it seemed alive with its sons and daughters. There appeared to be the utmost order and regularity in their encampment. And they held all things in common.
>
> —WILLIAM APESS

> This is the world
> so vast and lonely
> without end, with mountains
> named for men
> who brought hunger
> from other lands,
> and fear
> of the thick, dark forest of trees
> that held each other up.
>
> —LINDA HOGAN

In the 1829 edition of *A Son of the Forest*, Mashantucket Pequot writer William Apess briefly describes his itinerant life along the border between the United States and Canada at the close of the War of 1812. Apess had endured appalling violence during the conflict, having enlisted underage at fifteen to flee indentured servitude, and had witnessed the Battle of Plattsburgh in September 1814.[1] His testimony also illuminates the war's colonial contexts, as imperial nations fought over and devastated Native homelands.[2] Yet in one passage, Apess turns from the scenes of death that had stirred his prior portrayal of armed conflict to describe his inhabitance with the Mississauga and Tyendinaga Mohawk on the Bay of Quinte during the winter of 1815–16: "I then turned my eyes to the forest, and it seemed alive with its sons and daughters. . . . And they held all things in common."[3] Apess does not depict the Haudenosaunee in much detail in *A Son of the Forest*, but scholars have nevertheless traced their elusive presence in the text.[4] While he likely draws on early Christian history—"They had all things in common" (Acts 4:32)—this moment embraces a brief but powerful political ecology where woodlands *sustain* and are coextensive *with* human flourishing. In this sense, the linguistic background to Apess's chapter is particularly revealing: "Tyendinaga" denotes "placing the wood together" in the Mohawk language and echoes his image of an Indigenous community that exists interdependently with a vibrant forest world.[5]

At the Bay of Quinte, Apess may have also witnessed performances of the condolence rite that bound members of the Haudenosaunee Confederacy together—rites replete with gestures to trees.[6] In one story of the ritual's origin, Ayenwathaaa (Hiawatha) is in deep mourning after the loss of his daughters, which would have resonated with Apess's experiences of the War of 1812. When Deganawidah (the Peacemaker) encounters the distressed Ayenwathaaa, he heals him through a curative ceremony that clears his mouth, eyes, and ears of old wounds, as Seneca historian Arthur C. Parker recites: "When a person is brought to death by grief he seems to lose the sight of the sun, we therefore remove the mist so that you may see the sun rising over the trees or forest in the east."[7] Members of the Haudenosaunee Confederacy commemorate this healing with an exchange of wampum and pursue peace as an enduring relationship to Skarehhehsegowah, the Great Tree—indeed, the condolence ceremony often ritually begins "at the wood's edge."[8] After healing Ayenwathaaa, Deganawidah further counsels that if discord should ever again disrupt communal well-being, someone should climb Skarehhehsegowah and "look around over the landscape and . . . see if there is any way or place to escape . . . so that our children may have a home where they may have peace."[9]

A Son of the Forest illustrates that the path of peace is inseparable from practices of commoning. Lisa Brooks (Abenaki) argues that Algonquian ceremonies exemplified as much through a phrase—"the common pot"—that reverberates across practices of diplomacy.[10] In a 1789 petition, for instance, Mohegan leaders Henry Quaquaquid and Robert Ashpo testify to colonial evasions of these relations: "They had no contention about their lands, for they lay in common; and they had but one large dish, and could all eat together in peace and love. But alas! it is not so now; all our hunting and fowling and fishing is entirely gone."[11] Elizabeth Maddock Dillon's work on commoning in the early Atlantic world suggests that Indigenous figures like Apess, Quaquaquid, and Ashpo returned to this language to perform sovereignty at the very moment enclosure movements in Britain and its colonies were rapidly accelerating.[12]

And yet Apess would remove the sentence, "And they held all things in common," from the 1831 edition of *A Son of the Forest*. Barry O'Connell proposes that Apess may have wished to soften his condemnation of Christianity in order "to distinguish . . . between corrupt missionaries and those who might preach the Gospel in its true spirit."[13] He may have also wanted to temper his critique of property-formation and resource accumulation as modes of economic development Indigenous nations were increasingly pressured to participate within.[14] While these two explanations seem imminently plausible, this chapter extends a third possibility: that Apess desired to keep these customs, and the cosmogonies they derive from, hidden, for when Indigenous knowledge is visible, it risks becoming subject to colonial exploitation and erasure. In one Algonquian origin story, for instance, trees are more than resources, but are relatives: when the spirit Cautantowwit first creates humans from stone, he is not satisfied and then makes "another man and woman of a Tree, which were the Fountains of all mankind."[15] Read as cosmogony, "all things in common" rehearses a "dissent line," in Ngāti Awa/Ngāti Porou scholar Linda Tuhiwai Smith's words, a storied ancestry that roots bodies and bodies of knowledge in shared forest existence.[16] If woodlands constitute an "unspoken, enframing presence" for Apess's writings, as Mark Rifkin puts it, then "all things in common" also re-signifies practices of commoning away from European and American contexts and toward Indigenous emergence stories of coextensive sovereignty.[17] "All things in common" is more than a scriptural citation: it is a decolonial script—a small plot—that restores reciprocal relations between all woodland dwellers.[18]

The removal of "all things in common" thus resonates with tensions that would preoccupy Apess throughout his career: how to tell stories of Indigenous peoples and places when the onto-epistemic structures of modernity are premised on their political and imaginative erasure.[19] To bring Apess's decolonial scripts into relief in this chapter, I draw from *edge ecologies*—clearings cultivated through controlled burns—as a material analytic and palimpsestic figuration of commoning.[20] Broadly, Indigenous peoples used periodic fires to clear tangled undergrowth and return nutrients to the soil, creating an ecotone or "edge effect" that enabled a variety of plant and animal species to thrive, while facilitating hunting and trade routes.[21] Yet settlers often "unwitnessed," in Drew Lopenzina's words, these routines and interpreted woodland biodiversity as a flourishing "natural" to the Americas, which they were eager to extract through intensive farming, deforestation, and commercial hunting.[22] If few settlers recognized controlled burns *as* a valid cultivation practice, Roger Williams was nearly alone in arguing that these methods constituted "improvements" in a Lockean sense and protected Indigenous land title: "For the expedition of their hunting voyages, they burnt up all the underwoods in the Countrey."[23] Read in light of Indigenous subsistence practices and forest management, Apess's gesture to a woodland commons may reflect living memory of edge ecologies as zones of cultivated extension rather than discrete boundaries between Indigenous communities or their nonhuman relatives.

Put simply, Apess's writings survey what I am calling an *edge work*—a mode of figuration, a recuperative historiography, an epistemological throughline—that repudiates settler boundary-making, as well as modes of property-formation that accompanied enclosure. Throughout this chapter, I consider how edges mark an extralegal prerogative of boundary-making for the settler nation, but for Apess, edges refigure a mode of historical testimony that recovers scenes of Indigenous refusal to the extractive imposition of borders. These colonial borders take many iterations: in divisions between white and nonwhite skin color in racialized taxonomies, in separations of human and nonhuman cosmological kinships, and in impositions to Indigenous national borders and sovereignty.[24] While "all things in common" might appear always subject to erasure, the phrase counters the structural recursivity of dispossession, then, as Robert Nichols describes, where decolonial critiques of settler land theft can risk reifying Indigenous lands *as* property—where naming a colonial event "theft" implies proprietary interest. Because of this, he suggests that "the original proprietary interest" in Indigenous lands is sometimes "only visible after [it has] been lost."[25] Although Nichols primarily reads Apess as an "accommodationist" who develops an "immanent" critique of dispossession from within Methodist discourses—"all things in common" from the New Testament—I argue that his forest sensibility is closely, if sometimes subtly, embedded in Algonquian cosmogonies and customs that are partially hidden.[26] While we cannot always "know" Apess's forest commons overtly, we may nevertheless glimpse Indigenous relations with plant worlds as "they whisper quietly" from the edge of our sight, as Robyn Maynard and Leanne Betasamosake Simpson (Michi Saagiig) attest.[27] The cosmogony encoded by "all things in common" therefore refuses, as Audra Simpson (Mohawk) puts it, "to *let go of this knowledge*"—to let go of the cultivation of edges as a praxis for political life.[28]

Yet Apess's invocation of commons illustrates the formal challenges of representing Indigenous forest worlds to nineteenth-century publics when prevailing ecological rhetorics were rooted in teleologies of Manifest Destiny and Indigenous vanishing, which set into motion extractive economies leading to global warming today.[29] Across his writings, Apess's insistence that colonial expansion imperils not only Mashantucket Pequot peoples but also global communities of color renders him an early witness *to* and critic *of* these logics—indeed, as I explore in this chapter, renders him a theorist of racial capitalism and climate change *avant la lettre*.[30] In his citations of commons, Apess makes property-formation and land theft legible *as* racialized ways of being and knowing the world, anticipating Kathryn Yusoff's point that "coloniality cuts across both flesh and earth in the economies of valuation it established."[31] More specifically, Apess's writings often turn to intertwined images—branches and limbs, forests and flesh—to make visible how settler colonialism uproots Indigenous connections to homelands and grafts non-white populations onto the extractive economies of racial capitalism.[32] Apess's allusions to forest cosmologies as a ground for material and political life thereby reverberate with Tanana Athabascan scholar Dian Million's call to foreground Native "embodied ecologies," which reject a "settler imperative of emptying sacred places of Indigenous relations."[33] I read Apess, then, as a writer whose edge work—where commons illuminate an ongoing relation between human and nonhuman lives—opens new avenues for critiquing settler colonialism as *not* past but an onto-epistemic regime we now inhabit.[34]

In what follows, I trace Apess's meditations on climate and land-based knowledge in his four major texts—*A Son of the Forest* (1829/31), *An Indian's Looking-Glass for the White Man* (1833), *Indian Nullification of the Unconstitutional Laws of Massachusetts* (1835), and *A Eulogy on King Philip* (1836)—in order to show how he mobilizes multiracial and multispecies relations, where edges mark dense environmental *relations* rather than discrete *boundaries*.[35] By reading Apess this way, my intent is not to counter frameworks in Indigenous studies that center tribal–national knowledge but to attend to his solidarities with Mashantucket Pequot and Wampanoag Mashpee communities, with Native nations subject to displacement, and with antislavery politics.[36] For Apess, to live on the edge is not only to testify to uncertain existences under settler occupation, but also to cultivate Indigenous and interspecies intimacies as extant possibilities for a world held in common against ongoing acts of planetary dispossession.[37]

"The forest was alive with its sons and daughters"

In August 1635, a devastating hurricane swept along the coasts of Connecticut and Massachusetts, cleaving roofs from homes, uprooting trees, and flooding roads with its twenty-foot storm surge.[38] The tempest, moreover, ravaged Algonquian villages and fields, already under stress in the face of swelling English settlement at the onset of the Great Migration in 1630.[39] At Narragansett, at least eight men drowned while struggling to climb trees to escape from fourteen-foot flood waters.[40] In its cumulative effects, the storm exacerbated ongoing food insecurity, as unusually cold winters caused widespread challenges.[41] According to Katherine Grandjean, the hurricane illustrates how seemingly "chance" weather events—understood by settlers as providential—placed Indigenous communities at risk when colonial expansionist policies, accompanied by war, epidemic, and food insecurity, intensified Indigenous precarity.[42] Indeed, William Bradford testified to the ruins left in the storm's wake and prophesied longstanding effects: "Signes and marks of it will remaine this 100 years."[43] His words register an orientation to deep time, where ecological events leave impressions on the landscapes, even while he evades settler violences. At the same time, colonists interpreted extreme weather events or epidemics as manifestations of divine design, as John Winthrop muses: "If God were not pleased with our inheriting these parts, why did he drive out the natives before us? And why does he still make room for us, by diminishing them as we increase?"[44] The Great Hurricane intersects with critical debates on how to account for the political and environmental ruin of Indigenous places, then and now.

While the Anthropocene is often depicted in popular media as an imminent future yet to arrive, climate change's effects manifest at multiple scales and temporalities, what Rob Nixon defines as a "slow violence" that requires its witnesses to reimagine narrative forms to reckon with its myriad unfoldings.[45] For Indigenous nations, cataclysmic ruin to ecosystems has, in many cases, *already happened*. Anishinaabe scholar Kyle Powys Whyte contends that contemporary climate fiction often frames global warming through dystopian aesthetics that evade colonial complicity in disrupting Native ecologies: "Indigenous peoples challenge linear narratives of dreadful futures of climate destabilization with their own accounts of history that highlight the reality of constant change and emphasize colonialism's role in environmental change."[46] In tracing these ruptures, activists and critics have been turning to Native knowledge systems to reconceive environmental practices pursued between Indigenous and English settlements and their interventions on hemispheric ecosystems.[47] Read within these contexts, *A Son of the Forest* is more than a conversion narrative, prepared as part of Apess's ordination in the Protestant Methodist church, but an oblique meditation on Indigenous place-based knowledge. David J. Carlson reminds us that the spiritual autobiography requires "a critical inward turning that allowed limited opportunity for social criticism."[48] I argue that although *A Son of the Forest* takes up Apess's inner life, the text moves beyond a *telos* of spiritual transformation to portray vibrant glimmers of forest worlds. These are often brief scenes—a forest glen where Apess picks berries, a Haudenosaunee lake where he seeks healing after the War of 1812, a woodland clearing where Sally George preaches to Native congregants—but each site offers rich affordances for tracing Apess's orientations to Pequot embodied ecologies.

As Apess knew well, Pequot history grimly exemplified the violences of colonial genocide and ecological upheaval. By the 1630s, English settlers seemed possessed of an insatiable land hunger, while the region experienced rising precarities exacerbated by seventeenth-century global cooling, which increased the need to heat homes during unusually icy winters and contributed to the region's deforestation.[49] Intricate coastal ecosystems were also changing as free roaming livestock caused havoc, and English residents allowed their domestic animals to wander freely, where they trampled Indigenous fields.[50] Virginia DeJohn Anderson argues that while settlers occasionally offered restitution for destroyed crops, more often they condemned Native cultivators for not fencing their fields and used grazing to underline English claims to the land: "Colonists in effect appropriated Indian common lands to serve as their own commons."[51] Allan Greer further contends that British livestock engaged in a "multispecies assault" that accompanied colonial expansion, an ironic process of "dispossession-by-commons." Thus, while we typically imagine colonial land theft through property-formation, English animal husbandry practices contributed by destroying Indigenous agricultural fields, hunting paths, and foraging and gathering sites.[52] By contrast, Apess's interspecies idiom in *A Son of the Forest* gestures, if sometimes obliquely, to reciprocal partnerships with woodland animals and plant life.

Everyday colonial processes of dispossession erupted into open conflict in July 1635 in a struggle now known as the Pequot War—ostensibly over the murder of English trader John Oldham, who was an important figure in ferrying necessary provisions in seasons of scarcity, but also in response to long-standing settler incursions on Native territories.[53] In the war's most notorious incident, English soldiers set fire to the largest Pequot settlement on the Mystic River in May 1637, killing hundreds, including women and children. In the aftermath, settlers dispersed Pequot survivors to other Algonquian villages or transported them into slavery in Barbados and Bermuda, where they were coerced to labor on cotton and coffee, as well as nascent sugar, plantations.[54] For Pequots who remained, future reprisals of destruction and enslavement remained an ongoing worry. In September 1650, several Pequots came to John Winthrop Jr. over rumors that "some of the English threten to send them away to the Sugar Country, and that they shall not live no where in the Pequot Country."[55] Their agony over the specter of forced removal from "Pequot Country" powerfully contests English efforts to erase their people from living memory. John Mason, one of the leading perpetrators of the massacre at Mystic, pledged "to root their very name out of this Country . . . dunging the Ground with their Flesh," gruesomely rendering Pequot bodily remains as fertilizer in lands devastated by the intersecting catastrophes of war and weather.[56] The Treaty of Hartford, which concluded the conflict, was more explicit: "The Pequots were then bound by COVENANT, That none should inhabit their native Country, nor should any of them be called PEQUOTS any more."[57] In spite of the treaty, the Pequot nation endured, and Apess's writings bear witness to their resilience.

Born in Colrain, Massachusetts to William and Candace Apes, Apess's life was molded by historical conditions of land theft and enslavement that shaped the difficult labor of survival in Mashantucket Pequot country.[58] By the end of the eighteenth century, poor men like Apess's father were clearcutting forests for meager farms in the rocky hills that surrounded Colrain.[59] Candace's legal position posed an added vulnerability, as she was of Indigenous and African ancestry and enslaved. She would not be manumitted until 1805, when Apess was seven years old.[60] William and Candace's marriage was shaped by their desire to find a space where their children's freedom could be assured, and they continually moved across Connecticut and Massachusetts, whose legal codes differently regulated slavery and indentured servitude. William and Candace may have also attempted to reach Brothertown in New York, but the Brothertowners could offer no real safety, as they denied citizenship to residents of African descent in a vexed effort to protect sovereignty when settlers used any excuse to negate Indigenous land title.[61] With a partnership strained by poverty and slavery, William and Candace separated when Apess was a young child, leaving him and his siblings with their maternal grandparents.[62]

Apess's early life with his grandparents was punctuated by appalling abuse, but he stressed that settler brutality produced these bleak domestic conditions. In one of the most harrowing incidents he describes, his grandmother beat him until his arm broke "in three different places," all while asking him, "Do you hate me?"[63] Although Apess never fully absolves his grandmother, he argues that this experience was structurally shaped by colonialism: "But this cruel and unnatural conduct was the effect of some cause. I attribute it in a great measure to the whites, inasmuch as they introduced among my countrymen that bane of comfort and happiness, ardent spirits—seduced them into a love of it and, when under its unhappy influence, wronged them out of their lawful possessions—that land, where reposed the ashes of their sires."[64] Here, he characterizes alcohol as an instrument of occupation, one that "seduces" Indigenous peoples from generational attachments to their homelands and ancestors.[65] Even this early in *A Son of the Forest*, Apess transgresses the conventions of a conversion narrative's *telos*: he attributes guilt not to an individual sinner but to systemic regimes of settler violence. After white neighbors removed Apess from his grandparents' care, he was indentured by three Connecticut families (Furman, Williams, Hillhouse). All three profited from the expropriation of Indigenous lands, including William Hillhouse, the chief justice of the New London County Court and the great-grandson of John Mason.[66] The family of William Williams, moreover, stole and occupied over eighty acres of Mashantucket land, with Williams serving as overseer of the reservation until 1813, which led to the halving of the territory by the middle of the eighteenth century. The Pequot—including Apess's aunt, Sally George—strenuously advocated for Williams's replacement in the years that followed, but he only resigned the position in 1819. Apess would certainly have been aware of these struggles when writing *A Son of the Forest* less than ten years later.[67]

In *A Son of the Forest*, then, Apess's task is to portray his recovery of Pequot identity within the conversion narrative's constraints, an aporia intensified by growing up in a culture suffused with anti-Indigenous sentiments and by his legal subjugation as an indentured servant, which he believes is akin to slavery.[68] Mr. Furman, for instance, often beats Apess while calling him "you Indian dog," a racial epithet painfully proximate to Apess's tender affection for a real dog.[69] When Furman sells Apess's indenture to Hillhouse, Apess consents (believing he *can* consent) to join the household "on condition that I should take my dog with me."[70] Joshua Bennett argues that African American texts often unsettle "the dog as an example par excellence of *being-for-the-master*," and Apess's dog gestures toward a similar Indigenous inscription within a mode of servitude: "I had been *sold* to the judge."[71] While Apess expresses a creaturely communion that is resolutely predicated not on possession but rather on consensual coexistence, *A Son of the Forest* is silent on if he was separated from his dog, as he was from his Pequot relatives.

Everyday threats of racial violence inflect Apess's sense of disaffiliation, where anti-Native sentiment suffuses a punitive settler culture: "So completely was I weaned from the interests and affections of my brethren that a mere threat of being sent away among the Indians into the dreary woods had a much better effect in making me obedient to the commands of my superiors than any corporal punishment."[72] Acculturated to fear his "brethren of the forest," Apess describes a tense encounter with what he believes are Indigenous women gathering berries in the woods:

> One day several of the family went into the woods to gather berries, taking me with them. We had not been out long before we fell in with a company of white females, on the same errand—their complexion was, to say the least, as *dark* as that of the natives. This circumstance filled my mind with terror, and I broke from the party with my utmost speed, and I could not muster courage enough to look behind until I had reached home. By this time my imagination had pictured out a tale of blood.[73]

The "tale of blood" has principally been read by scholars as an instance of deracination that Apess struggles to think and feel beyond.[74] This psychic condition compels people of color to identify either with the prerogatives of whiteness or with dark skin as abnegation, as Frantz Fanon argues, where Apess has seemingly so internalized racial paradigms that he misrecognizes white women in the forest—and fears them greatly.[75] To this point, I add that the woodland encounter also illustrates Apess's palpable ecological estrangement, an affective disposition to forests that renders them a perilous landscape almost wholly unintelligible to him—"the dreary woods." That this scene in the forest concerns berry picking is also not incidental, given that many berry species required periodic fire (controlled through slash-and-burn practices) to bloom.[76] That the gatherers are perhaps benefiting from the continuing effects of Algonquian cultivation routines may bear witness to an edge ecology, but if it does, it is one Apess cannot read because the only tales of Indigeneity available to him are distorted by settler brutality.

Because this scene gestures to settler ideologies of race and the environment, I believe that Apess anticipates Jennifer Fay's point about climate change's assumed teleologies in popular discourses: present conditions of capitalist exhaustion and its attendant anticipatory fears of disaster coalesce in the specter of a future "inhospitable world" at the Anthropocene's end.[77] Yet Apess locates this threat of an "inhospitable world" as a present exigence for Indigenous peoples, who are separated from rich entanglements of human and nonhuman relation and from their traditional woodland routines. In this sense, Apess presses on settler teleologies of Indigenous vanishing that often end either in physical removal and genocide or in Christian conversion and cultural assimilation (which is, itself, a form of disappearance: "Save the man, kill the Indian," as Richard H. Pratt, founder of the Carlisle Indian Industrial School, infamously put it later in the nineteenth century).[78] Apess's writings delineate how American teleologies of continental expansion require Indigenous people to create what Anna Lowenhaupt Tsing names "refugia," or sites where ecologies and the peoples who inhabit them improvise worlds that exceed the enclosures of imperial and industrial projects.[79]

Apess's itinerancies after the War of 1812 introduced him to just such an Indigenous refugia, when his "brethren were all around [him]" in Haudenosaunee territory—where "brethren" could signify both multitribal solidarities and nonhuman relatives, as well as a healing of his separation from home. Indeed, Mohawk waterways and woodlands shape Apess's developing vocabulary of animate matter—of a "forest alive with its sons and daughters." He offers, for instance, a tender description of the Lake of the Mountain, which overlooks Lake Ontario one hundred feet below, and, without any apparent sources, appears bottomless and miraculously sustained: "On the very top of a high mountain in the neighborhood there was a large pond of water, to which there was no visible outlet—this pond was unfathomable."[80] Here, Apess draws from Mohawk geographies in his challenges to settler presumptions of sovereignty over all Indigenous territories.[81] Within Haudenosaunee stories, this "great body of water" is more than a praxis for political dissent but a setting in the Peacemaker's journeys and thus a resonant site for the condolence ceremony that binds the Confederacy together.[82] Read this way, Apess's inhabitance with the Haudenosaunee, as well as his encounters with their cosmogonies and ceremonies, enable him to acknowledge what Lisa Brooks calls an "obligatory reciprocity to the forest that gave him birth and to its sons and daughters, whom he now fully recognize[s] as his relations."[83] That is, Mohawk lakes and forests summon material and metaphoric possibilities for Apess to revise the conversion narrative's *telos* to reflect his recovery of Indigenous kinships, human and otherwise.

Once Apess returns to Connecticut after the War of 1812, he carries this woodland sensibility to his orientation to place. In Connecticut, he lives with his aunt, Sally George, a Pequot medicine woman and lay preacher who possessed deep knowledge of the region's ecosystems. Apess describes this period in his life as a flourishing of his own desire to preach, animated by George's approach to worship: "These seasons were glorious. We observed particular forms, although we knew nothing about the dead languages, except that the knowledge thereof was not necessary for us to serve God. We had no house of divine worship, and believ[ed] 'that the groves were God's first temples.'"[84] Indeed, George may have preached in the Pequot language, suggesting a level of irony in Apess calling Indigenous dialects "dead."[85] Lurking beneath the irony, however, his representation of forest communion flickers with the survivance of Mashantucket Pequot cosmogonies as another kind of edge work. Apess's movement into woodland clearings delineates his reconnections not only with human and forest kin, but also with himself as a member of the Pequot community, relations ruptured by displacement, war, and servitude. In this sense, A Son of the Forest extends what Donna Haraway names the "thick, ongoing presence" of a form of life that "requires learning to be truly present, not as a vanishing pivot between awful or edenic pasts or apocalyptic or salvific futures" but as human and nonhuman kin in "myriad unfinished configurations of places, times, matters, meanings."[86] Even in brief passages, A Son of the Forest depicts Apess's recuperation of dense partnerships—dogs, berries, lakes, forests—as "unfinished configurations" of shared being and belonging.

Histories Made Flesh

Because Indigenous relational cosmogonies center people and place as historically and materially connected, for Apess the figure of settler exceptionalism is often located in flesh and forest as conjoined sites where white property violently emerges.[87] To extend this point, here I consider how Apess depicts embodied and ecological relations in his sermon, An Indian's Looking-Glass for the White Man, which turns to the rhetorical trope of the mirror to reflect and refract racial hierarchies. An Indian's Looking-Glass builds on nascent themes developed in A Son of the Forest, where Apess's edge work—as political praxis and narrative form—subverts settler presumptions of racial superiority exemplified in a telos of national expansion and Christian atonement. A Son of the Forest, for instance, early holds up a mirror to colonial exercises of theft and war: "But let the thing be changed. Suppose an overwhelming army should march into the United States for the purpose of subduing it and enslaving the citizens; how quick would they fly to arms, gather in multitudes around the tree of liberty, and contend for their rights. . . . And who would blame them for it?"[88] Given Apess's experiences during the War of 1812—"I could not think why I should risk my life and limbs in fighting for the white man, who had cheated my forefathers out of their land"—his use of "let the thing be changed" rhetorically reflects scenes of military and economic exploitation that contoured nineteenth-century Indigenous histories.[89]

An Indian's Looking-Glass further gestures to Mashantucket Pequot survivance elliptically reported in *A Son of the Forest*, where Apess at one point portrays his homecoming to his *"first love"*—"I went then to my native tribe, where meetings were still kept up."[90] Jack Campisi argues that these meetings were significant cultural and political gatherings: "Available evidence indicates that tribal members maintained a council house, met frequently on tribal business, and took an active part in community affairs."[91] Apess appended *An Indian's Looking-Glass* to *The Experiences of Five Christian Indians of the Pequot Tribe* (1833), a collection of spiritual biographies for four Pequot women, including Apess's wife, Mary Wood, and his aunt Sally George, who would have been participants or matriarchs within the seven extended clans who attended these meetings. Although the print history of *An Indian's Looking-Glass* suggests its importance as a revision to the genre of the conversion narrative, it also, as the title implies, holds up a mirror to a semiotics of skin color, what Fanon would later call a "racial epidermal schema."[92] *An Indian's Looking-Glass* therefore intersects with Indigenous scholarship on refusing the paradigms of settler recognition, which interpellate Native nations within colonial definitions of racialized blood quantum and citizenship.[93]

As a challenge to settler taxonomies of skin color, Apess's mirror refracts the racialized modes of address that whiteness hails into being, which he repudiates for solidarity with global people of color.[94] Skin trembles as both sign and substance of racialized violence in *An Indian's Looking-Glass*, perhaps most famously in the following passage, where Apess trenchantly illuminates racial hierarchies deliberately cultivated under global imperialism. To that end, Apess begins with an urgent call to "assemble all nations together in [the] imagination":

> [S]uppose these skins were put together, and each skin had its national crimes written upon it—which skin do you think would have the greatest? . . . Can you charge the Indians with robbing a nation almost of their whole continent, and murdering their women and children, and then depriving the remainder of their lawful rights, that nature and God require them to have? And to cap the climax, rob another nation to till their grounds and welter out their days under the lash with hunger and fatigue under the scorching rays of a burning

sun? I should look at all the skins, and I know that when I cast my eye upon the white skin, and if I saw those crimes written upon it, I should enter my protest against it immediately.[95]

Here, skin is the border settlers use to sever historical Indigenous relations to peoples and places, but in response, Apess rereads that boundary—that edge—as a place where white colonists are marked by and with their own violence. What Apess describes is, in essence, a skin book—an epidermal archive—that refuses an array of cultural discourses denoting whiteness as an unmarked sign of "civilization." Legislative policies materialized these discourses during the era of Indigenous removal (1828–39), when Andrew Jackson opened his administration with laws designed to displace Muscogee, Cherokee, Chickasaw, Choctaw, and Seminole nations from their homelands, while local white mobs and land speculators persistently harassed Native families—a coordination of legal and extralegal violence. Although the Constitution located the regulation of Native sovereignty with the federal government, Chief Justice John Marshall in *Georgia v. Cherokee* (1831) redefined Indigenous communities as "domestic dependent nations" in need of paternalistic guardianship.[96] Southern states capitalized on these decisions to displace Native nations and further develop plantation agriculture—sites of enslavement and the source for paper (made from cotton rags) in the early nineteenth century.[97] In the face of the numerous thefts, Apess speculates on histories occluded by settler exceptionalism and urges a perspectival shift in favor of what people of color *see*—the "skin-deep" prejudices of white people." John Kucich argues this shift enables Apess to configure "an embodied archive . . . of histories entrenched in flesh," to produce "an alternative kind of evidence."[98] Building on this point, I argue that while Apess's skin books write another history into legibility, his command, "let *us look* for the whites," is also a collective judicial decision, affording a global history from below (or outside) the law at a moment when many enslaved or nonwhite persons faced restrictions or outright prohibitions on their court testimony.[99] In this, his witness resonates with contemporary literary accounts of removal. Aiden Wildfire, an Irish Seminole character in Andrea Hairston's novel *Redwood and Wildfire* (2011), evocatively critiques these legal and extralegal events: "For gold in the mountains, for cotton and corn in the fields. They stole the sunrise and the distant sea breeze. They tore the people from the place of their ancestors, leaving spirits to roam and no one to take heed."[100]

As a generational survivor of the Pequot massacres and the son of an enslaved mother, Apess understands what it means for settlers to disregard brutality committed on communities of color, including "robbing a nation almost of their whole continent, and murdering their women and children, and then depriving the remainder of their lawful rights."[101] Apess's portrayal of white skin as an archive of colonial violence revises tropes in some dominant traditions of white abolitionist activism, where Black figures were often required to display scars as evidence of slavery's atrocities.[102] William Grimes, for instance, inverts this requirement by proposing: "If it were not for the stripes on my back which were made while I was a slave, I would in my will, leave my skin a legacy to the government, desiring that it might be taken off and made into parchment, and then bind the Constitution of glorious happy *and free* Americans."[103] In an incisive reading of Grimes, Lindon Barrett argues: "There is no better parchment, Grimes seems to say, than the lacerated skin of an American slave to gird the nation's prized but hyperbolically false self-declaration and self-knowledge."[104] Contra this hyperbolic self-declaration, Apess and Grimes summon *white* skin as evidence of settler atrocity, a perspective at odds with American nationalist discourses that overdetermine Black and Indigenous peoples as the "ghostly matter" that haunts sovereignty, as Avery Gordon puts it.[105] Instead, skin reflects a raw edge of vulnerability through which settler violence is materially and discursively embodied. In this way, *An Indian's Looking-Glass* shows how discourses of Black and Brown skin emerge from within the plantation's crucibles of fungibility and accumulation, where flesh signifies the wounding through which the body is constituted in Black studies and a site of ruptured relations to land and kin in Indigenous studies.[106] To read *white* skin clearly is to refuse American "national crimes" in favor of reconnecting with colonized peoples and places across the globe. Apess thus gathers a critical archive where Black and Indigenous histories *matter* again.

As a revisionist theology, the sermon moves from legal and political histories to the racial disaffiliations that suffuse everyday life, encapsulated in Apess's question, "What is love, or its effects?"[107] In line with other chapters in this book, here I consider love in the context of settler regulations of intimacy, which tend to imbricate racial hierarchy within rhetorics of Christian civilization. Apess deliberately counters these moves by retrieving Christ from white supremacist theology: "Jesus Christ being a Jew, and those of his Apostles certainly were not whites—and did not he who completed the plan of salvation complete it for the whites as well as for the Jews, and others?"[108] By emphasizing Christ's brownness, Apess reverses a dominant theological schema that understood dark skin as a sign of divine punishment—the "curse of Ham"—and was used to justify slavery and settler expansion.[109] Yet *An Indian's Looking-Glass* appeals to a decolonial incarnational theology—God made brown—that opens a new horizon of ethical regard, extending what Hannah Arendt would later call "the great and incalculable grace of love, which says with Augustine '*Volo ut sisi*' (I want you to be)."[110] Against settler recognition as an originary site of ethical regard, which hinges on whiteness, Apess envisions Indigenous skin impressed with Christ's brownness: "Now let me ask you, white man, if it is a disgrace for to eat, drink, and sleep with the image of God, or sit, or walk and talk with them. Or have you the folly to think that the white man, being one in fifteen or sixteen, are the only beloved images of God?"[111] Where, in other words, can love arise when there is (and has been) no regard, when no one says, "I want you to be"? Here, Apess's vernacular theology—which lingers with eating, sleeping, and all quotidian actions needed to sustain life—grapples with what happens when a "settler common sense," as Rifkin puts it, is taken as self-evident, when colonial Christian notions of subjectivity and intimacy are dominant and become internalized.[112] Settler discourses frequently condemn Indigenous peoples to vanish and separate their nations from the bounds of sovereignty, while also coercing people of color to live within its intimate logics, which, when turned inward, collapse into self-hatred. A mirror to Apess's "What is love, or its effects?" is the question his grandmother once so painfully asked, "Do you hate me?" *An Indian's Looking-Glass* asks if love can arise in resurgent practices of Indigenous self-regard, a perspective that echoes the agonized question Samson Occom posed near the end of the *Sermon on the Execution of Moses Paul* (1772): "If we don't regard ourselves, who will regard us?"[113]

To further probe these questions, near the sermon's end Apess isolates prejudice against interracial marriage and preachers of color as indexes for interpersonal and psychic conditions of settler violence.[114] Indeed, he writes from his position as a biracial figure intimately experienced with servitude, as well as a witness to his mother's enslavement, and from a historical moment when a mob burned effigies of Cherokee leader Elias Boudinot and his white wife, Harriet R. Gold, in 1826 over their interracial alliance. He speaks from within a political context where Indigenous kinships and multiracial solidarities measure the edges between legal and extralegal violences: "I ask if a marriage or a funeral ceremony or the ordinance of the Lord's house would not be as acceptable in the sight of God as though he was white."[115] Apess's critique illustrates how "a possessive logic of white patriarchal sovereignty," as Aileen Moreton-Robinson (Dandrubin Goenpul of the Quandamooka

Nation) puts it, subtends these violences, which are at work in some fashion in all colonized territories.[116] Apess's refusal of this logic, moreover, radiates to challenge the planetary reach of colonialism, with the sermon showing how conflicts over the meaning(s) of skin mediate and diffuse imperial affects across time and space. While Apess argues that global communities of color outnumber the earth's white residents, he is also concerned with more than merely invoking numeric plenitude when he turns to planetary populations and their resistant intimacies. Instead, Apess contends that when people of color regard each other as "beloved . . . of God," then it might be possible to approach what Fanon calls "true authentic love—wishing for another what one postulates for oneself, when that postulation unites the permanent values of human reality."[117] *An Indian's Looking-Glass* meditates on flesh to consider how everyday existence under settler governance compels global Indigenous peoples to assemble socialities on the edge: to cultivate a love that can, against all odds, survive colonial aggression.

Although love, as Richard Iton suggests, can be "a significant political act, particularly among those stigmatized and marked as unworthy of love," I also recognize that turning to love as an anticolonial exercise is a move that can too swiftly move past brutal suppressions of Indigenous relations, while sentimentalizing traditions of care work.[118] Even Apess hints at the hazards of loving in the ruins when he pleads for his congregation to endure at the sermon's close: "Do not get tired, ye noble-hearted—only think how many poor Indians want their wounds done up daily . . . [I] pray you stop not till this tree of distinction shall be leveled to the earth."[119] Here, he summons one of his only negative figurations of forests, where the "tree of distinction" signifies embodied and ecological hierarchies that oppose the curative work of Skarehhehsegowah, the Haudenosaunee Great Tree.[120] Can we, then, recover a sense for how Apess practices "communitism," in Cherokee scholar Jace Weaver's words, or a "proactive commitment" to "healing . . . the grief and sense of exile felt by Native communities" by reimagining love as a recuperation of flesh?[121] Can his skin books afford an "indigenous reading" praxis, what Chumash and Esselen critic Deborah Miranda calls a mode of interpretation that does not turn exclusively to idioms of unrelenting tragedy to describe colonialism, but rather "[enriches] Native lives with meaning, survival, and love"?[122] If so, then as figurations for alternative practices of intimacy, Apess's skin books document the difficult stakes of endurance under regimes of racialized terror—"national crimes" written on white skin—but perhaps also archive possibilities for living *otherwise*.

"Freeborn Sons of the Forest"

Throughout this chapter, I have been improvising a critical methodology to show how Apess retrieves Indigenous commoning routines as an historical ethos that derives from his memories *of* and participation *in* Algonquian and Haudenosaunee customs, even while recognizing that these moments sometimes only flicker on the edge of a page—a sense of history, revealed and occluded, that I have been calling Apess's edge-work. By reading this way, we may be able to trace how Apess's writings subtly cultivate what Keith Basso calls a "place-world" or "a means of exploring not merely how things might have been but also how, just possibly, they might have been different from what others have supposed," by "reviving and revising" former traditions.[123] Understood this way, his descriptions of the Lake of the Mountain and Haudenosaunee woodlands in *A Son of the Forest* revive place-worlds *as* commons.

Broadly, commons balance vernacular customs for collective land usage with political values of access and exclusion—or the ability of local coalitions to determine subsistence practices against outside influence.[124] These protocols have rarely been prominent in surveys of American literature, which Dana Nelson argues have overdetermined the emergence of a liberal democratic politics serving both a territorially expanding federal unity and an ideal of propertied citizenship. This critical aporia results in a familiar narrative of self-making, a *telos* proleptically read onto early American literature that occludes performances of commoning that may have been extant.[125] In addition, literary and historical criticism often schematizes English settlement as always organized through property and Indigenous tenure through commons, which evades complex negotiations of land usage in the early modern period.[126] These insights illuminate how Apess's approach to commoning in *A Son of the Forest* mediates not only struggles over historically contested practices of land ownership and resource use, but also revisionary possibilities for plural sovereignty toward which Indigenous woodlands implicitly gesture. Moreover, Apess's focus on the material imbrication of racial hierarchy within a *nomos* of settler expansion in *An Indian's Looking-Glass* reflects waves of displacement, which contoured an emergent global modernity coextensive with economic extraction on Native lands and anthropogenic climate change.

Apess's *Indian Nullification of the Unconstitutional Laws of Massachusetts* (1835) extends these emphases to reveal palimpsestic improvisations of Indigenous land usage under shifting conditions of expropriation in the 1830s. These crises, by the very nature of their systemic force, often require narrative frames that exceed generic boundaries, meaning the text itself is a collage, juxtaposing multiple records to represent the political and environmental exigencies circumscribing Mashpee survivance.[127] While Apess first publicized the Mashpee struggle in a series of sermons and in communally written formal documents, including petitions to the Massachusetts legislature and governor, *Indian Nullification* includes articles about the conflict (positive and otherwise) that appeared in local newspapers.[128] Hannah Manshel argues that *Indian Nullification* is thus a "formally experimental" text whose purpose is to "nullify" settler title to Mashpee lands: "Nullification is a more profound undoing of law than a mere refusal to follow it . . . [but] abolishes the very conditions that allow such laws to exist: in this case, the property form."[129] Nullification, of course, carried intense political freight, as South Carolina's resistance to federal tariffs and slavery legislation nearly led to war during the Nullification Crisis (1832–33). Building on Manshel, I want to consider how Apess's recourse to a language for commoning affords a conceptual frame for *living* Indigenous sovereignty in a moment of acute political crisis.

Indian Nullification begins by laying out the centuries of colonial exploitation of Wampanoag Mashpee lands. In 1763, the British crown categorized Mashpee land as a "plantation" under the governance of Massachusetts Bay. Although Mashpee inhabitants still had the right to elect local officials, their authority was heavily circumscribed. After the American Revolution, a 1788 state treaty revoked the nation's self-governance and appointed five white stewards to administer the reservation. In the following decades, these stewards rented land to white residents, expropriated timber and other resources, and occupied civic positions (teacher, pastor) without seeing to Mashpee needs.[130] Moreover, Harvard College had the authority to assign a minister for the community—here, Phineas Fish—but Fish angered Mashpee residents by primarily serving white families in the area.[131] Aware of these histories, Apess first preaches at the local chapel, a "sacred edifice" built in 1684 in the Wampanoag Mashpee "noble forest," knowing that his congregation would be primarily white: "Look to what quarter I would, most of those who were coming were pale faces, and, in my disappointment, it seemed to me that the hue of death sat upon their countenances."[132] Early in *Indian Nullification*, then, Apess associates whiteness with mortality—"the hue of death"—embodied by white congregants who "[steal] from the Indians their portion in the Gospel."[133]

More specifically, in his challenge to settler property-formation, Apess occupies what Kevin Bruyneel terms a "third space of sovereignty," a site where Native jurisdictions undermine American presumptions of authority over state borders: Indigenous sovereignty, like the blurred boundaries of edge ecologies, is a "supplemental space, inassimilable to the institutions and discourses of the modern liberal democratic settler-state."[134] While Bruyneel principally traces Indigenous sovereignty struggles after the Civil War, *Indian Nullification* surveys an earlier site of activism, when the Wampanoag Mashpee demarcate a form of governance inassimilable to the settler nation. Throughout this conflict, Apess grounds Mashpee sovereignty and relationship to ancestral lands in a divinely gifted earth—"God has given to all men an equal right to possess and occupy the earth"—where a planet held in common authorizes a politics of the commons.[135] Although Apess draws occasionally from the language of nineteenth-century US treaty rights, *Indian Nullification* roots Mashpee sovereignty in longstanding political rites and subsistence routines, which "treated all the plantation as lands owned in common."[136] Here, Apess's political vernacular echoes nineteenth-century Indigenous texts that challenge a settler *nomos* of sovereignty *as* property, including *The Life of Black Hawk* (1833), where Sauk leader Black Hawk asserts: "My reason teaches me that *land cannot be sold*. The Great Spirit gave it to his children to live upon, and cultivate, as far as is necessary for their subsistence; and so long as they occupy and cultivate it, they have the right to the soil."[137]

In the summer of 1833, Apess and Mashpee citizens took this anticolonial rhetoric to their drafting of documents for self-governance, namely a Constitution "suited to the spirit and capacity of freeborn sons of the forest, after the pattern set us by our white brethren. There was but one exception, viz., that *all* who dwelt in our precincts were to be held free and equal, *in truth*, as well as in letter."[138] Shadowing Apess's strategic recognition of white political example is a critique of racial hierarchy codified in American political texts, perhaps most memorably in the Declaration of Independence's invocation of Indigenous peoples as "savages." Instead, the Mashpee Constitution retrieves Native woodland practices to produce a freedom "in *truth*, as well as in letter." By relating "truth" to "letter," Apess demonstrates a deep respect for botanic life, given that cotton rags (and later trees) produce the paper on which many American laws are composed and archived.[139] If in *A Son of the Forest*, Apess suggests that paper often embodies "scenes of sanguinary vengeance which have too often stained the pages of colonial history," then here he may be implying that the US Constitution is a waste of paper, a desecration of the animal and botanic materials on which many governing documents are written.[140]

Given Apess's attention to settler resource extraction and writing as constitutive violences, perhaps it is no surprise that Mashpee nullification also begins with resistance to wood theft. While walking through the forest on July 1, Apess comes across two white settlers cutting timber on reservation grounds. The date was significant: in the "Nullification Ordinance" posted in the reservation, the Mashpee called for an end to timber theft by July 1 and had likely organized patrols to survey the territory.[141] In the encounter, Apess cautioned those who accompanied him "to do no bodily injury to any man, unless in their own defense, but to stand for their rights."[142] The Mashpee unloaded the wagon, while the trespassers "used very bitter language at being thus, for the first time, hindered from taking away what had always been as a lawful spoil to them."[143] On July 4, the Mashpee broke into their church (Fish had denied access to the building), and Apess preached a blistering sermon that catalogued the abuses the community had suffered under white protectorship. This date, too, was significant, with Apess calling for July 4 to be a day "of fasting and lamentation . . . for surely there is no joy in [it] for the man of color"—a remark that anticipates Frederick Douglass's 1852 speech, "What to a Slave is the Fourth of July?"[144] Apess was arrested for disturbing the peace and sentenced to thirty days in jail. Always conscious of how fantasies of democratic self-making occlude racial violence, he wryly deployed a rhetorical mirror to describe his protest: "Now if I had taken any neighbor's wood without his leave, and he had thrown it out of my cart, and told me to go away, and had given me no farther molestation, I should think I had gotten off very easily."[145] These events were intensely debated in the local press, as Mashpee self-determination and civil disobedience unsettled deeply cherished myths of American democracy.[146]

Although Mashpee demands for restorative justice embraced a field of local exploitations, Apess's calls for sovereignty reverberate within hemispheric histories of ecological destruction and land enclosure. He argues, for instance, that Wampanoag Mashpee resistance intersects with other Native freedom struggles in the removal era, suggested in his citation of Benjamin Hallett's arguments on behalf of Cherokee sovereignty in *Indian Nullification*: "We now see how unjust we have been to . . . the Cherokees, and if we persist in oppressing the Marshpee Indians, let us hasten to *unresolve* all the glowing resolves we made in favor of the Georgia Indians."[147] Apess's purpose, moreover, is animated by both denials of Mashpee wood rights and Indigenous removal policies as actions that reflect long histories of extraction.[148] Indeed, by the seventeenth century, deforestation in the Northeast was proceeding on scales never seen before, with early settlements likely consuming more than two hundred million cords of firewood by the time Apess was born in 1798.[149] Settlers knew that practices of clear cutting woodlands were changing climate systems, as Strother E. Roberts argues: "Early modern theorists of climate believed that local environmental actions—most notably the clearing of wooded land—could transform first local conditions, then regional weather patterns, and finally the climate of entire continents. In part, this belief in the malleability of nature rested on early modern systems of thought that tied political morality firmly to the physical environment."[150] Forests prevented excess evaporation and contributed to what settlers believed were unhealthy, damp environments—"savage" ecologies that English colonists were eager to revise.[151] Yet by the end of the seventeenth century, English colonists understood that felling timber had noticeably shifted weather patterns, with William Howard Tucker, a local historian in Hartford, Vermont, drawing on virulently racialized terms ("scalping") to describe these changes: "Since the hills have been literally scalped of trees, drouths are more frequent . . . Most of the streams have diminished in size as the forests have been cleared up, and some are entirely dry in the summer time."[152] By the 1830s, steam-powered shipping also drastically expanded the nation's fuel requirements and deforestation accelerated, even as its center moved to western parts of the United States.[153] Andrew Jackson tellingly invoked these economic priorities in his 1830 State of the Union speech: "What good man would prefer a country covered with forests and ranged by a few thousand savages to our extensive Republic[?]"[154] Yet Jackson's words are ultimately a settler fantasy that unwitnesses edge ecologies, for the continent was *never* an endless forest, but rather a series of interconnected ecologies shaped by longstanding Indigenous cultivation. At the same time, even while Apess condemns American removal policies and the over-consumption of resources on Indigenous lands, he recognizes that Mashpee sovereignty might require a pragmatic interaction with national economic priorities, for as Nick Estes (Lower Brule Sioux Nation) points out, Indigenous nations must sometimes "actively participate in resource extraction and capitalist economies in order to strengthen their self-determination."[155] Read in light of these difficult histories of Indigenous cultivation and settler extraction, Apess extends a rhetoric of rights to safeguard Mashpee economic development—which includes nonhuman relatives like trees: "We will not permit any white man to come upon our plantation, to cut or carry off wood or hay, or any other article."[156] Here, *Indian Nullification*'s expansive gestures to rights discourse counters a settler "replacement narrative that argued for a glorious and honorable New England history entailing the rightful replacement of Indian peoples," as Jean M. O'Brien (White Earth Ojibwe) argues.[157]

Although *Indian Nullification* clearly draws from nineteenth-century economic and political vocabularies—treaties, rights, self-determination, sovereignty—to enunciate the Mashpee's claims to land title, Apess also seems to deny an instrumental orientation to forests as resource reservoirs in the text. If so, then does his view align with Robert Nichols's contention that Indigenous critiques of land theft sometimes reinterpret "dispossession" as something more like "desecration" or the "defilement of some object of concern whose moral worth cannot be measured in purely anthropocentric terms"?[158] In asking this, I wish to take care not to portray Apess's language of commoning as an "autochthonous discourse" in which Indigenous sovereignty, as Nandita Sharma and Cynthia Wright describe, is framed as "*metaphysically . . . of* the land colonized by various European empires."[159] Such claims can risk cohering around mythologized and sentimentalized assertions of Indigenous land inhabitance from "time immemorial"—assertions that risk abstracting living communities from material ecologies and reifying cultural lifeways as static rather than reflections of historically negotiated and shifting practices.[160] Instead, I want to make clear that when Apess articulates traditions of coexistence with generational landscapes, he expresses them as *lived* relations. For this point, I am influenced by Eduardo Kohn's contention that Quechua orientations to Amazonian forests and their animal inhabitants counter settler ontologies of personhood: "Life thinks, thoughts are alive. . . . Wherever there are 'living thoughts,' there is also a 'self'. . . . 'We' are not the only kind of *we*."[161] Although Kohn turns to Quechua cosmogonies to reassesses the human-centered analytics vital to anthropology, I have been considering how *Indian Nullification* not only refuses resource extraction on Mashpee lands as a legal and political matter but also hints at Algonquian stories of trees as relatives, rendering dispossession an existential and ontological threat.

In taking seriously Apess's arboreal vocabulary, I am posing this question: What comes into relief if we read his commoning perspective with broader Algonquian convictions of forests as *relatives* to live with?[162] For this, I am drawing from Kim Tallbear (Dakota), who describes settler epistemic norms as an "animacy hierarchy" incompatible with Indigenous practices of mutually obligated bodies, what she calls "being in good relation," and from Robin Wall Kimmerer (Potawatomi), who analyzes Anishinaabemowin verb structures to recover "a grammar of animacy" ascribing personhood to more-than-human entities.[163] Although carrying this line of inquiry to Apess's different linguistic context in Mashantucket Pequot and Wampanoag Mashpee cultures requires caution, their points may still open up his attention to a "forest . . . alive with its sons and daughters" as an epistemological orientation *toward* "being in good relation" with human and nonhuman beings.[164] Indeed, this is the perspective Lisa Brooks brings to Apess's portrayal of Haudenosaunee commoning: he acknowledges an "obligatory reciprocity to the forest that gave him birth and to its sons and daughters, whom he now fully recognize[s] as his relations," a gloss on *A Son of the Forest* I earlier cited.[165] In the context of *Indian Nullification*, Apess's use of familial metaphors like "freeborn sons of the forest" establishes ways of being in the world at odds with settler extractive practices, which deny Indigenous recognitions of nonhuman personhood and the cosmogonies they are rooted within: "Doubtless there are many who think it granting us poor natives a great privilege to treat us with equal humanity. The author has often been told seriously, by sober persons, that his fellows were a link between the whites and the brute creation."[166] Here, Apess's phrase "brute creation," as with Occom's "brutal creation," counters a settler biopolitics that assembles Indigenous peoples and places as raw resources to be removed and consumed.

Reading Apess as a theorist of woodland cosmology brings into relief an edge work incommensurate with settler modernity, suggested in the ways the Mashpee nation has been compelled to respond continually to existential crises provoked by shifting policies at the state and federal level. In 1842, the Massachusetts legislature forcibly divided much of the remaining commons into individual plots, preceding by several decades the disastrous allotment of reservation lands under the Dawes Act (1887).[167] In the 1970s, the Mashpee worked to recover land through a series of court cases, which were decided against them.[168] The Mashpee only gained federal recognition in 2007, an acknowledgement limited in reach, however, as officials under Donald Trump's administration informed the Mashpee Council that its sovereignty status would be rescinded and over three hundred acres of land removed from trust under the Department of the Interior. The Mashpee strenuously resisted these decisions by pursuing legal action and publicizing their history in the press. On June 6, 2020, a US court reversed the Department of the Interior's decision, while in February 2021 the federal government, under Joseph Biden's administrative priorities, dropped its case against the Mashpee Nation.[169] These ongoing political conflicts index the economic priorities of woodland clear-cutting and the forcible containment of Indigenous commons into private property—all processes that underlie the extractive contingencies of racial capitalism and anthropogenic climate change.

Locating a nineteenth-century conflict over Indigenous commoning within histories of extraction and anthropogenic climate change necessarily takes us to Apess's images of wildfire—the opposite of the controlled burns that created edge ecologies—to describe settlers' insatiable land hunger. In the *Eulogy on King Philip* (1836), for instance, Apess calls colonial occupation a "fire, a canker, created by the Pilgrims from across the Atlantic, to burn and destroy my poor unfortunate brethren."[170] Yet it would be a mistake to read Apess's fiery idiom as a prophetic anticipation of an "inevitable" future of Indigenous dispossession and global warming, for such a critical move reproduces a colonial *telos* that his writings otherwise disavow. As Daniel Hartley argues, discourses on the Anthropocene often impose a "retrospectively projected necessity" on events and deny alternative possibilities for orienting to the future: "The Anthropocene can only ever think the past in its proleptic trajectory toward our present. Its specific narrative mode translates the time of initiative and praxis into the time of pure physical necessity. For precisely this reason, it can only think *our own present* as part of the empty homogeneous time of linear succession, which increasingly contracts as catastrophe approaches."[171] In *Indian Nullification*, however, Apess charts his clearest resistance to the seemingly "inevitable" destruction of Indigenous peoples and places, as well as the systems—ontological, political, epistemological, economic—that produce settler sovereignty and its extractive routines of accumulation and exploitation. In this sense, *Indian Nullification* presses on alternative cosmogonies for arranging Wampanoag Mashpee and Mashantucket Pequot relations—all things held in common for all the sons and daughters of the forest—as historically extant and ongoing practices. As Osage scholar Robert Warrior argues, with his perspectives on commoning, Apess "projects himself out of that history as a reminder of his time as well as ours of the awful human price paid by those on the underside of modernity," and because he does, "we [may be] able to glimpse and to grasp the shape of our own liberation, even if that liberation lives in generations yet to come."[172]

To Carry a Common World

> We gather up these strands broken from the web of life. They shiver with our love, as we call them the names of our relatives and carry them to our home made of the four directions and sing.
>
> —JOY HARJO

Commemorating the life and death of the Wampanoag sachem Metacom, or Philip, Apess's *Eulogy on King Philip* (1836) situates Metacom's resistance to colonial occupation in a conflict now called King Philip's War (1675–76) within a broader consideration of settler historiography and Indigenous placemaking: "It will be well for us to lay those deeds and depredations committed by whites upon Indians before the civilized world."[173] The deadliest conflict per capita in American history, King Philip's War saw Wampanoag, Narragansett, Wabanaki, Nipmuck, and Pocumtuck allies engaged in resistance against British settlers from Rhode Island in the south to Maine in the north.[174] In *The Name of War* (1999), historian Jill Lepore contends that the conflict became the crucible out of which the English transformed their anxieties over colonial violence into a cultural identity of exceptionalism through an excess of historical writing: "However remarkable for the magnitude of its destruction and the depth of its cruelties, King Philip's War is almost as remarkable for how much the colonists wrote about it: more than four hundred letters written during the war survive in New England archives alone, along with more than thirty editions of twenty different printed accounts."[175] However, Lepore goes on to (in)famously elide Indigenous perspectives on the conflict: "We would do well to investigate why some colonists wrote so much while [Indigenous peoples] wrote nothing at all."[176] *Our Beloved Kin* (2019), Lisa Brooks's recent field-defining history of the war, challenges Lepore's claim and foregrounds Indigenous archives of the war invisible in *The Name of War*. She does this by pursuing "a decolonizing process of expanding the strategies through which we might do the work of history, which in the Abenaki language is called *ôjmowôgan*, a cyclical activity of recalling and relaying in which we are collectively engaged."[177] For Apess, telling the story of King Philip's War—and of centuries of colonial dispossession—similarly requires a reindigenization of *place*, a critical process that recalls longstanding Native relations to space and time.[178] Apess's historiographic imperative anticipates Christine Delucia's contention that the act of remembering King Philip's War and the conflict's violence occurs in what she terms a "memoryscape" or "constellations of spots on the land that have accrued stories over time, transforming them from seemingly blank or neutral spaces into emotionally infused, politically potent places."[179]

Drawing from Brooks and Delucia, I close this chapter by considering how Apess's portrait of Metacom, an "all-accomplished son of the forest," roots the *Eulogy*'s memory-work in sovereign relations to land, where the text itself functions as a performance of Indigenous commoning. Indeed, Apess spoke the *Eulogy* multiples times in settings across the Northeast, most notably at the Odeon Theater in Boston on January 1 and again on January 8, 1836, and then at Boylston Hall on January 26, 1836, opening with a series of questions that index Indigenous memory through both flesh and geography: "[I] bring before you beings made by the God of Nature, and in whose hearts and heads he has planted sympathies that shall live forever in the memory of the world, whose brilliant talents are shown in the display of natural things. . . . Those noble traits that marked the wild man's course lie buried in the shades of night; and who shall stand?"[180] Given the text's significance as a performed witness to Indigenous experiences of colonial war and violence, Apess here *embodies* the decolonial work of remembrance that Brooks and Delucia powerfully delineate.

To that end, Apess lingers with colonial practices that mutilate Indigenous relations to place by denying burial, exemplified in Puritan minister Increase Mather's *A Brief History of the Warr with the Indians in New-England* (1676) and Thomas Church's *Entertaining Passages Relating to King Philip's War* (1716). Church relates how his father, Benjamin Church, led the military expedition that captured Metacom and refused him a proper burial: "That for as much as he had caused many an English man's body to lie unburied and rot above ground, that not one of his bones should be buried."[181] Near the close of *A Brief History*, Mather also gruesomely portrays Metacom's death as a communal feast, which authorizes Puritan claims of sovereignty over the continent's lands and waters: "[There] was he . . . cut into four quarters, and is now hanged up as a monument of revenging justice. . . . Thus did God break the head of that Leviathan, and gave it to be meat to the people inhabiting the wilderness."[182] Here, Mather tarries with the brutal spectacle of Metacom's dismembered body, a monument to God's seeming providential favor, to justify Puritan occupations of a land reconfigured as "wilderness" in need of English improvement. In his metaphor of consumption, moreover, Mather figures Metacom as a substance that sustains a "people inhabiting the wilderness," where "wilderness" denies historical Native idioms for inhabiting the land. Kathleen Bragdon argues that Algonquian languages frequently used eating (*meechu* and its cognates in Wampanoag) to denote forms of inhabitance, as well as the subsistence needs of home and close kin. In a 1673 land transaction, for instance, Wampanoag resident Sabiah Jootes observed, "For we have eaten it [the land] all, I and my children."[183]

In the *Eulogy*, Apess likewise seems to draw from these Indigenous cultural contexts in his refusals of colonial historiography: "Accordingly, he was quartered and hung up upon four trees. . . . His head was sent to Plymouth and exposed upon a gibbet for twenty years; and his hand to Boston, where it was exhibited in savage triumph; and his mangled body denied a resting place in the tomb. . . . I think that, as a matter of honor, that I can rejoice that no such evil conduct is recorded of the Indians, that they never hung up any of the white warriors who were head men."[184] In this moment, Apess pointedly reverses the rhetoric of consumption deployed by English historians after King Philip's War—Metacom's bodily remains and the extended afterlife of their display in Boston, rather than sustaining the Puritans' mission, bears witness to colonial brutality instead. By doing so, Apess not only repudiates settler claims of exceptional authority as a directive toward territorial occupation but also contests the belief that Indigenous peoples have no presence in historical archives beyond the moment of erasure. Of course, one form of presence Apess describes is an absence—"no such evil conduct is recorded" of Indigenous communities in their wars with the English. By returning to Indigenous place-based perspectives of the conflict, Apess rereads Metacom's dismemberment not as a sign of providential care but as a violence that requires a decolonial historiography, one that can access Indigenous epistemologies outside of encounters with settler sovereignty.

As the *Eulogy* ponders practices for remembering and re-membering Indigenous relational and place-based histories, the performance unfolds in two parts—an overview of early English settlement and an Indigenous account of King Philip's War—while using the war as an analytic to bring into relief the unliveability of colonial modernity.[185] In one of the text's most poignant moments, Apess pauses to tell the story of a father who loses his son to illness, in some ways an utterly unremarkable occurrence given Native experiences with epidemic diseases. Yet this brief story also reflects a reality where the mode of being-in-common under colonialism *is* violence, as Ariella Aïsha Azoulay observes: "Imperial violence is our commons."[186] That is, Apess turns to this father and child to meditate on how colonialism lays waste to Indigenous worlds as a shared experience of agony:

> History informs us that in Kennebunk there lived an Indian, remarkable for his good conduct, and who received a grant of land from the state and fixed himself in a new township. . . . Though not ill treated, yet the common prejudices against Indians prevented any sympathy with him, though he himself did all that lay in his power to comfort his white neighbors, in case of sickness and death. But now let us see the scene reversed. This poor Indian . . . now vainly looks for help, when sickness and death comes into his family. Hear his own words. He speaks to the inhabitants thus: "When white man's child die, Indian man he sorry; he help bury him. When my child die, no one speak to me; I make his grave alone. I can no live here." He gave up his farm, dug up the body of his child, and carried it 200 miles, through the wilderness, to join the Canadian Indians.[187]

Apess first locates the Indigenous father within the civic spaces of the settler state, where he has "received a grant of land"—land stolen from his own community. In this, he traces how colonial institutions insidiously fracture Indigenous polities, as well as how the "common prejudices" of white in- habitants inflect quotidian life. If the father has been interpellated within an inhospitable settler sociality, he also (if less overtly) is compelled to struc- ture his interactions with his neighbors according to *their* notions of com- munal morality. The father is "known" for his "good conduct," a character recorded under the hostile gaze of his neighbors, and still he shares in their sorrow when incidents of sickness and death fracture communal well-being.

Apess does not, however, close the story here: what begins as a narrative of one Indigenous father's inscription within the affective and political ar- rangements of "common prejudices" turns into a trenchant indictment of white apathy. When Apess charges us to "hear [the father's] own words," he summons his audience, both the listeners of his speech and the generations of readers who encounter the *Eulogy*, to bear witness to this father's agony. Even so, the father's words offer as many questions on what "history" can and cannot "inform us" as it answers, given settler historiographic aporias. What are their names, this father and child of Kennebec? How old was this beloved son when he died, and from what did he perish—or does this matter at all in the face of his father's suffering? Where is the child's mother: has she, too, been separated from her kin by disease or by the dislocations of war? How might Apess turn to his audience and speak *as* this father? What tone of voice could express the devastating experience of burying a child? What gesture could convey the harrowing task of carrying—of beholding—his child's bodily remains for over two hundred miles? What cosmological eth- ics derived from "an earth given to the children of men" can possibly account for this child carried so far from home? And what can any historiographic perspective hope to remedy if this single and singular child is lost? To ask these questions is to recognize the impossibility of following in the father's path or of reconstructing any complete narrative of this child's life and death. This is history at its limit.

The father's final exhausted declaration that he cannot "live here" indicts colonial displacements of Indigenous peoples from ancestral lands and re- lations, what Apess in *A Son of the Forest* earlier called "that land, where re- posed the ashes of [my] sires."[188] I have often pondered whether Apess's story of this bereaved father anticipates Jacques Derrida's meditation on a poetic fragment by Paul Celan in *The Beast & the Sovereign II* (2011): "The world is gone, I must carry you."[189] Derrida would no doubt insist on the child's utter singularity, whose death heralds an end of the world: "Each time, and each time singularly, each time irreplaceably, each time infinitely, death is nothing less than the end of the world."[190] At first glance, Derrida's scale— the apocalypse of any one person's death—appears too small to encompass Indigenous losses in the midst of the ongoing catastrophes of settler colonialism and climate change, but he urges that the interlocking units of ethical regard—personal, planetary—begin as a response to an imperative—*must*. The world is gone, and I *must* carry you, which "seems to sign a commitment . . . like the seal of a love that, at the moment of good-bye, of good-bye to the world, salutes or swears to work for your safety . . . [or] to save you without salvation."[191] Even so, the loss of *the* world inherent in any one person's death would seem to foreclose holding much of anything in common (and Derrida is notoriously skeptical of the possibility of community). Indeed, his meditation depends on an unbridgeable abyss between *earth* and *world*—on the difference between material ground and shared socialities. Kelly Oliver argues that because of this skepticism, Derrida strives to locate "the ethical import of 'I must carry you' on the groundless ground of the earth, insofar as it remains our only home," even if a common world is ultimately impossible.[192] Yet Apess's argument throughout the *Eulogy* suggests that the "groundless ground" of Derrida's earth may be far too abstract—far too distant from both ancestral Indigenous ties to storied landscapes and the brutal exigences of displacement that disrupt historically located Algonquian placemaking. This is worldmaking at the end of the world.

From the perspective of this limit case, then, what can "world" mean? The *Eulogy*'s answer is that the father must, impossibly, improvise a world out of a shattering loss and an unsettled grave. This requires exposing a historical system in which Native communities, as Chickasaw scholar Jodi Byrd argues, are conscripted as colonized subjects who can be bound and displaced— where settler occupation reformats Indigenous life and livelihood as moveable, and because moveable, disposable. At the same time, colonial policies deliberately render these violences illegible and, because illegible, *ungrievable*.[193] For the father, to tenderly bear his child when the world is gone requires "[gathering] up these strands broken from the web of life," in Muscogee poet Joy Harjo's words.[194] For Apess, the small-scale apocalypse of this child's death did not and could not end Indigenous community, reflected in his decision not to locate the father within an identifiable point in history: given the *Eulogy*'s temporal span, the father could have lived at any point from the seventeenth to the nineteenth centuries. He may have been displaced not only by his English neighbors' cruelty, but also by armed conflict along the northern front of King Philip's War. If so, then he may have sought a haven with the Abenaki at Odanak or further north at a Haudenosaunee village.[195] However, Apess's invocation of "Canadian Indians" may also reflect a more recent historical scene, when national borders were formalized between the United States and Canada, and thus anticipates the shelter offered by the Haudenosaunee when his own life was ruptured by violence during the War of 1812. In either case, Apess's point seems to be that the father must turn elsewhere for comfort in his great grief, but that his journey north, while a profound unsettlement, is also a kind of homegoing to extended kin.

Although Apess surveys the geographies of world-destroying colonial violence as he rehearses the father's long crossing to reinter his child, the *Eulogy*'s iteration of his passage summons something more than loss. The father's utter refusal to accommodate to settler apathy measures the distance between colonized territories of seemingly empty "wilderness" and their final worldly limits by reminding us that Indigenous persons marked by itinerancy and dispossession still demand a piece of earth, not merely a "grave alone." Rather than locating a common world in a colonial "grant of land" or in Christian social attachments, as the Puritans might, the father improvises new relations with the "Canadian Indians," and, along the way, gathers a mode of witnessing otherwise: a way of making legible (and hence grievable) colonial structures of un/survival that were (and are still) constraining Indigenous sovereignties and their traditions of land tenure across the globe. Apess's sensitivity to *ground*, as material reservoirs of commoning in practice and in memory, suggests a recuperative ethics cultivated in shared testimony, as he indicates near the end of the *Eulogy*: "Did you ever know of Indians hurting those who was kind to them? No. We have a thousand witnesses to the contrary."[196] Here, Apess shows how colonial elisions of Indigenous witnessing are also elisions of dense relations to specific places—worlds that "a thousand witnesses" testify to. Here, too, he repudiates the political and discursive erasures of human and more-than-human kinships that have carried on apace under settler colonialism. For Apess, this father is one of "a thousand witnesses" who challenge the world-destroying regimes of exploitation and extraction that define the Anthropocene's longue durée. Instead, the father *endures*—in a different Indigenous territory, among a different Indigenous community—while bearing the remains and the memories of his beloved son. The *Eulogy* therefore extends a series of (im)possible questions: What could it mean to remember (and re-member) Indigenous loss and survival while continuing to live on the edge of colonial dispossession? And what could it mean to carry this child's history into a reconstituted future?

CHAPTER FOUR

Robert Wedderburn, Prophet of Unfinished Revolution

> Prepare for flight, ye planters, for the fate of St. Domingo awaits you. . . . Recollect the fermentation will be universal. . . . They will slay man, woman, and child, and not spare the virgin, whose interest is connected with slavery, whether black, white, or tawny. O ye planters, you know this has been done; the cause which produced former bloodshed still remains, — of necessity, similar effects must take place.
>
> — ROBERT WEDDERBURN

> When there is no more rest except in the land of midnight, then prophetic speech, which tells of the impossible future, also tells of the "nonetheless" that breaks the impossible and restores time.
>
> — MAURICE BLANCHOT

Early in *The Axe Laid to the Root, or A Fatal Blow to Oppressors, Being an Address to the Planters and Negroes of the Island of Jamaica* (1817), Robert Wedderburn not only predicts an imminent uprising against slavery—that Jamaica will experience the "same fate" as St. Domingue during the Haitian Revolution (1791–1804)—but goes much further.[1] He anticipates that when insurgency erupts in Jamaica, it will spread across the globe in a "fermentation [that] will be universal." Moreover, he warns that the coming conflagration will "not spare" those "whose interest is connected with slavery": it will, in other words, utterly transform the world, but only for a remnant divested from regimes of Black subjugation. Yet the passage's temporal schema unexpectedly shifts between "recollect" and "will be," rendering an insurrection that, in some sense, has already happened and is still to come.[2] *The Axe Laid to the Root* thus lingers in an acute chronological tension: Wedderburn's citation of the Haitian Revolution as a victory against slavery nonetheless questions what "success" means for those still living in a historical moment when imperial powers are accelerating the formation of plantation industries in Jamaica and around the globe.[3] And he presses on what "success" means when Haitian sovereignty continues to be circumscribed by exploitative global political and financial systems, including forced reparations to France, international refusals to recognize Haitian statehood, and foreign invasion. If, as Jeremy Matthew Glick reminds us, for many Black writers the Haitian Revolution summoned an "unfinished" horizon for imagining "a transformative future," then *The Axe Laid to the Root* extends an urgent question: what political horizons open up if "universal" revolution is considered not in its failure to arrive, but as merely—and perhaps forever—incomplete?[4]

While Wedderburn's conjuring of an imminent revolution in 1817 reflects a surge of millenarianism in the wake of the American, French, and Haitian Revolutions, his urgency also derives from his familiarity with brutal violence in Jamaica.[5] Wedderburn was born in 1762, the son of a Scottish doctor, James Wedderburn, and an enslaved woman, Rosanna. His visionary rhetoric, exemplified in his anti-Trinitarian pamphlet *Truth Self-Supported* (1802), his periodicals *A Forlorn Hope* (1816) and *The Axe Laid to the Root* (1817), and his autobiography *The Horrors of Slavery* (1824), assesses the global expansion of the plantation and connects Caribbean slavery to the ongoing dispossession of agricultural laborers and the emergence of industrial systems in Britain.[6] Wedderburn's history in Jamaica and his indigent existence in London continually left him on the margins of respectable society, but his activities remain unusually well documented, both in his own prolific writings and in government surveillance records.[7] After escaping Jamaica and settling in London, he earned a scarce living as a journeyman tailor and became involved with forms of popular insurgency driven, in part, by postwar recessions. By 1813, he was drawn to the communitarian politics of Thomas Spence, a radical activist and bookstall proprietor who operated in High Holborn.[8] Across his oratory and pamphlets, Spence advocated for the abolition of property, a position he advanced after witnessing the threatened enclosure of Newcastle's Town Moor in 1771.[9] By April 1819, Wedderburn licensed his own radical club, the Hopkins Street Chapel, where members debated strategies for popular revolt in London and the Caribbean, activities that swiftly led to his imprisonment for blasphemy and sedition.[10] But while the Caribbean remained a touchstone for Wedderburn throughout his peripatetic career, he never returned to Jamaica, believing those in power "would most certainly have trumped up some charge against me, and hung me."[11] Because of this, critics have situated Wedderburn within the London underworld, placing him within a radical lineage that includes the Levellers and the Diggers during the English Civil War, and the Luddites and the United Irish in his own day.[12] More recently, however, scholars have worked to locate Wedderburn within transatlantic insurgencies against slavery and colonialism.[13] I extend these critical threads by arguing, in line with previous chapters on Black and Indigenous cosmogonies, that for Wedderburn the Haitian Revolution extends not only an exemplar for politics but also an emergence narrative of what the world *might* be otherwise.

In this way, I am interested in how Wedderburn's career extends the worldmaking insights of the Haitian Declaration of Independence (1804): "We have dared to be free, let us be thus by ourselves and for ourselves. . . . Let us walk down another path."[14] Here, the Declaration draws from kinesthetic routines of Black fugitivity, what Fred Moten calls "walking in another world while passing through this one," to imagine forms of life beyond the plantation.[15] In addition, the Declaration dares to make revolutionary dreams thinkable when European philosophies made the specter of Black insurgency unthinkable, as Michel-Rolph Trouillot argues: "The contention that enslaved Africans and their descendants could not envision freedom—let alone formulate strategies for gaining and securing such freedom—was based not so much on empirical evidence as on an ontology, an implicit organization of the world and its inhabitants."[16] As Frederick Douglass poignantly argued in an essay that resonates with my consideration of Indigenous cosubstantial worlds in Chapter 1, Haiti was "the work of a people, bone of our bone, and flesh of our flesh."[17] In his conviction that the coming Jamaican insurrection will equal the Haitian Revolution in reshaping Black being and belonging, Wedderburn, as Ifeoma Nwankwo suggests, therefore joins other Black activists attempting to "[foment] a massive revolution that might overturn the whole Atlantic slave system."[18]

In particular, I argue that Wedderburn formally conceives the Haitian Revolution as a cosmogony by inventing revolutionary personas—by practicing a prophetic form of prosopopoeia—which collectively decry property holdings in land and flesh.[19] Performing figures who occupy diverse positions of privilege and precarity, Wedderburn sometimes writes as his sister Elizabeth and at other times as enslaved laborers, insurgent Maroons, or radical prophets. His impersonation of Elizabeth, in letters purportedly by her included in *The Axe Laid to the Root*, is exceptionally vital, as it centers a Black woman's dissent from slavery.[20] Elizabeth, who inherits a plantation, frees enslaved captives on the estate after an encounter with Wedderburn's anti-property and abolitionist convictions, further shaped by her kinship ties with the Windward Maroons and her grandmother Amy, a conjure woman and practitioner of Obeah. To be sure, Elizabeth's relinquishing of her status as a landowner and enslaver in favor of antislavery priorities threatens to spark widespread revolt in Jamaica, a possibility extensively narrated in *The Axe Laid to the Root's* final issues. By attending to Wedderburn's performance as Elizabeth, I am less interested in whether his portrait of her as a landowner is historically plausible, given her status as a biracial woman, but rather in how he *deploys* her voice to disavow property.[21] Put more simply, I turn to *The Axe Laid to the Root*'s layering of plural voices as a radical abolitionist and feminist praxis inspired by Black women's commoning traditions in the Caribbean.[22]

To that end, I contend that Wedderburn's rehearsals of revolution's ignored actors and incomplete aims speculate on un/thinkable histories from below, enabling him to improvise a critical practice that Lisa Lowe names "what could have been." This perspective "revisit[s] times of historical contingency and possibility to consider alternatives that may have been *unthought* in those times," but which may allow us "to imagine different futures for what lies ahead."[23] When Wedderburn in *The Axe Laid to the Root* disperses the energy of Black resistance to multiple voices, he signals that others should speak even if he perishes as a casualty of state execution or revolt. At the same time, *The Axe Laid to the Root* also measures the difficulty—even impossibility—of fully instantiating a radical future when revolutionary openings are impeded by the genres of colonial modernity, which often compel Black archives, and the political praxes they assemble, to follow a liberal *telos* that ends in legal gains but not always in real freedom.[24] Indeed, *The Axe Laid to the Root*'s print history bears witness to these embattled conditions: the periodical is incomplete, ending midsentence.[25] Although Wedderburn yearns to ignite political ruptures through insurgencies against property and slavery, his career thus intersects with recent meditations on what futures are recoverable at *all* in "the continuous and changing present of slavery's unresolved unfolding," as Christina Sharpe names it, which Saidiya Hartman reminds us may deny possibilities for reconstructing "useable pasts" in the present.[26] Formally, I want to suggest that Wedderburn's writings evoke a mode of "metaleptic history," which Stephen Best defines as a queer attentiveness to "people and utterances that appear to be not available for recovery."[27] Because Wedderburn is a witness to a liberation in Haiti not yet fulfilled elsewhere, he implicates history's impossible recoveries in visions of an imminent—but perhaps foreclosed—future.

In what follows, I trace Wedderburn's improvisation of feminist and metaleptic modes of speech in *The Horrors of Slavery* and *Truth Self-Supported*, which seek to recover Black women's dissent to slavery even while the texts relinquish a conviction that slavery's violences can ever be fully restored—a mode of prophetic adjustment that shapes his evocation of an interrupted global revolution in *The Axe Laid to the Root*. As I will show, because Wedderburn preaches out of a sense of "forlorn hope" rather than ecstatic certainty, he refuses "a politics of despair brought about by a failure to lament a loss, because it is not rooted in hope of winning," as Jared Sexton has put it.[28] Instead, Wedderburn dwells with revolution's ensnared temporalities—belated, recursive, deferred—which are not "rooted in" anything, as Joseph Albernaz reminds us, for the axe has been laid to *every* root.[29] Indeed, by embracing an irreconcilable ethos of uprooted expectation, Wedderburn faces time much like Walter Benjamin's materialist historian in "Theses on the Philosophy of History" (1940), who grasps the past "as it flashes up in a moment of danger"—who confronts history not as it *was*, but as it could *be* otherwise.[30] Ultimately when Wedderburn speculates that the future requires a restless dispersal of radical speech, he attests to something beyond the violences that continually halt Black political (and hence revolutionary) formations: where the single voice may be ephemeral, voices speaking as ensembles do more than "flash up"—they *endure*.

A Radical Inheritance

Broadly, Wedderburn's prophetic expectation in *The Horrors of Slavery* is refined by his dismay at the expropriation of Black women's bodies, sexualities, and labor, a perspective Jennifer L. Morgan argues attends to "the real and imagined reproductive potential of women whose 'blackness' was produced by and produced their enslavability."[31] Wedderburn witnessed the brutal violences that his mother and grandmother lived under, and the memory of their captivity remained with him for the rest of his life.[32] *The Horrors of Slavery* first appeared in Holborn and Smithfield bookshops in late 1824, but it originated as a series of letters in the populist weekly *Bell's Life in London*. Inspired by a February 1824 article censuring the proslavery lobby, Wedderburn submitted letters attacking his father for failing to support his children born of enslaved mothers. Andrew Colville, Wedderburn's half-brother, attempted a refutation, but an editorial that concluded the series declared Wedderburn won the dispute.[33]

Although *The Horrors of Slavery* appears late in Wedderburn's oeuvre, I begin here because it centers Black women's experiences as a matter of political and ethical obligation—indeed, the text depicts revolution as an utterly necessary response to the intimate violations suffered by Wedderburn's kin. To that end, his rhetorical impetus depends on a powerful fabulation of prenatal manumission, a social relation brought into being when his mother negotiated for his freedom before he was born: that Rosanna rebelled so persistently against James that he chose to sell Rosanna to a Lady

Douglas, and that Rosanna, who was pregnant, insisted on her son's freedom as a condition of the sale, which Douglas honored.[34] In this act, Rosanna exemplifies "a life-sustaining definition of blackness" that Jessica Marie Johnson contends enslaved African women demanded on behalf of their descendants.[35] While scholars like Ryan Hanley and Nadine Hunt have discovered that Wedderburn likely *was* enslaved as a child, he nonetheless portrays his mother as the origin of his liberation, an act made real through her voice and rage.[36]

Put differently, I am tracing how Wedderburn employs features of emphatic typography to signal feminist and nonpatrilineal genealogies of revolutionary rage, exemplified in his mother and grandmother's lived practices of Obeah and care work. In this, I build on Peter Linebaugh and Marcus Rediker's claim that *The Horrors of Slavery*'s typography "bend[s] the King's English to his oral mode and distinctive vernacular dialect."[37] Alan Rice argues that in its development of a "subaltern typography," *The Horrors of Slavery* "cannot be related in the plain prose of normal typography; the enormity of the horror must be challenged with a vernacular discourse that lies outside the traditional literary language . . . and estranges the basis of its authority."[38] Wedderburn begins, for instance, by recalling how Rosanna was "FLOGGED IN THE MOST INDECENT MANNER" for not "acquainting her mistress that her master had *given her leave to go to see her mother in town*," using italics and capitals to accentuate slavery's profound disruptions of Black kinship.[39] Wedderburn gestures at similar disavowed relationships in his stories of his grandmother's life, a conjure woman named Talkee Amy, whose full name highlights the significance of her voice. He reports that "such was the confidence the merchants of Kingston had in her honesty, that she could be trusted to any amount; in fact, she was the regular agent for selling smuggled goods."[40] Yet Amy suffered brutal treatment by her enslaver Joseph Payne, who feared her adherence to Obeah (magnified in the aftermath of Tacky's Rebellion and Obeah's criminalization in Jamaica after 1760).[41] Payne, "an old and avaricious merchant," outfitted a vessel to smuggle mahogany from Honduras, but Spanish privateers captured the ship and sentenced Payne "to carry stones at Fort Homea, in the bay of Honduras, for a year and a day."[42] Payne, by then in his seventies, survived the imprisonment but died on the return journey and "was tossed overboard to make food for fishes," a vengeful counterpoint to the harrowing deaths experienced by African captives during the Middle Passage.[43]

Wedderburn relates that Amy was "flogged for a witch" by Payne's nephew and heir, a brutal punishment he witnessed as a young child: "The ill-success of old Payne's adventures was owing to my grandmother's having bewitched the vessel. The old miser had liberated five of his slaves before he set out on his unlucky expedition; and my grandmother's new master being a believer in the doctrine of Witchcraft, conceived that my grandmother had bewitched the vessel out of revenge."[44] By framing Payne's death as an "unlucky expedition," Wedderburn defends his grandmother from the charge of occultism, no doubt well aware that enslaved communities practiced Obeah for healing and protection, and lingers with these events to contest colonial governance over Black women's bodies, sexualities, and knowledges.[45] As Wedderburn also recalls: "Now, what aggravated the affair was, that my grandmother had brought up this young villain from eight years of age, and, till now, he had treated her as a mother."[46] Although Wedderburn scorns Payne's superstitious understanding of Obeah as "witchcraft," he is particularly derisive of the nephew's disregard for Amy's care, calling attention to patterns that entrench the ontological brutality and terror of slavery into everyday relations.[47]

Broadly, Wedderburn's witness resists trafficking in European stereotypes in their depictions of Black women's rituals and knowledges as objects of ridicule.[48] Rather, he portrays Obeah as a ground for the "political power" of "slave rebellions and the incursions and revolts of West Indian Maroons," as Alan Richardson puts it.[49] Moreover, Wedderburn turns to Obeah to disavow Christian frameworks of forgiveness, where contrition should rouse clemency. Indeed, he recalls that his grandmother "could never forget the whipping" before offering his own response to her punishment, which fuses a Shylockian protest that all recognize the humanity of African captives to a refusal to accommodate himself to the mandate of reconciliation: "Hath not a slave feelings? If you starve them, will they not die? If you wrong them, will they not revenge?"[50] Wedderburn echoes this conviction in a scathing passage from *The Axe Laid to the Root*: "My heart glows with revenge, and cannot forgive. Repent ye christians, for flogging my aged grandmother before my face, when she was accused of witchcraft by a silly European."[51] Wedderburn ultimately contends that his anger has come to him as a generational inheritance from Rosanna and Amy. When Rosanna responded with fury to James's abuse, for instance, he claims: "I have not the least doubt, but that from her rebellious and violent temper during that period, that I have inherited the same disposition—the same desire to see justice overtake the oppressors of my countrymen—and the same determination to lose no stone unturned, to accomplish so desirable an object."[52] In *The Horrors of Slavery* and *The Axe Laid to the Root*, his accounts of Black women's resistant practices—Obeah, smuggling, challenges to regimes of sexual violence—took shape in a post-Haitian Revolutionary world, which, as Marlene Daut argues, often featured narratives of biracial protagonists seeking vengeance from "colonial fathers" who refused to "recognize or pass down to them the rights of citizenship."[53]

While *The Horrors of Slavery* lingers with Black feminist dissent to slavery, *The Axe Laid to the Root* turns to Elizabeth to figure possibilities for revolution's emergence. Wedderburn recalls that Elizabeth's acts of devotion to her relatives—such as facilitating their brother John's emancipation—are "beyond the power of princes to imitate."[54] Elizabeth's witness ultimately inspires his own sense of prophetic office: "Oh, Miss Campbell, the greatness of the deed has inspired me with a zeal to extend freedom beyond present conception: Yes, the slaves shall be free, for a multiplied combination of ideas, which amount to prophetic inspiration and the greatness of the work that I am to perform has influenced my mind with an enthusiasm."[55] Here, Elizabeth's fidelity to abolition has the potential to transform a global order premised on the exploitation of Black women and families: "While they hold my innocent fellow a slave, I will kindle wrath in their inmost souls which the eternal God himself, whose throne is founded on the bed of justice will not be willing to take away until they make a public confession. . . . Fast bound by eternal truth, I have hold of the God of Israel, like a Jacob, and will not let him go."[56] His citation of Jacob, who wrestles with "the God of Israel" in Genesis, is perhaps the most radical, for it enunciates what Robin D. G. Kelley would call a "freedom dream"—Wedderburn's sense that before a world "beyond present conception" can come into being, it must first be *envisioned*.[57] His citation of Genesis, moreover, animates a new future: Jacob is renamed "Israel" ("contended with God") for prevailing in the struggle, an act of stamina Wedderburn both attributes to Elizabeth and predicts for his own son Jacob, born in 1822 just prior to the publication of *The Horrors of Slavery*.[58] For Wedderburn, then, Black women—Rosanna, Amy, and Elizabeth—defiantly dream an anti-patrilineal horizon of Black kinship, one that refuses the exploitative conditions of racialized production and reproduction under slavery.[59] And as Wedderburn argues at his trial for sedition in 1819, this future requires a repudiation of all patriarchy: "Acknowledge no King—Acknowledge no priest. Acknowledge no Father."[60]

Wedderburn's "freedom beyond present conception" informs not only his relations to Black women but also his experiences as an impoverished father.[61] Late in *The Horrors of Slavery*, he describes how he applied to Colville for assistance in a time of "extreme distress" after he first moved to London: "I was out of work," and his wife Elizabeth, whom he married in 1781, was "lying in."[62] When Colville refused, Wedderburn appealed to Deuteronomy: "If a man have two wives, one beloved and another hated, and they have borne him children . . . he shall acknowledge the son of the hated for the first-born, by giving him a double portion of all."[63] Here, Wedderburn limns radical insurgency with an alternative model of inheritance: beloved by Amy, Rosanna, and Elizabeth, yet hated by his father, he revises the patrilineal implications of Psalm 115:16 — "an earth given to the children of *men*" — to enact revolution as a legacy of Black maternal and sororal support. In this sense, Wedderburn's vision echoes José Esteban Muñoz's claim that queer intimacies may open a mode of historical recovery, where "the past is a field of possibility in which subjects can act in the present in the service of a new futurity."[64] Across his oeuvre, Wedderburn similarly revises his own past to challenge a logic of patriarchal property ownership and inheritance in order to marshal the residents of Stefano Harney and Fred Moten's "undercommons" — those who "plan without a pause, rebel without a policy, conserve without a patrimony" — and announce that the earth is not a territory to own.[65] Even so, Wedderburn's turn to recovered histories and redeemed kinships is nearly always a fraught undertaking: even if revolution arrives, he knows that no force can fully restore what has been lost to slavery.

"This DEAD MAN a Hiding-Place"

If Wedderburn's late writings situate radical insurgency within a matrilineal genealogy, his earliest work, the contentious pamphlet *Truth Self-Supported* (1802), details his brief conversion to Wesleyan Methodism and rejections of orthodox theology, including Christ's divinity and resurrection.[66] While *Truth Self-Supported* might seem like a counterintuitive text for thinking with unfinished revolution, there Wedderburn reconceives the affordances of *hope*.[67] His emphasis on Christ's irrecoverable mortality, for instance, approaches something like Gustavo Esteva's contention that "hope is not the conviction that something will happen, but the conviction that something makes sense, whatever happens."[68] *Truth Self-Supported* offers possibilities for extending investigations of Black radical traditions within and against evangelical formations. Although Elie Halévy and E. P. Thompson famously theorized that the Methodist movement impeded revolutionary outbreak in Britain, more recent studies have delineated how popular Methodism assembled a wide spectrum of heterodox discourses and unruly practices, enabling us to locate Wedderburn within radical undertakings of antinomian dissent.[69] Even so, I am less interested in situating Wedderburn within cultures of evangelical piety than in exploring how his emphasis on Christ's mortality is at odds with the spiritual ecstasies scholars are so attuned to in textual representations of African diasporic spirituality.

For Wedderburn, conversion initially marshals an internal reanimation of a believer's spirit, which can also, perhaps counterintuitively, provoke intense skepticism against religious authority.[70] More radically, the event of personal conversion can prompt a believer to refuse creeds that do not align with inner experience, and Wedderburn describes his conversion to Methodism as a prelude to a more extensive dislocation of evangelical doctrine: "Passing the Seven-Dials one Lord's day, the author stopped to hear a preacher of Mr. Westley's connection. The words that he spoke, struck his mind with strong conviction of the awful state he was in, both by nature and practice . . . and he was enabled, by the Holy Spirit, to accept with joy, the offered Grace."[71] Joanna Brooks notes that to undergo conversion "was to enact the spiritual content of the slave experience, to radicalize the relationship between past and present, and to negate the assumed finality of enslavement and white domination."[72] As the pamphlet unfolds, Wedderburn uses conversion to similarly challenge the generational scope of slavery and reimagine a new future by arguing that churches are culpable for sustaining colonialism, a far more devastating legacy than denominational strife. *Truth Self-Supported* targets three distortions within evangelical doctrine: Christ's divinity, substitutionary atonement, and ecclesiastical authority. Because Wedderburn rejects Christ's divinity and his resurrection, he improvises a new theological language for finitude, which he deploys not only to counter the "finality of enslavement," but also to recover a prophetic view of history as unfinished:

> It is generally taught by professors of the present age, that, the atonement of Christ, was to satisfy the Justice of God—the assertion is unscriptural, —they also assert, that, God could not be reconciled to a sinner without his justice was satisfied by the death of Christ—this is also contrary to scripture; the word atonement signifies *covering*—so, the atonement of Christ, is, for the use of the awakened sinner, who sees himself exposed to the judgement of God, and who would despair, were it not for this Covering, or City of Refuge—it is a fact, though strange, that the Spirit directs the awakened sinner to this DEAD MAN, as an Hiding-place, and there, he experiences such safety, that his fears are calmed.[73]

Here, Wedderburn targets a substitutionary model of the atonement where Christ dies as a "substitute" for sin, thereby satisfying God's justice, a legalistic approach that reads the work of the cross as transaction for sin's debts.[74] But in his psychological reading of salvation, Wedderburn emphasizes not the appeasing of God's wrath but the calming of the "awakened sinner," who perceives that she is "exposed to judgment" and may hide from God *in* Christ.

Provocatively, Wedderburn calls it a "fact, though strange" that sinners are covered by Christ, a "DEAD MAN." He revises Romans 6:11's idiom of redemptive embodiment, where newly awakened believers are "dead to sin" but "alive in Christ." For Wedderburn, however, conversion is a haunting. The sinner clothes herself within Christ's bodily remains, for his version of Christ does not rise at all. Instead, it is Christ's *death* that paradoxically enables the "awakened sinner" to face the future. From the perspective of Caribbean traditions, Wedderburn's denial of the resurrection may be a little unusual. Early African diasporic literature frequently recurs to images of bodily regeneration, for instance, which reflect Black and Indigenous struggles to survive the unlivable conditions of colonialism. These images then shaped the development of everyday religious performances and rituals, such as baptism by immersion and "falling out" during moments of spiritual ecstasy.[75] In Jamaica, however, resurrection ran counter to many West African cosmogonies and their New World adaptations, which tended to emphasize the presence of spirits and ancestors.[76] The dead, Vincent Brown reminds us, "were an undeniable presence" for Black communities who believed in "the continuing presence on earth of the spirits of the dead," including ghosts, shadow souls, and duppies.[77] Wedderburn seems to draw on these Caribbean traditions when he names Christ's bodily remains a place of communal safety and a house for spirits—a "City of Refuge" and a "Hiding-Place"—which is a resonant parallel to Joseph Roach's "City of the Dead," or sites where Black and Indigenous performance traditions circulate and center anticolonial views of history.[78] Indeed, Wedderburn's language may reflect circumstances where the bodies of captives are denied final resting places, especially across the Middle Passage or in the plantation's killing fields. For impoverished communities in England, too, the indigent could expect their bones' removal from burial plots, if space was needed. Wedderburn's text reflects a profound unsettling of the oppressed, in life and in death.

Broadly, Wedderburn conceives of conversion in *Truth Self-Supported* as a conjuring of a limited redemption—a never fully recovered world.[79] More simply, the spiritual conviction he embraces is certainly not ecstasy, but something more like forlorn hope—indeed, perhaps he echoes the affect evoked in what Paul calls *hōs mē*: "the appointed time is grown very short," and believers must live "as if" (or *hōs mē*) Christ's coming is nigh (I Cor. 7:29). Recently, critics who have taken up Paul have grafted the structure of *hōs mē* to immanent experiences of history, revisiting revolutionary longing as the expectation of an impossible future whose belated arrival is anticipated "as if" it were nigh.[80] In "Theses on the Philosophy of History," for instance, Walter Benjamin summons a nonlinear history where every event in the present is pregnant with past fulfillments of promise or catastrophe, indexed in what he calls *jetztzeit* or "now time," or "a revolutionary chance in the fight for an oppressed past"—a fight for a present that is not *yet* present.[81] Benjamin formalizes *jetztzeit*'s impossible call in a meditation on Paul Klee's painting *Angelus Novus*, or the angel of history, who witnesses the past as a "single catastrophe which keeps piling wreckage and hurls it in front of his feet."[82] Confronted by ruin, the angel yearns "to awaken the dead, and make whole what has been smashed."[83] Similarly, Wedderburn reckons with the "fight for an oppressed past" when he imagines those like Rosanna and Amy speaking against exploitation. At the same time, Wedderburn's prophetic acts are just as often fractured by loss, exhaustion, and exile—for every moment where *The Horrors of Slavery* reimagines his past to invest his mother with emancipatory rage, *Truth Self-Supported* closes without a resurrection or *The Axe Laid to the Root* ends midsentence. Wedderburn's efforts to speak *as* and *with* Rosanna, Elizabeth, and Amy thus extends a resonant counter to Paul de Man's claim that prosopopoeia can work as a literary critical practice "by which the dead are made to have a face and a voice."[84] In the arena of transatlantic slavery, what could it mean to "awaken the dead"—or give the dead "a face and a voice"—in a past that must be perpetually reinvented? Or, to paraphrase Katherine McKittrick, what future can the ruins of plantation pasts bring forth?[85]

From the perspective of the angel of history, Wedderburn's antiresurrection ethos reverberates with a pervasive concern in Black studies—the impetus to name the systemic forces that consign Blackness to nonbeing and nonrelationality. Orlando Patterson argues, for instance, that Blackness emerged through procedures in which the enslaved African is "violently uprooted from his milieu" and "desocialized and depersonalized" in a world of "social death," which Achille Mbembe takes to mean that to be enslaved is to be existentially dead—in other words, is to experience "death-in-life."[86] For scholars who have traced the legal and social determinants of slavery, its relational disruptions occasion "the isolation of being severed from . . .

kin and denied ancestors," as Hartman suggests, with Frank B. Wilderson adding that slavery denies generational time and prevents people of African descent the opportunity to meaningfully assemble a past, present, or future: "The capacity to redeem time and space is foreclosed to the Black because redemption requires a 'heritage' of temporality and spatiality, rather than a past of boundless time and indeterminate space."[87] Building on these scholarly genealogies, I contend that in *Truth Self-Supported*, Wedderburn portrays relations forged by death that nevertheless possess a form of lifegiving power: to be atoned, after all, is to claim kinship with God's executed and mortal son. Moreover, Wedderburn suggests that the only way to "wake the dead" is to be covered by Christ's bodily remains, which offer a "Hiding-Place" for those living in a precarious present. No prophet, not even Christ, returns from the dead to remake the world.

Wedderburn's orientation to a shadowed future and a forlorn hope carries into *The Horrors of Slavery*, which recognizes the abnegation of Black being and belonging under slavery, even while his mother's rage invents a scene of diasporic worldmaking in the ruins. In other words, Wedderburn denies conviction in the future's total renewal, even while he cannot help but anticipate a "universal" revolution against slavery and property. Because of this, I am inclined to read him as a figure who echoes elements of plural worldmaking rehearsed in philosopher Isabelle Stengers's notion of "cosmopolitics": if we adjust to the cosmos as the material ground for "multiple divergent worlds," whose fullness evades our grasp, we may then renounce "the temptation of a peace intended to be final"—or finished.[88] In his gestures to unfinished worlds, Wedderburn refuses a capitalist regime premised on seemingly hegemonic and unrelenting routines of extraction. Instead, he repudiates all efforts to reconstitute the governed subjectivities and linear temporalities central to colonial administration in a world after the revolution.[89] In *The Axe Laid to the Root*, when Wedderburn imagines a global commons with the potential to reshape politics, he still remains wary of radical projects that portend a fully redeemed future.

". . . Tenants at Will to the Sovereignty of the People"

As in *Truth Self-Supported*, in *The Axe Laid to the Root*, Wedderburn deliberately grounds his political vernacular within a cosmogony of finitude—in a recognition of the earth's limited lands, resources, lives—to interrupt an accelerating capital accumulation that depends on fictions of seemingly unending colonial growth and expansion.[90] For Wedderburn, the earth and its human and nonhuman inhabitants instead share in "the fact of finitude," as Eduardo Kohn terms it.[91] By denying the Enlightenment's cunning myths of property-formation, possessive individualism, and the "civilizing" aims of missionary projects, he repudiates modernity's vision of linear progress.[92] In this section, I trace how Wedderburn invokes commoning traditions in *The Axe Laid to the Root* to materialize a political ecology of finitude, especially in his gestures toward *tenancy*—or his refusals of property claims and land titles. While chapters one and two of this project focused on Indigenous and African diasporic exercises of collective witness against colonial exploitations of local ecologies and communities, and chapter three on an alternative history of Native commoning, here I argue that although Wedderburn's worlding praxis does not center on discrete configurations of material existence in the same way as Samson Occom (plants and waterways), Mary Prince (salt), and William Apess (forests), he uses a tenant commons as an epistemic framework to imagine a revolutionary pathway out of racial capitalism and toward a kind of planetary communalism.

Broadly, *The Axe Laid to the Root* extends Thomas Spence's radicalism to conceive forms of political tenancy as a ground for plural worlds. Spence's platform, delineated in pamphlets like *The Rights of Man* (1793) and *The End of Oppression* (1795), and in periodicals like *Pigs' Meat* (1793–94), was relatively straightforward: he called for land to be held in common and equated a rejection of private property with popular sovereignty. Elaborating on this basic principle of communal agrarianism, Spence called for the end of landlords and the organization of self-governing parishes as local, democratic bulwarks for representative institutions at the national level in Great Britain. Spence believed equal payment of land rents and a "social guarantee" to provide income for those unable to work could sustain this system—both of which would be institutionally protected through universal suffrage. Most importantly for Wedderburn's emphasis on the reproduction of antipatrilineal futures, Spence acknowledged the rights of infants and children to live free from abuse and poverty.[93] Wedderburn gives an overview of Spenceanism in the first issue of *The Axe Laid to the Root*, whose priority of place indicates its significance: "The Spenceans presume that the earth cannot be justly the private property of individuals, because it was never manufactured by man; therefore, whoever first sold it, sold that which was not his own, and of course there cannot be a title deed produced consistent with natural and universal justice."[94] His summary constitutes a sustained assault on the relationship between property and civil society clarified in early modern texts like John Locke's *Second Treatise on Government* (1690), which argued: "Whatsoever then he removes out of the state that nature hath provided . . . he hath mixed his labor with, and something that is his own, and thereby makes it his property."[95]

The Axe Laid to the Root is committed to a planetary commons *and* to the development of political plurality and consensus governance. Wedderburn grounds this sense of plurality in a revision of the Jubilee, which resets history by inaugurating a sacred time where all debts are forgiven, prisoners and captives are freed, and agricultural labor is suspended: "You shall neither sow nor reap what grows of itself nor gather the grapes from the undressed vines. For it is a jubilee. It shall be holy to you" (Lev. 25:10–12).[96] Although the Jubilee offers Wedderburn a resonant language for expressing "vengeance on behalf of the afflicted, the bound, the brokenhearted, the captive, and the grieving," he also takes this idiom even further: "The Spenceans recommend a division of rents, in preference to a division of lands:—as Moses's system failed. Spence's plan is an improvement upon that system which came from heaven. It admits no mortgages; it needs no jubilee."[97] Throughout *The Axe Laid to the Root*, Wedderburn argues that Mosaic law is flawed because it materially divides what is not fungible—the earth itself—and demands a periodic eschatological event to restore economic and political justice. By insisting that Spencean precepts require no jubilee at all, he instead contends that the underlying causes of expropriation never gain historical momentum.[98]

In addition, Wedderburn urges a kind of dwelling in the world that rejects property attachments formalized in hierarchal relationships between landlords and agricultural workers: "When you are exhorted to hold the land, and never give it up to your oppressors, you are not told to hold it as private property, but as tenants at will to the sovereignty of the people."[99] By invoking "tenants at will," a legal term for tenants who can be evicted without notice, his vision of sovereignty anticipates Michel Serres's in *Malfeasance* (2010), which argues that to "practice . . . the dispossession of the world" is, at its core, to inhabit a kind of "tenancy."[100] For Serres, this embraces a recognition that "we live as transients or tenants, deprived of a fixed abode."[101] He arrives at this conception out of his reading of Christian pilgrimage—a spiritual practice in which "a person *leave[s] no trace whatsoever that would allow us to infer a history*."[102] Anahid Nersessian contends that Serres's form of tenancy constitutes more than a mode of politics but "an almost penitential practice of not simply minimizing but actively relinquishing our real and metaphysical stakes in the appropriation of a planetary environment."[103] Yet Wedderburn draws from more than Christianity for his challenges to colonial consumption of bodies and lands, but also from Indigenous and Maroon traditions of commoning, as well as Black practices of fugitivity. These practices constitute "a metaphysical system that [has] never allowed for property in either the physical, philosophical, temporal, legal, social, or psychic senses," a denial of racial capitalism vital to the Black radical tradition, as Cedric Robinson describes.[104]

Wedderburn's conception of sovereignty *as* tenancy may constitute his most vital extension and revision of Spence. When Spence imagines a post-revolutionary and multiracial society in *The Reign of Felicity* (1796), he idealizes Indigenous peoples as "the only free-men remaining on the face of the earth."[105] Here and elsewhere, Spence portrayed a commons equally available to dispossessed Indigenous and African diasporic communities, as well as disenfranchised people of European descent.[106] Although Wedderburn recognizes that Spence's revolutionary societies are extraordinarily sensitive to Caribbean violence, he also maintains that Caribbean residents could arrive at Spencean philosophy through their own experiences of exploitation, regardless of their familiarity with British radical culture. He says as much in *The Axe Laid to the Root* in a passage where he ventriloquizes Elizabeth: "The land is yours, not because Wedderburn, the Spencean says so, for I have read the word of God, and it says, the Lord gave the earth to the children of men. You are the children of men as well as others."[107] Elizabeth's exhortation functions as a vibrant "commoning practice," reflecting a praxis that Elizabeth Maddock Dillon maintains "articulate[s] relations of mutual belonging in a collective whole."[108] Here, Dillon echoes Silvia Federici, who argues that "commons are not things but social relations"—a point of clarification that resists the reification of commons.[109] In the same way, Elizabeth situates the commons not in the written archives of British radicalism, but in embodied and ecological traditions assembled by enslaved and Maroon communities, especially women of color.

Although Spence occupies a significant place as political theorist of Atlantic proletarian freedom, he is not always able to transcend imperialist geographies, as Wedderburn indicates.[110] Spence's short pamphlet *A Supplement to the History of Robinson Crusoe* (1782), a radical epilogue to Daniel Defoe's *Robinson Crusoe* (1719), illustrates how he cannot *quite* relinquish the language of possession even when envisioning a Caribbean utopia free from property ownership. Spence structures the *Supplement* as a dialogue between two figures, an unnamed English "Captain" and a resident of Crusonia called "Mann." The pamphlet's dialogic structure echoes the forms of polyvocality Wedderburn would use in his writings, a collaborative and communal ethos that suffuses working-class rhetoric in Great Britain in the 1820s.[111] Crusonia's multiethnic citizens represent the revolutionary possibilities for plural worlds Spence sometimes conjured in his writings. As the mouthpiece for Spencean doctrine, for instance, Mann might signify either a European citizen or the Indigenous captive Friday, whom Crusoe sometimes hails as "Man Friday." Because of this, when Mann narrates the island's history, Crusoe's and Friday's names index a troubling imperial geography:

> This puts me in mind to tell you of the names given to this famous island, and these are Cruson or Crusonia, from Robinson Crusoe, the founder of the empire; and the inhabitants Crusons or Crusonians. . . . They name the continent, which they have colonized, Fridinea, from his Man Friday, because it was his country, but this is only a provincial name, to distinguish the continent, from the island, for the general name, of the whole nation, both on the island and continent, is the United Parishes of Crusonia.[112]

Spence's cartographic nomenclature includes Caribbean Indigenous histories within his egalitarian reimagining of Caribbean sovereignty—it was "his" and Friday's "country." But while Spence's description of the island's structure of governance as "united parishes" is a familiar part of his political ideology, his deployment of the Crusoe narrative is a potentially counterproductive choice. Even the seemingly incidental matter of names makes this clear. In Defoe's novel, Crusoe does not ask Friday's name, but *imposes* one: "And first I made him know his Name should be *Friday*, which was the Day I sav'd his Life. . . . I likewise taught him to say *Master*, and then let him know, that was to be my Name."[113] Friday's name signifies his enslavement, a history retained in Spence when he calls Crusoe the "founder of an empire." Moreover, while Crusoe's naming of Friday purportedly testifies to his rescue from "cannibals," Friday's name also exists in the text as the result of an archival error. When Crusoe finally leaves the island, he discovers that the calendar he has been using to mark time is incorrect, meaning Crusoe did not encounter Friday *on* a Friday.[114] Spence's cartography retains this error, signaling how histories of colonial dispossession endure as traces. The alternative future to Defoe's novel envisioned by Spence is thus haunted by Friday's domination in both name and body.

Spence's *Supplement* neatly captures a tension inherent to radical British politics, when Mann proclaims, "You could not in any country possess a place more properly."[115] Mann's use of "possess" is disconcerting, for it implicitly retains a mandate for colonial occupation. Yet Wedderburn's invocation of tenancy implies that the persistence of any language for possession, even one significantly refined by Spence's agrarian communalism, risks reproducing these logics. When Wedderburn summarizes Spencean doctrine, he defines European possession of Caribbean territory as a matter of "force or fraud": "Any person calling a piece of land his own private property, was a criminal; and though they may sell it, or will it to their children, it is only transferring of that which was first obtained by force or fraud."[116] A colonial genealogy of "force or fraud" is the historical legacy Wedderburn hopes a global revolution will eradicate. He does this to offer, as David Worrall observes, a "green" future in the face of capitalist extraction: "Instead of nineteenth-century imperialism, there might have been a self-sufficient and equable nation decentralized into parishes, perhaps even into a welfare state. . . . It did not have to be the way it is now."[117] Building on Worrall, I argue that Wedderburn entrenches sovereignty within a deterritorialized, even itinerant, form of dwelling that *can* continue into a future because it fully divests from property, primogeniture, and slavery. In Wedderburn's conflicted recounting of Spence, it is possible to glimpse two postrevolutionary prospects—a new order founded on "proper" possession and an insurgent form of tenant life. Wedderburn's politics of tenancy thus aligns with his practice of prosopopoeia in this and other texts—plural speakers, plural worlds. Yet it is his very emphasis on collective voices that government surveillance records archive as the most dangerous aspects of his activism, as I explore in the next section.

"A Government . . . Open Mouthed and Ready To Devour"

A broad network of government spies reported on Wedderburn's political work in the 1810s and 1820s. As a member of the Society of Spencean Philanthropists, Wedderburn joined a coalition of pamphleteers, preachers, and activists centered in impoverished neighborhoods of London, where poor Black residents tended to live.[118] Iain McCalman calls this network "a tiny, informal underground, which gradually rallied the survivors of Jacobin revolutionary cadres smashed in the government repression of 1798–1803, then gained a fresh batch of recruits during the partial radical revival" in the final years of the Napoleonic wars.[119] After the war, popular unrest intensified in the wake of the Peterloo Massacre in 1819, when English cavalry notoriously charged a crowd that had gathered to demand parliamentary reform, killing fifteen and injuring dozens. Members of Parliament responded by passing the repressive "Six Acts," measures aimed at suppressing radical assemblies, on December 30, 1819. Wedderburn himself was arrested for blasphemy and sedition in late November 1819 and sentenced to two years' imprisonment at Dorchester Gaol, leaving his wife and six children without his support.[120] During the trial in February 1820, Wedderburn defended his radical activities by reminding the court that he did not grow up with the influence of a "Christian father." The jury recommended clemency "in consequence of his not having had the benefit of *parental care*" — an assessment that elides Rosanna and Amy's roles in his life.[121] In a grim irony, Wedderburn's time in jail may have inadvertently saved his life.[122] Several of his Spencean comrades, including his fellow Jamaican, William Davidson, were arrested in 1820 for their involvement in the Cato Street Conspiracy, a plot to assassinate members of the Cabinet, including the Prime Minister, Lord Liverpool. Government officials learned of the scheme through George Edwards, an informer who infiltrated the group, and Davidson was among the five conspirators executed on May 1, 1820.[123] Wedderburn's life during these dangerous years remains unusually well documented, largely because of the efforts of spies like Edwards, who reported on dissident meetings.[124]

Nevertheless, members of the Hopkins Street Chapel worked to promote measures for resisting state suppression and surveillance. These efforts at collective strategy are evident in spy reports from the period, even (or especially) in passages where they embellish radical speech with the intent to shock or horrify bureaucrats. Deformed and warped by state agents, Wedderburn's dissident speech contains evocative details of how he interacted with listeners.[125] Yet we must be careful to read spy reports with methods developed in Black studies: as with many narratives of enslavement, surveillance records are shaped by observers, editors, and amanuenses.[126] Despite the hostile conditions of their origins, it is still possible to trace scenes of political solidarity in these reports. At a speech given during a November 1819 debate, for instance, one spy writes that Wedderburn ventriloquizes three different speakers — a Black preacher, a Jewish radical, and an English heretic — who form a revolutionary coalition out of discrete millenarian traditions:

> [Wedderburn] began his discourse about Blacks in Jamaica and said that a black who had a chapel at Kingston who preached to the slaves that all men were Christians ought to be free they pulled down his Chapel and put him in prison and sent to know whether he was free his master did set him free at sixteen then they said that it was not lawful to be set

free before twenty and on[c]e however he got out of prison and being determined to preach no one would allow him ground to build a Chapel upon but a Jew who did not believe in him [Christ] and said that as their Government was sanctioned by the Princes and his ministers they ought to be made way with. . . . for it is said in scripture that he that stealeth a man and selleth him ought to be put to death and that the missionaries dare not preach that and another sentence in Jamaica Do not own yourselves masters and that he did not think on him so much his enemy as Government who were looking at him open mouthed ready to devour him or emprison him as they did Richard Brothers who had preached for years but when he began to launch out against government they had him confined as a madman.[127]

In this extraordinary speech, Wedderburn first rehearses the charged sermon of the Black preacher, that "all men [who] were Christians ought to be free," who draws from Biblical precedent to argue that conversion and fidelity to Christian creed confers legal freedom. The Black preacher, furthermore, believes access to the chapel affords him the opportunity to voice this dangerous message. The spy's emphasis on both the preacher and the chapel suggests how closely Wedderburn tied his conception of prophetic office to local institutions and buildings in Jamaica. Finally, Wedderburn refuses to close his narrative with only the Black preacher's resistant speech. Instead, he moves to voice a Jewish revolutionary who offers ground for a new chapel, regardless of his own lack of commitment to Christianity: "no one would allow him ground to build a Chapel upon but a Jew who did not believe." Despite their different religious affiliations, the Jewish revolutionary echoes the preacher's populist political theology, going so far as to promote total state overthrow: "As their Government was sanctioned by the Princes and his ministers they ought to be made away with."[128] The call to do "away with" an imperial order instituted on slavery reverberates throughout the different speakers' layered vernaculars. The Jewish revolutionary grounds his political aims within a reciprocal ethics, "for it is said in scripture that he that stealeth a man and selleth him ought to be put to death," recalling that in the Pentateuch the legal punishment for enslaving another person is death (Ex. 21:16). In channeling these voices, Wedderburn's speech invokes a *longue durée* of anticolonial resistance, one that connects Caribbean revolutionary efforts with millenarian traditions from other times and places. Indeed, if his first two speakers appeal to shared sacred texts to condemn slavery, then the final speaker foregrounds the threat of future revolt in the heart of the British metropole.

According to the surveillance record, Wedderburn concludes his speech by invoking the British heretic Richard Brothers. A contemporary of Wedderburn, Brothers famously claimed in *A Revealed Knowledge of the Prophecies & Times* (1794) that a remnant of diasporic Jewish peoples have "descended of Israel" and survived in Britain—and will create the world anew.[129] Yet for Brothers, before this new social order can come into being, the British Empire must fall: "A little time longer, and England will be so much entangled as not to be able to go forward without feeling the pains of the *Colonial Conquest* which is to be the cause of her death."[130] Mary Favret argues that Brothers depicts the British Empire as inextricably ensnared by pressing financial and military commitments, prompting Brothers to urge all citizens to "inhabit time differently."[131] Brothers's "a little time longer" resonantly echoes a passage in *The Axe Laid to the Root*, when Wedderburn warns that a "time is fast approaching, when such rulers must act righteously, or be drawn from their seats; for truth and justice must prevail—combined armies cannot stop their progress."[132] Brothers's "a little time longer," as with Wedderburn's "time . . . fast approaching," warns that an oncoming revolution is imminent and will end the British Empire. Wedderburn further intensifies Brothers's "pains" of empire, summoning a visceral vernacular of imperial cannibalism to dissect how surveillance destroys both politics and community. Rather than an embattled institution, his colonial government stands ready to imprison and consume those who voice dissidence: it "look[s] at him open mouthed ready to devour him." In all these ways, Wedderburn's personas in this surveillance record respond to and build upon the previous persona's claims: the preacher's egalitarian message becomes the Jewish radical's call for violent revolution, which then instantiates the powerful prophecy of empire's end that Brothers voices. The surveillance record thus archives a colonial order profoundly vulnerable to the heterodox collaborations Wedderburn so often prophetically calls into being.

In addition, George Cruikshank's *The New Union Club* (1819), a virulently racist satirical image, visually recoils from the collective energy Wedderburn's speeches frequently assembled, while closely associating him with events in Haiti. The print depicts a meeting of the African Institution that degenerates into a sexual orgy (figure 2). Prominent members of the antislavery movement, including William Wilberforce, Zachary Macaulay, and William Smith, are present throughout the room.[133] The threat of miscegenation is particularly prevalent, as many of the men caress African women or are surrounded by biracial ("piebald") children. *The New Union Club* draws on conventions of both religious painting and political satire to represent the

FIGURE 2 George Cruikshank, "The New Union Club" (1819). Courtesy of the Lewis Walpole Library and Yale University.

menace of a multiracial present, as Marcus Wood argues, and "constitutes both an apotheosis of black chaos and a vision of hell for white people; it is a last judgement for abolition."[134] As the prophet of this last judgement, Wedderburn stands at the center and gestures to the crowd.

Although scholars like Jenna Gibbs and Ryan Hanley have addressed the sexual and racial dimensions of *The New Union Club*'s composition, I am interested not only in how Wedderburn's posture embodies the specter of Black insurgency but also in how the print signals British anxieties about the Haitian Revolution in its peripheral iconography, where artwork lining the back wall of the print alludes to Haiti as a postrevolutionary nation.[135] Along the left-hand side, for instance, is a newsprint depicting the "The [Haitian] king royal family sitting," with the script, "King Henry of Hyti [is] to be drunk [to] 3 times 3." This scene perversely invokes traditions of toasting a sovereign, with this public performance of patriotism directed at Henry Christophe, then King of Haiti, until his suicide less than a year later under threat of a coup (October 8, 1820). As with the spy report, the print brings into relief critical problems for grappling with its racist imaginary: Can the print extend possibilities for recovering a Black sovereignty that exceeds the visual norms of British satire? Tina Campt argues that *listening* to, rather than merely *seeing*, antiblack images may enable us to subvert the ocular hierarchies of colonial surveillance, affording opportunities for hearing diasporic conceptions of time and space.[136] Indeed, on the right-hand side, one painting represents "The King of Hayti and his Black-guards" on the brink of movement, with the implication that the sounds of imminent revolutionary activity are just out of frame. Listening to *The New Union Club*, then, may summon Wedderburn's charismatic voice as he speaks a decolonial future into existence, an instance where the sounds of his speech constitute a radically polyphonic act of worldmaking.

"You Are No Longer Slaves . . ."

When Wedderburn turns from the Haitian Revolution to future revolt, he often reconfigures with and extends working-class periodical and performance repertoires to express a Black radical tradition. In one context, *The Axe Laid to the Root* formed part of broader efforts by the Society of Spencean Philanthropists to cheaply disseminate political pamphlets and newspapers in the manner of the corresponding societies of the 1790s.[137] Examples include editions of Paine's *Rights of Man* (1790) and Thomas Spence's *Pigs' Meat* (1793–94) and *Important Trials* (1801), which were republished for Society members, as well as original texts like Wedderburn's periodicals *A Forlorn Hope* and *The Axe Laid to the Root*. Printed by Arthur Seale in Houndsditch, *The Axe Laid to the Root* first appeared in six installments, suggesting that Wedderburn designed the periodical to be read as a series of sermons to radical audiences gathered in alehouses and dissenting clubs.[138] As such, Wedderburn directs these sermons to the dual reading and listening publics he imagines encountering the periodical: members of the London underclass and those enslaved in Jamaica.[139] But while Wedderburn opens *The Axe Laid to the Root* by proclaiming the primacy of the newspaper in the work of revolution—"The press is my engine of destruction"—the last two issues are entirely comprised of letters between Wedderburn and Elizabeth.[140] Elizabeth portrays the illicit flow of news into Jamaica, sending letters to Wedderburn via a Black cook rather than the official post. She further warns that the circulation of radical periodicals invites discussions of the Haitian Revolution, portraying reading and rumors as interconnected inspirations for resistance: "The free Mulattoes are reading Cobbett's Register, and talking about St. Domingo."[141] Generically layered, *The Axe Laid to the Root* rehearses the kinds of clandestine rumors that circulated as both oral intelligence whispered from ear to ear and printed news read aloud.[142]

Although *The Axe Laid to the Root*'s individual issues also included articles, hymns, and poems, the letters between Wedderburn and Elizabeth offer insight into epistolary texts' ability to archive in their quotidian details "heterodox performances of the very meaning of freedom," as David Kazanjian has argued in a different context.[143] Their letters exhort readers to practice fidelity to the Haitian Revolution as an event that animates the continuing work of abolitionist resistance. Wedderburn at one point asserts that the Haitian Revolution remains incomplete because imperial expansion threatens Haiti as a nation: "You will have need of all your strength to defend yourself against those men, who are now scheming in Europe against the blacks of St. Domingo."[144] Against present "schemes" to retake Haiti, Wedderburn purposely turns to marronage as a tactic for contesting British rule.[145] Elizabeth emphasizes her kinship ties to the Windward Maroons because they empower her to inhabit Spence's radical ideals, even when colonial patriarchal systems circumscribe her agency: "I, who am a weak woman, of the Marroon [*sic*] tribe, understood the Spencean doctrine directly: I heard of it, and obey, and the slaves felt the force directly."[146] Moreover, this generational legacy to marronage closely ties Elizabeth to Haiti, given that many, in Kamau Brathwaite's words, would have understood the Haitian Revolution as "the greatest and most successful Maroon polity of them all."[147] In view of these histories, I argue that Elizabeth's ties to Haiti and the Maroons—and implicitly to the early Maroon leader Nanny—assemble renegade paths away from colonial domination. In this way, Wedderburn renders Elizabeth a navigator of fugitive pathways that are constitutive of Black radical worldmaking.[148] *The Axe Laid to the Root* thus depicts a world where marronage constitutes not only an escape from a specific colonial locale, but also a retreat from the *world as it is lived*.[149] Indeed, this worldmaking capacity shapes Wedderburn's claim that Maroon botanic knowledge enables Black resistance to a Jamaican colonial order and, more importantly, subverts the circulations of global capital itself: "Their store of provisions is every w[h]ere in abundance; you know they can live upon sugar canes, and a vast variety of herbs and fruits, — yea, even upon the buds of trees. You cannot cut off their supplies. They will be victorious in their flight, slaying all before them."[150] Building from Wynter's claim that enslaved provision grounds and Maroon enclaves were sources "of cultural guerrilla resistance to the plantation system," Katey Castellano further argues that Wedderburn's agrarian perspective reflects a reality where enslaved persons could "cultivate commons in creative relationship to land, plants, and animals."[151] Ultimately, Wedderburn portrays Elizabeth's plantation as a "sacred plot of land where slaves wd plot," as Brathwaite defines it, where collective embodied and ecological knowledge enables Black insurgency.[152]

That Wedderburn centers this praxis of fugitivity in his prosopopoeia of Elizabeth, however, is not without vexed social and political implications. While a historical person named Elizabeth Campbell likely existed, Wedderburn probably ghostwrote her letters, and he never gives any details on how Elizabeth, a biracial woman, came to inherit a plantation in Jamaica.[153] Moreover, his ventriloquism of Elizabeth is grounded in the messy histories of coercion and resistance fostered by plantation exploitation along the Caribbean littoral. For one, Elizabeth's position as a plantation owner and a descendent of Maroons illustrates Mavis Campbell's point that colonial governments sought to constrain the provocation extended by marronage to the entire system of slavery.[154] As societies that drew primarily from Akan culture, Maroon towns disrupted plantation economies, but after signing treaties with colonial governments in the mid-eighteenth century, they were also required by law to return Black freedom seekers to their enslavers and assist British militias during insurrections against slavery—priorities that Maroon communities sometimes complied with or resisted in different ways. Elizabeth's heritage as the daughter of an enslaved woman and Maroons illustrates Neil Roberts's point that an "underlying maxim of marronage" is that "freedom is perpetual, unfinished, and rooted in acts of flight that are at moments evanescent, durable, and overlapping."[155] In this figuration of unfinished freedom, Wedderburn uses Elizabeth's complicated position to imagine an opening for abolition itself: his feminist vision of a Black woman liberating an estate expresses a possibility that Richard Waswo calls "the history that literature makes," where "fictional imaginings, themselves a response to past events, can become a cause of future ones."[156] Wedderburn's narrative of Elizabeth's act of emancipation, then, is a fantasy of abolition that he hopes will ignite *actual* revolution. In other words, Elizabeth's choice to manumit everyone on her plantation—a decision rooted in her relationships to the Haitian Revolution and Jamaican marronage—portends a revolutionary history that Édouard Glissant calls a "prophetic vision of the past" or a way of envisioning history as it *could be*, rather than as it *was*.[157]

These complexities take center stage in *The Axe Laid to the Root*'s final issues, which describe Elizabeth's manumission of all laborers on the plantation she has inherited. On the one hand, it might be too easy to interpret these issues as Wedderburn refusing to render freedom an outcome of revolutionary self-emancipation, but as an act that originates in the voice of the property owner. On the other hand, I want to suggest that these letters function as a corollary to his all-encompassing denunciation of all forms of complicity with plantation violence, including every "man, woman, and child . . . whose interest is connected with slavery, whether black, white, or tawny." Put more simply, Elizabeth exemplifies a refusal to live in collusion with economies of stolen labor and land, even though she inherits a measure of privilege within this economic system.[158] Even so, at the very moment of Elizabeth's act of liberation, Wedderburn portrays an elderly man who dies after hearing her words of manumission, suggesting his profound awareness of the contingent nature of freedom itself:

> You are no longer slaves my conscience is free from guilt, but the blood of my ancestors, who fell for freedom's cause will be required at the hands of the white men, who, against knowledge, refuse obedience to nature's law, The unexpected sounds, you are no longer slaves, deprived them of speech; some fainted with joy, the rest were amazed, an old man, whose head was white as snow, cried out, Lord help us! Missy, Missy, you sall sit on de same seat wid de Virgin Mary; may God make dee his servant. I will go to toder country in peace. He then dropped, like Palmer, on the stage: by this time, the rest of the slaves recovered from their stupor, four young men with solemn respect, bore the corpse away.[159]

Here, Elizabeth's words of manumission momentarily "[deprive]" the freed captives "of speech"—unusual in Wedderburn's representations of radical projects—but then an old man "[cries] out" in valediction and rapture, and then in pain. Indeed, his death complicates the letter's vision of abolition, for his incomplete speech and untimely loss confront readers with circumstances where mortality limits the transformative reach of radical revolution.

From one perspective, what Wedderburn offers is a script: he situates an elder's death within British performance history, alluding to John Palmer's sudden onstage death in 1798 while acting in August von Kotzebue's tragedy *The Stranger* (an English translation of *Menschenhass und Reue*, or *Misanthropy and Repentance*). Palmer's premature death, an intrusion of the real on stage, accrued its own peculiar legend, with theatergoers reporting that he died after speaking the portentous line, "There is another and a better world."[160] Wedderburn, however, alters this apocryphal line to "I will go to toder country in peace," revising a spectral utopia that *may* exist elsewhere to a country the old man promises he will certainly *see*. By naming Elizabeth an equal to the "Virgin Mary," moreover, the old man inscribes her within Catholic iconography, where she, like Mary, gives birth to something wholly new. The old man's cry is inextricably entangled with British stage history and Christian theology, where both offer a vocabulary that renders visible the violences that shaped the old man's life and death under slavery, as well as possibilities for a transformed world. As a further meditation on performance, it is significant that Wedderburn ends the scene with the newly freed inhabitants moving with "solemn respect" toward another shared ritual: a funeral. Even so, because readers are not able to follow the elder's passage from the plantation to his burial place, this passage marks an incomplete performance that accompanies his unfinished speech. In other words, both comprise a metaleptic history, or unresolved events that are not fully available for closure or recovery.

A Maroon's vengeance. A Black woman's act of liberation. An elder's loss. At these scenes, Wedderburn struggles with his own inability to fully speak abolition into being. In this sense, *The Axe Laid to the Root* resonates with C. L. R. James's *The Black Jacobins* (1938), which grapples with the vexed career of Toussaint L'Ouverture, whose position within systems of extractive capitalism circumscribed his political horizon.[161] As James discusses, L'Ouverture was faced with the choice of imagining Haiti's future when the island was circumvented by economic networks predicated on Black exploitation. L'Ouverture could support subsistence agriculture or plantation monocultures, knowing that either decision would indelibly shape Haiti's future—indeed, in several paragraphs James added to the second edition of *The Black Jacobins* in 1963, he suggests that L'Ouverture struggled to identify an extant pathway beyond these constraints. James's meditation has lingered with me as I have grappled with Wedderburn's words. Would a different script have assured revolutionary outbreak in Jamaica—and the survival of formerly enslaved elders—or is Wedderburn contending with hegemonic systems that circumvent Elizabeth's choices? This question has brought me to David Scott's point that James improvises a theory of revolutionary tragedy—that L'Ouverture inhabited a global order that he could "neither simply claim as his own nor completely disavow," that he was "a conscript of modernity."[162] Read similarly, Wedderburn is also concerned with conceiving radical revolution's contingencies under a global regime of racialized terror and capitalist extraction.

Yet I also wonder if *The Axe Laid to the Root* is less an account of his position as a conscript of modernity and more an insight into the exigencies of radical exhaustion, what Fred Moten calls "exhaustion as a mode or form or way of life" under racial capitalism.[163] This is not to say that the old man's death is *not* an example of revolutionary tragedy, occurring as it does just after he cries out in freedom, but that his loss exposes a "mortal vulnerability" predicated on *systems* of plantation enslavement. These systems index the calculations of value and loss that shape the elder's life and death, which are formally replicated in colonial archives.[164] Thus, while *The Axe Laid to the Root*'s shattering of the scene of emancipation certainly challenges Elizabeth's (and, because Wedderburn is voicing her, his own) proclamation of a revolutionary future for all, the single death of this elder represents an eschatological return to the anti-resurrection theology Wedderburn espoused so trenchantly in *Truth Self-Supported*, an ontology of human finitude in which history cannot be fully repaired. But if Christ's death counterintuitively enables a kind of communal deliverance, then perhaps what *The Axe Laid to the Root* formally models in Elizabeth and Wedderburn's letters is not a "superseded future," as Scott terms it, but what Ariella Aïsha Azoulay calls a practice of "potential history": "Potential history does not mend worlds after violence but rewinds to the moment before violence occurred and sets off from there. . . . Such rehearsals of nonimperial political thinking and archival practice are not undertaken in preparation for an imminent day of reckoning, but rather as a mode of being with others differently."[165] By inventing Elizabeth's Jamaican insurgency as a point of historical departure, Wedderburn disavows the hegemonic conscriptions of capital modernity and rehearses a way of "being with" formerly enslaved persons on the cusp of living emancipated lives, even if a full abolition still remains on the horizon. Because of this, he seeks to make this elder—and the radical insurgency he responds to—an extant *present*, rather than a future always already lost.

A Suspended Now

> But when does one decide to stop looking to the past and instead conceive of a new order? When is it time to dream of another country . . . or to make an opening, an overture, where there is none? When is it clear that the old life is over, a new one has begun, and there is no looking back?
> —SAIDIYA HARTMAN

> I would like to think that this new world is still to come.
> —MARLENE DAUT

Across his speeches and writings, Wedderburn maintains that a world without slavery is a historical inevitability, but in his dual recognition of revolution's contingency and certain approach, he anticipates Benjamin's materialist historian, who must inhabit a *kairos* of revolutionary possibility by "[establishing] a conception of the present as the 'time of the now' which is shot through with chips of Messianic time."[166] Paul K. Saint-Amour argues that this materialist historian's orientation to revolution's contorted and recursive unfoldings must also encompass a refusal to turn away from the dead: "What if some of the most trenchant critiques of violence we possess were mounted by those faced with a future they believed already lost to violence? In response, the angel of history would need, while facing the past, to bear witness to the past, to bear witness to past apprehensions of the *future* as the disaster or the storm oncoming."[167] To pose this question differently: for Wedderburn, can a *kairos* of unfinished revolution likewise afford a rehearsal of witnessing—a practice of waiting while watching for—a future already lost to violence?

As a witness to a history that could be, *The Axe Laid to the Root* marshals in its formal structure the possibilities of a revolutionary "now" in the last letter sent by Elizabeth to Wedderburn. Here, Elizabeth describes a terrifying acceleration of plantocratic paranoia in response to her efforts to popularize Spenceanism and advocate for emancipation. The letter's prosopopoeia is exceptionally layered, for Wedderburn speaks as Elizabeth, who relays the threats of white colonists, in this case a planter named James MacPherson: "Miss Campbell should be considered as a lunatic, and be treated as such; for, if this assembly was to countenance such a degree of madness, as to tolerate, by law, any individual giving liberty to their slaves, and a right to the soil, we should then become actual Spenceans."[168] Yet Elizabeth refuses the hysteria underpinning efforts to constrain either her actions or those of her fellow insurgents, as she retorts: "It is in vain for you to inflict death on the slaves for preaching."[169] For Elizabeth, not even capital punishment can contain revolutionary outbreak, asserting that liberation—and perhaps a global commons—will arrive no matter the violent retaliation of colonial governments. In this way, *The Axe Laid to the Root*'s final letter rehearses a politics of expectancy that portends the end of imperial sovereignty, a performance of "prophetic time" that Deborah Thomas contends "validates the expectancy of faith in a future in a way that creates a sense of an already existing freedom rather than one that is always one or two steps away."[170]

Even so, Elizabeth's last letter to Wedderburn implicitly recognizes that not all will live to see the revolution to come. The material history of *The Axe Laid to the Root* supports the text's conviction that human mortality, the result of either colonial brutality or revolutionary contingency, limits any anticolonial future. Ominously, the periodical ends midsentence, with

Elizabeth repeating the words of James McPherson, who is planning swift and wholesale reprisals against Black insurgents, who now live on Elizabeth's emancipated plantation:

> You will recollect, gentlemen, the slaves are not so ignorant as the Marroons were, when, after they had gained their own liberty, became instruments to guard the woods from being a harbour for other runaway slaves. You will also recollect, we have broken the treaty with the Marroons, by punishing one of their tribes without trial by their own judge and jury, for which they went against us. . . . [Besides], we transported the whole of that tribe into a cold climate, which destroyed the chief part of them. Now, gentle—*To be continued*.[171]

Here, Macpherson alludes to the Second Maroon War (1795–96), when members of Trelawny Town, a Maroon village on the leeward side of Jamaica, revolted in response to the unjust punishment of three Maroon men, who were accused of stealing two pigs in Montego Bay. British soldiers finally defeated the insurgent Maroons only after months of conflict. Over 580 members of the community were banished to Nova Scotia and transported in the fall of 1796.[172] Wedderburn's invocation of these events, via his prosopopoeia of Elizabeth, who is herself ventriloquizing a white Jamaican official, performs several roles: it foregrounds the Maroons as an object lesson for the dangers of surrender and urges future revolutionaries to never compromise, for colonial governments make use of the very earth and weather in their reprisals. Indeed, the British transport the Maroons to a "cold climate" in Nova Scotia, which Wedderburn interprets as an act of environmental genocide because it "destroyed the chief part of them."[173]

Although this historical context is significant (and suggests how attentively Wedderburn followed events in Jamaica after leaving in 1779), I want to close this chapter by lingering with his use of the dash. After MacPherson urges colonial duplicity against the Maroons as a political template for dealing with African insurgents, he concludes, "Now, gentle—," followed by "*To be continued*." Yet *The Axe Laid to the Root* suspended publication in late 1817, and another issue never subsequently appeared. We could read this textual rupture as an outcome of British repressions of the radical press—as a sign that the periodical could not continue because state agents dispersed the equipment needed for publication.[174] However, this midsentence interruption could also elusively signal that the revolution has already begun—that Elizabeth's accuser cannot complete his sentence because he has been cut down by an insurgent force. Fran Botkin and Paul Youngquist name such open ended moments in Caribbean texts the "anarchival," a Maroon "ambush" that preserves a line of flight away from the imperial violence that suffuses Jamaican scenes.[175] At the same time, because *"To be continued"* is not quite an ambush, but the pause before the strike, it concisely marks the sense of breathless expectation that Wedderburn so often prophetically registers — that he lives on the cusp of insurrection, on the precipice of an imminent revolt. The dash grammatically attests that the "time is fast approaching" but stops just short of announcing that the awaited future has finally arrived. In this way, *The Axe Laid to the Root* evinces a Benjaminian "model of Messianic time [that] comprises the entire history of mankind in an enormous abridgement," one that prompts readers to occupy the infinitive of *"To be continued."*[176] Put differently, Wedderburn's readers must come to inhabit the dash — they must survive in a stalled archive and continue in the perpetual "now" of revolution's belated approach.

Wedderburn's readers are waiting, in short, for a *rejoinder* to the dash — we are waiting for someone to speak what Maurice Blanchot calls "the 'nonetheless' that breaks the impossible and restores time."[177] Because *The Axe Laid to the Root* ends midsentence, it becomes a periodical in perpetuity, preserving Elizabeth's interrupted voice as a prophetic repertoire, a small plot to carry as we wait for revolution's beginning. In its formal structure, *The Axe Laid to the Root* resonates with critical preoccupations in Black studies that have taken up "now time" as constitutive of diasporic archives. Tina Campt, for instance, contends that African American art marshals "a politics of prefiguration that involves living the future *now* — as imperative rather than subjunctive — as a striving for the future you want to see, right now, in the present."[178] By inhabiting this temporal rupture, "Now gentle —" also illustrates Michelle M. Wright's contention that "now" chronologies are "*not* directly borne out of" the past, but coordinate past, present, and future in new, nonlinear relations.[179] In other words, Wedderburn anticipates that not everyone will survive to see the revolution, but urges all — from their varied locations in time and space on this finite earth — to speak a new world into existence *now*. And *The Axe Laid to the Root*'s abbreviated ending is perhaps one reason why Wedderburn has seen such a surge of critical interest in Black studies and Romanticism studies. "Now," Wedderburn's term for a worlding praxis that puts pressure on the seemingly impossible reparation of Black being and belonging, radiates to embrace the unruly discourses of the London underworld, the transatlantic solidarities of proletarian commoning, the agrarian projects of a green future, and the queer and feminist undertakings of diasporic performance.[180]

Embattled and abbreviated, *The Axe Laid to the Root* archives Wedderburn's efforts to develop a prophetic vernacular that can instigate new solidarities in the wake of the Haitian Revolution. In its attentiveness to the liberatory potential of language, the text seeks to reimagine planetary life beyond slavery and the structures of antiblackness and patriarchy that undergird it. Even so, in the final years of Wedderburn's life, no truly "universal" insurrection ignited to carry on the promise of the Haitian Revolution, in Jamaica or elsewhere, although insurgencies like Bussa's Rebellion in Barbados (1816), the Demerara Revolt in Guyana (1823), and the Baptist War in Jamaica (1831–32) promised much—indeed, Bussa's Rebellion and the Demerara Revolt informed the exigence of *The Axe Laid to the Root* and *The Horrors of Slavery*, as Wedderburn published each text in the wake of these resistance movements. According to one line of critical interpretation, however, Wedderburn became disenchanted with the possibility of disarticulating modernity from its accomplices in property and slavery. In a recently discovered pamphlet, *An Address to the Right Honorable Lord Brougham* (1831)—likely Wedderburn's final text—he advocates a gradualist approach to abolition with accompanying compensation to enslavers.[181] Ryan Hanley speculates that Wedderburn's rhetoric was circumscribed by the growing pressure toward respectability in popular, proletarian, and antislavery movements in the 1830s, which shifted away from unruly anticlericalism and toward evangelical sentimentality—historical processes that similarly constrained *The History of Mary Prince*, also published in 1831.[182]

Still, I wonder if perspectives like Hanley's perhaps begin with the wrong question. Rather than reading *An Address to the Right Honorable Lord Brougham* as exemplifying a conservative agenda, what if we read the text as a reflection on the demands of political stamina that preoccupied Wedderburn throughout his career? In the face of revolution's harrowing deferrals, he consistently modeled a prophetic itinerancy that could disrupt—and perhaps undo—colonial dominion over land and flesh, even in instances where one person could no longer speak because of poverty, illness, war, or death. Understood this way, Wedderburn's work confronts his readers (then and now) with an urgent realization: if we are to see his radical vision—an earth in common, worlds in plurality—come to pass amid accelerating climate catastrophe and antiblack violence, then revolution will approach through a shared announcement within unexpected coalitions and will sound forth even if Wedderburn approached the end of his life shuddering with exhaustion. We should ask then: Who will speak next in a future that is "*to be continued*"? Will it be Robert Wedderburn? Elizabeth Campbell? Or a prophet not yet known?

Coda

To travel without a map, to travel without a way. They did, long ago. That misdirection became the way. After the Door of No Return, a map was only a set of impossibilities, a set of changing locations. A map, then, is only a life of conversations about a forgotten list of irretrievable selves.

—DIONNE BRAND

An imperfect map will have to do, little one.

—JOY HARJO

Throughout *The Rich Earth Between Us*, I have turned to Samson Occom, Mary Prince, William Apess, and Robert Wedderburn to retrieve modes of desiring otherwise. In their dense elaborations of "an earth given to the children of men," they challenge one origin narrative of private property, land theft, and colonial expansion. By engaging with their citations of a gifted earth, I have also interrogated another, more recent origin story—that of a planet in crisis. Confronted by an acceleration in global warming, climate scientists have increasingly searched for a "golden spike" when expropriations of human and earthly reserves began reshaping material existences on a planetary scale.[1] This body of research has surveyed the early years of colonial discovery to identify when the Holocene transitions to a "red / Round Globe, hot burning," in William Blake's lyric script—when the Holocene shifts to the Anthropocene.[2] Simon L. Lewis and Mark A. Maslin propose 1610 as the year that heralds our ongoing climate emergency, arguing that a devastating decline in Native populations, and hence a waning in the human activities that shape weather patterns, produced historically low carbon levels, while setting into motion the extractive systems driving increasing levels of atmospheric carbon today.[3] Put simply, 1610 recognizes colonial massacre as central to the story of a heating planet.[4]

Even so, an emphasis on 1610 could risk overdetermining Indigenous vanishing by beginning with the most colonial of genres: a set of statistics, a double-entry account of demographic collapse. While 1610 reflects the mathematics of deficit and loss occasioned by an unlivable history of racial capitalism, its procedures of qualified abstraction threaten to reproduce the boundary-making imperatives inherent to colonial subjugation of land and life.[5] Kathryn Yusoff argues that 1610 thereby marks a "fabulation of beginnings" that "coheres around an exclusive notion of humanity"—a "reduction to matter, of what is supposed not to matter," in Fred Moten's elegant gloss.[6] Building from these interventions, in this project I have traced performances of diasporic survivance and dissent not by mediating between terms for the geologic era we now inhabit (Anthropocene or otherwise) as more epistemically accurate, nor by offering my own name for it, but by lingering with Black and Indigenous responses to these histories as they were unfolding. If colonial conquest delineates one plot for understanding a globe in crisis, then "the earth was given to the children of men" longs for another vision of planetary inhabitance. And the conceptual weight given to these stories *matters*—as Occom, Prince, Apess, and Wedderburn all knew well.

Tracing sensuous practices of diasporic worldmaking brings into relief Black and Indigenous refusals of colonial teleologies of racialized extraction, both then and now. Yet in my efforts to unearth these small plots against the hegemonic forces of global extraction, I have perhaps also reflected an impossible longing: a desire to approach, if only fleetingly, alternative ways of being in the world that *seemed* conceivable once—but can they be extant forms of life again? To ask this question is to confront the incompleteness of diasporic archives—they remain secret knowledge, exercises of unfinished social assembly, and practices of being with the earth that exceed the reach of imperial records. Indeed, these epistemological confrontations inextricably shape not only our engagements with the past, but also our perceptions of what lies ahead. In this coda, I wish to speculate with imagined cartographies in recent Black and Indigenous writing to extend an additional series of questions: How can we *re*-imagine what it might mean to dwell in a rich earth when a shared globe is itself at risk? How could a return to past practices of worldmaking sustain present and future plural cosmogonies, when the felt effects of violence against Black and Indigenous communities continue to structure the spaces we live and write within? And how can we inhabit these questions in such a way that our quest toward something like an answer nevertheless refuses the impulse to achieve a satisfactory arrival—a structure of desire too reliant on colonial logics of measurement and progress? While Benedict Anderson once argued that colonial cartography emerged as one of the key institutions through which imperial powers named, imagined, and governed the world, Black and Indigenous maps ask what it might look like to undo the onto-epistemic regimes that undergird racial capitalism and anthropogenic climate change.[7] By way of a conclusion and as a resistance to en/closure, then, I turn to diasporic maps as pathways for what we might do to survive in the days ahead.

In *A Map to the Door of No Return* (2002), Dionne Brand meditates on imagined belonging across African diasporic worlds. These are belongings improvised against and between colonial orientations to time and space, shaped by what Saidiya Hartman calls the "afterlife of slavery," in which the historical weight of the Middle Passage and of *partus sequitur ventrem* is felt. This history inextricably "conditions an afterlife that bears it, that extends it," as Fred Moten also argues.[8] A yearning for a reprieve from slavery's perpetual unfolding emerges most forcefully in a citation of Derek Walcott: "*Pray for a life without plot, a day without narrative,*" which Brand glosses: "I cannot know precisely what he means but I recognized something in it. Or perhaps something in it called me. It described perfectly my desire for relief from the persistent trope of colonialism. To be without this story of captivity, to dis-remember it, or to have this story forget me."[9] For Brand, the task for thought is to sever the material and mythmaking exercises of slavery, which unfurl as ruptures to Black kinship and history—to move, somehow, toward "a life without plot." Yet Brand recognizes that this unplotted life is still framed by a continual wounding in diasporic communities and their relations to a past: "Having no name to call on was having no past; having no past pointed to the fissure between the past and the present." Here, I want to suggest that Brand's point about the *ongoingness* of severed relations to history is anticipated by Mary Prince when she mourns, "The salt water come[s] into my eyes when I think of the days in which I was afflicted—the times that are gone; when I mourned and grieved with a young heart for those whom I loved!"[10] If "the times . . . are gone," and if having no recoverable past only maps "a set of impossibilities," what futures then? Can small plots, perhaps counterintuitively, improvise pathways *away* from "this story of captivity" and *toward* a kind of plotlessness?

Muscogee poet Joy Harjo takes up similar questions in the titular poem from *A Map to the Next World* (2001), which plumbs the affordances of decolonial desires at a moment of transition to "the fourth world." As such, Harjo develops the central conceit of the map by drawing on Muscogee cosmology—on traditional teachings that times and seasons do not unfold linearly, but are, as Angelique V. Nixon contends, "intersecting, mutually dependent, and perpetually moving in and out of each other."[11] Instead of a settler-national sense of what is progressive "history," Harjo represents cyclical transitions to new worlds: "Crucial to finding the way is this: there is no beginning or end."[12] For Harjo, this multidimensional orientation to time embraces what Ariella Aïsha Azoulay calls "unlearning imperialism"; as the poem puts it, "We do not want your version of progress."[13] This refusal of ideologies of historical progress undergirds the poem's collective worldmaking, enunciated with clarity in the first lines: "In the last days of the fourth world I wished to make a map for / those who would climb through the hole in the sky."[14] In the following lines, however, the speaker recognizes that her longings are interpellated within institutional settler violences, which seep into intimate scenes of everyday life: "My only tools were the desires of humans as they emerged / from the killing fields, from the bedrooms and the kitchens."[15] Because of this, Harjo's stanzas remind me of Occom's haunting reflection on what must have felt like the "last days of [this] world" during the American Revolution: "We have a Violent World to oppose."[16] Read this way, Occom's deepest desires for Brothertown also inflect Harjo's lyrical perspective: the charge to "carry fire to the next tribal town, for renewal of spirit."[17] To that end, Harjo does not map the world as it *is* but as it *will be*, assuring her listeners that in their journey into the next world, they will not have "a guidebook with words you can carry," but only "an incomplete map"— only a hope of what the cosmos *might be otherwise*. In its prophetic orientation, then, "A Map to the Next World" echoes Wedderburn's palpable urgency in *The Axe Laid to the Root* (1817), where he warns that a "time is fast approaching, when such rulers must act righteously, or be drawn from their seats; for truth and justice must prevail."[18]

Ultimately, I believe that Black and Indigenous maps show that unlearning imperialism is a difficult task, as any route toward recovered geographies, revitalized cultures, and renewed sovereignties must grapple with what settler expansion has tried to sever, elaborated by Harjo as a pained recognition of disrupted relations to Indigenous languages, land-based teachings, and nonhuman relatives: "We no longer know the names of the birds here, how to speak to / them by their personal names."[19] Yet we must perpetually remind ourselves that diasporic worlds are not wholly and irretrievably lost, as Chickasaw poet Linda Hogan suggests in her poem "Maps." They may only be asleep—only dreaming:

> There are names each thing has for itself,
> and beneath us the other order already moves.
> It is burning.
> It is dreaming.
> It is waking up.[20]

Notes

Introduction

1. Robert Wedderburn, *The Axe Laid to the Root* (1817), in *The Horrors of Slavery and Other Writings*, ed. Iain McCalman (Princeton, NJ: Princeton University Press, 1991), no. 1, 81–88; 82.

2. Jean-Jacques Rousseau, *Second Discourse on the Origin and the Foundations of Inequality*, ed. Susan Dunn (New Haven: Yale University Press, 2002), 69–148; 113. Jimmy Casas Klausen argues in *Fugitive Rousseau: Slavery, Primitivism, and Political Freedom* (New York: Fordham University Press, 2014) that Rousseau was preoccupied with primitivity as an idea and largely silent about the slave trade. Yet historical marronage still shaped his theories of property (53–86). See also Jane Anna Gordon's discussion of decoloniality and Rousseau in *Creolizing Political Theory: Reading Rousseau through Fanon* (New York: Fordham University Press, 2014), especially chapter 2.

3. On primitive accumulation, see chapters 26–33 of Karl Marx, *Capital* (Vol I), eds. Ben Fowkes et al. (London: Penguin Books, 1992). For theoretical engagements with primitive accumulation and colonialism, see Silvia Federici, *Caliban and the Witch: Women, the Body, and Primitive Accumulation* (New York: Autonomedia, 2004), 8–17; 21–60; and Paula Chakravartty and Denise Ferreira da Silva, "Accumulation, Dispossession, and Debt: The Racial Logic of Global Capitalism: An Introduction," *American Quarterly* 64, no. 3 (September 2012): 361–85.

4. John Locke, *Second Treatise on Government*, ed. Ian Shapiro (New Haven: Yale University Press, 2003), 111. Siraj Ahmed contends that tropes of dispossession "[reflect] the Enlightenment's profound ambivalence toward the origins of private property, of civil society, and hence of European modernity itself" (153). See Siraj Ahmed, "Dispossession and Civil Society: The Ambivalence of Enlightenment Political Philosophy," *The Eighteenth Century: Theory and Interpretation* 55, no. 2–3 (Summer/Fall 2014): 153–74. Ahmed's insights have influenced my reading of Wedderburn as a theorist engaged in similar priorities as eighteenth-century European philosophers, but also as an activist in the Black radical tradition who goes much further in his challenges to property.

5. See Robert Nichols, *Theft is Property!* (Durham: Duke University Press, 2020), 157.

6. Eric Williams in *Capitalism and Slavery* (Chapel Hill: University of North Carolina Press, 1944) and Cedric Robinson in *Black Marxism: The Making of the Black Radical Tradition* (Chapel Hill: University of North Carolina Press, 1983) trace capitalism's emergences in slavery and land theft. For racial capitalism, see Robinson, *Black Marxism*, 9–28, as well as *Cedric Robinson: On Racial Capitalism, Black Internationalism, and Cultures of Resistance*, ed. H. L. T. Quan (London: Pluto Press, 2019); *Futures of Black Radicalism*, eds. Gaye Theresa Johnson and Alex Lubin (New York: Verso, 2017); Gargi Bhattacharyya, *Rethinking Racial Capitalism: Questions of Reproduction and Survival*

(Lanham, MD: Rowman and Littlefield International Press, 2018); and *Histories of Racial Capitalism*, eds. Destin Jenkins and Justin Leroy (New York: Columbia University Press, 2021).

7. See chapter 7 in Cedric Robinson's *Black Marxism* for a description of the Black radical tradition, 167–75.

8. Wedderburn, *The Axe Laid to the Root*, no. 1, 84. Samuel Sewell's pamphlet *The Selling of Joseph* (1700) likewise invokes a gifted earth in an early condemnation of slavery: "It is most certain that all Men, as they are the Sons of *Adam*, are Coheirs; and have equal Right unto Liberty, and all other outward Comforts of Life. *God hath given the Earth* [with all its Commodities] *unto the Sons of Adam.*" See Sewell in *The Norton Anthology of American Literature: Beginnings to 1820*, eds. Robert S. Levine, et al., 8th ed. (New York: W. W. Norton, 2017), 323–26; 323.

9. Immanuel Kant, *Perpetual Peace: A Philosophical Sketch*, in *The Political Writings of Kant*, ed. H. S. Reiss (Cambridge: Cambridge University Press, 1991), 93–129; 106.

10. For Kant and international law, see Kelly Oliver, *Earth and World: Philosophy after the Apollo Missions* (New York: Columbia University Press, 2015), 52–53.

11. Wedderburn, *The Axe Laid to the Root*, no. 1, 84.

12. Robert Wedderburn, *The Horrors of Slavery*, in *The Horrors of Slavery and Other Writings*, ed. Iain McCalman (Princeton, NJ: Princeton University Press, 1991), 99.

13. Allan Greer, *Property and Dispossession: Natives, Empires, and Land in Early Modern North America* (Cambridge: Cambridge University Press, 2018), 1–5.

14. On colonial enclosure, see Francis Jennings, *The Invasion of America: Indians, Colonists, and the Cant of Conquest* (Chapel Hill: University of North Carolina Press, 1975); Jean M. O'Brien, *Dispossession by Degrees: Indian Land and Identity in Natick, Massachusetts, 1650–1790* (Lincoln: University of Nebraska Press, 2003); Stuart Banner, *How the Indians Lost Their Land* (Cambridge, MA: Harvard University Press, 2005); and Michael Witgen, *Seeing Red: Indigenous Land, American Expansion, and the Political Economy of Plunder in North America* (Chapel Hill: University of North Carolina Press, 2022). For commoning, see Peter Linebaugh and Marcus Rediker, *The Many-Headed Hydra: Sailors, Slaves, Commoners, and the Hidden History of the Revolutionary Atlantic* (Boston: Beacon Books, 2000); Derek Wall, *The Commons in History: Culture, Conflict, and Ecology* (Cambridge, MA: Harvard University Press, 2014); Peter Linebaugh, *The Magna Carta Manifesto: Liberties and Commons for All* (Berkeley: University of California Press, 2009), and *Stop, Thief!: The Commons, Enclosures, and Resistance* (Oakland: PM Press, 2014). For colonial and early American literature and commoning, see Elizabeth Maddock Dillon, *New World Drama: The Performative Commons in the Atlantic World* (Durham: Duke University Press, 2014); and Dana D. Nelson, *Commons Democracy: Reading the Politics of Participation in the Early United States* (New York: Fordham University Press, 2016). For contemporary theories of the commons, see Silvia Federici, *Re-Enchanting the World* (Oakland: PM Books, 2019), 85–98; and Stefano Harney and Fred Moten, *The Undercommons: Fugitive Planning and Black Study* (New York: Autonomedia 2013).

15. Sylvia Wynter, "Novel and History, Plot and Plantation," *Savacou*, 5 (June 1971): 95–102; 101.

16. Ariella Aïsha Azoulay, *Potential History: Unlearning Imperialism* (New York: Verso 2019), 388.

17. Sarah Jane Cervenak, *Black Gathering: Art, Ecology, Ungiven Life* (Durham: Duke University Press, 2021), 3–5.

18. Cervenak, *Black Gathering*, 5.

19. Mary Prince, *The History of Mary Prince, a West Indian Slave, Related by Herself*, ed. Moira Ferguson (Ann Arbor: University of Michigan Press, 1997), 94. On the freedom as a gift of white liberal humanism, see Mimi Thi Nguyen, *The Gift of Freedom: War, Debt, and Other Refugee Passages* (Durham: Duke University Press, 2012), 1–32.

20. Robin D. G. Kelley, *Freedom Dreams: The Black Radical Imagination* (Boston: Beacon Press, 2003), 3–6.

21. Prince, *The History*, 58.

22. See Cheryl Harris, "Whiteness as Property," *Harvard Law Review* 106, no. 8 (June 1993): 1707–91; Joanne Barker, *Native Acts: Law, Recognition, and Cultural Authenticity* (Durham: Duke University Press, 2011); Colin Dayan, *The Law is a White Dog: How Legal Rituals Make and Unmake Persons* (Princeton: Princeton University Press, 2013); and Aileen Moreton-Robinson, *The White Possessive: Property, Power, and Indigenous Sovereignty* (Minneapolis: University of Minnesota Press, 2015).

23. Cervenak, *Black Gathering*, 4.

24. For the American Revolution and Indigenous lands, see Colin G. Calloway, *The American Revolution in Indian Country* (Cambridge: Cambridge University Press, 1995), and *One Vast Winter Count: The Native American West Before Lewis and Clark* (Lincoln: University of Nebraska Press, 2003); and Michael Witgen, *An Infinity of Nations: How the Native New World Shaped Early North America* (Philadelphia: University of Pennsylvania Press, 2013).

25. Wedderburn, *The Axe Laid to the Root*, no.1, 86.

26. For African oceanic crossings, see Paul Gilroy, *The Black Atlantic: Modernity and Double Consciousness* (Cambridge: Cambridge University Press, 1993); and Stephanie E. Smallwood, *Saltwater Slavery: A Middle Passage from Africa to the American Diaspora* (Cambridge, MA: Harvard University Press, 2007). Scholars such as Tim Fulford, Kevin Hutchings, and Robbie Richardson also have taken up representations of Indigenous peoples in anglophone literatures of the long eighteenth century, while critics like Jace Weaver and Coll Thrush remind us that Native figures moved across the transatlantic world, and Nikki Hessell has added that Romantic texts circulated widely in Indigenous translations in the nineteenth century. See Tim Fulford, *Romantic Indians: Native Americans, British Literature, and Transatlantic Culture* (Oxford: Oxford University Press, 2006); Tim Fulford and Kevin Hutchings, eds., *Native Americans and Anglo-American Culture, 1750–1850* (Cambridge: Cambridge University Press, 2009); Robbie Richardson, *The Savage and the Modern Self: North American Indians in Eighteenth-Century British Literature and Culture* (Toronto: University of Toronto Press, 2018); Jace Weaver, *The Red Atlantic* (Chapel Hill: University of North Carolina Press, 2017); Coll Thrush, *Indigenous London: Native Travelers at the Heart of Empire* (New Haven: Yale University Press, 2016); and Nikki Hessell, *Romantic Literature and the Colonised World: Lessons from Indigenous Translations* (London: Palgrave Macmillan, 2018).

27. Sidney Mintz, *Sweetness and Power: The Place of Sugar in Modern History* (London: Penguin, 1986), 97–99.

28. On eighteenth-century literature and Native studies, see the special issues on "The Indigenous Eighteenth Century," *Eighteenth-Century Fiction*, ed. Eugenia Zuroski vol. 33, no. 2 (Winter 2020–21); "Re-Indigenizing Romanticism: A Forum," *Studies in Romanticism*, eds. Nikki Hessell and Elizabeth Potter, vol. 61, no. 4 (Winter 2022); and "Indigenous Studies and the Eighteenth Century," *Eighteenth-Century Studies*, ed. Ramesh Mallipeddi vol. 56, no. 2 (Winter 2023). For hemispheric studies that engage with race, see Tiya Miles and Sharon Holland, eds., *Crossing Waters, Crossing Worlds: The African Diaspora in Indian Country* (Durham: Duke University Press, 2006); Joselyn M. Almeida, *Reimagining the Transatlantic, 1780–1890* (Burlington, VT: University of Vermont Press, 2011); Tiffany Lethabo King, *The Black Shoals: Offshore Formations of Black and Native Studies* (Durham: Duke University Press, 2019); and Kathryn Walkiewicz, *Reading Territory: Indigenous and Black Freedom, Removal, and the Nineteenth-Century State* (Chapel Hill: University of North Carolina Press, 2023).

29. Alexander X. Byrd traces Equiano's shift from Ibo to African identity in *Captives and Voyagers: Black Migrants across the Eighteenth-Century British Atlantic World* (Baton Rouge: Louisiana State University Press, 2008).

30. On Indigenous revitalization movements, see Anthony Wallace, *Death and Rebirth of the Seneca* (New York: Vintage, 1969); R. David Edmunds, *The Shawnee Prophet* (Lincoln: University of Nebraska Press, 1983); Gregory Evans Dowd, *A Spirited Resistance: The North American Indian Struggle for Unity* (Baltimore: Johns Hopkins University Press, 1992); and Susan Juster, *Doomsayers: Anglo-American Prophecy in the Age of Revolutions* (Philadelphia, 2003), 210–13.

31. On cosmologies as resistant politics, see Marisol de la Cadena, "Indigenous Cosmopolitics in the Andes: Conceptual Reflections beyond 'Politics,'" *Cultural Anthropology* 25, no. 2 (April 2010): 334–70; 345.

32. On philosophical ruptures between subject and object, and life and matter in European philosophy, see Kathryn Yusoff, *A Billion Black Anthropocenes or None* (Minneapolis: University of Minnesota, 2018), 3–7; and Elizabeth Povinelli, *Geontologies: A Requiem to Late Liberalism* (Durham: Duke University Press, 2016), 1–29.

33. For thing theory and literary studies, see Deidre Lynch, *The Economy of Character: Novels, Market Culture, and the Business of Inner Meaning* (Chicago: University of Chicago Press, 1998); Bill Brown, *A Sense of Things: The Object Matter of American Literature* (Chicago: University of Chicago Press, 2004); Elaine Freedgood, *The Ideas in Things: Fugitive Meaning in the Victorian Novel* (Chicago: University of Chicago Press, 2006); Mark Blackwell, "The People Things Make: Locke's *Essay Concerning Human Understanding*," *Studies in Eighteenth-Century Culture* 35 (June 2006): 77–94; Julie Park, *The Self and It: Novel Objects in Eighteenth-Century England* (Stanford: Stanford University Press, 2009); Jonathan Lamb, *The Things Things Say* (Princeton: Princeton University Press, 2011); Elizabeth Kowaleski Wallace, "The Things Things Don't Say: *The Rape of the Lock*, Vitalism, and New Materialism," *The Eighteenth Century: Theory and Interpretation* 59, no. 1 (Spring 2018): 105–22; and Lynn Festa, *Fiction Without Humanity: Person, Animal, Thing in Early Enlightenment Literature and Culture* (Philadelphia: University of Pennsylvania Press, 2021). For recent work in eighteenth-century animal

studies, see Tobias Menely, *The Animal Claim: Sensibility and Creaturely Voice* (Chicago: University of Chicago Press, 2015); Heather Keenleyside, *Animals and Other People: Literary Forms and Living Beings in the Long Eighteenth Century* (Philadelphia: University of Pennsylvania Press, 2016); and Lucinda Cole, *Imperfect Creatures: Vermin, Literature, and the Science of Life, 1600–1740* (Ann Arbor: University of Michigan Press, 2016).

34. Settler epistemologies accompanied incipient scientific vocabularies that emphasized the ostensibly inherent nature of phenotypical difference. Hortense Spillers and Lindon Barrett have argued, however, that Blackness is *not* an ontology, but a set of grammatical propositions materially instantiated within racial capitalism — perhaps most memorably expressed in Prospero's hailing of Caliban as "this thing of darkness I call mine" in William Shakespeare's *The Tempest*. Because of this, Fred Moten asserts that "blackness is ontologically prior to the logistic and regulative power that is supposed to have brought it into existence" (739). Global systems of power are rooted in material and linguistic orders of racial difference that continue to render vulnerable Black life. On race and ontology, see Hortense Spillers, "Mama's Baby, Papa's Maybe: An American Grammar," *Black, White, and in Color* (Chicago: University of Chicago Press, 2003), 203–29; Fred Moten, "Blackness and Nothingness (Mysticism) in the Flesh," *South Atlantic Quarterly* 112, no. 4 (Fall 2013): 737–80; Lindon Barrett, "The Experiences of Slave Narratives: Reading Against Authenticity," in *Conditions of the Present*, ed. Janet Neary (Durham: Duke University Press, 2018), 48–60; Denise Ferreira da Silva, *Toward a Global Idea of Race* (Minneapolis: University of Minnesota Press, 2007); Calvin Warren, *Ontological Terror: Blackness, Nihilism, and Emancipation* (Durham: Duke University Press, 2018); and Frank B. Wilderson III, *Afropessimism* (New York: Liveright, 2021).

35. John Law, "What's Wrong with a One-World World?," *Distinktion: Scandinavian Journal of Social Theory* 16, no. 1 (August 2015): 126–39; 126. For recent scholarship on Black, Indigenous, and decolonial cosmologies, see Kimberly Blaeser, "Centering Worlds: Writing a Sense of Place," *Wicazo Sa Review* 14, no. 2 (Autumn 1999): 92–108; Isabelle Stengers, *Cosmopolitics I*, trans. Robert Bononno (Minneapolis: University of Minnesota Press, 2010); Joni Adamson, "Environmental Justice, Cosmopolitics and Climate Changes," in *The Cambridge Companion to Literature and Environment*, ed. Louise Westling (Cambridge: Cambridge University Press, 2013), 169–83; Eduardo Kohn, *How Forests Think: Toward an Anthropology Beyond the Human* (Berkeley: University of California Press, 2013); Povinelli, *Geontologies*, 1–29; and Marisol de la Cadena, *Earth Beings: Ecologies of Practice across Andean Worlds* (Durham: Duke University Press, 2015).

36. See Dennis Tedlock, *Popol Vuh: The Definitive Edition of the Mayan Book of the Dawn of Life and the Glories of Gods and Kings*, 2nd Ed. (New York: Touchstone Books, 1996). On the destruction of Mayan libraries, see Daniel Heath Justice, "'Go Away Water!': Kinship Criticism and the Decolonizing Imperative," in *Reasoning Together: The Native Critics Collective*, eds. Craig S. Womack, Daniel Heath Justice, and Christopher B. Teuton (Norman: University of Oklahoma Press, 2008), 147–68.

37. Marisol de la Cadena and Mario Blaser, "Pluriverse: Proposals for a World of Many Worlds," in *A World of Many Worlds*, eds. Marisol de la Cadena and Mario Blaser (Durham: Duke University Press, 2018), 1–22; 3.

38. Zoe Todd, "An Indigenous Feminist's Take on the Ontological Turn: 'Ontology' Is Just Another Word for Colonialism," *Journal of Historical Sociology* 29, no. 1 (March 2016): 4–22.

39. Walter D. Mignolo and Catherine E. Walsh, *On Decoloniality: Concepts, Analytics, Praxis* (Durham: Duke University Press, 2018), 1–5; 240. See also Linda Tuhiwai Smith, *Decolonizing Methodologies: Research and Indigenous Peoples* (London: Zed Books, 2012), 12–13.

40. Cass Turner, "Disposable World(s): Race and Commerce in Daniel Defoe's *Captain Singleton*," Conference Presentation, 90–117; 111. Indiana Center for Eighteenth-Century Studies Workshop: "Networks and Ecologies," May 13–14, 2021. I am grateful to Cass for sharing work in progress with those of us who attended the workshop.

41. On the problematic valences of OOO and strands of new materialism, see Zakiyyah Iman Jackson, *Becoming Human: Matter and Meaning in an Antiblack World* (New York: New York University Press, 2020), 21–34.

42. See Martin Heidegger, "The Origin of the Work of Art," in *Poetry, Language, Thought*, trans. Alfred Hofstadter (New York: Harper Perennial Modern Classics, 1975), 15–86; 43; Michel Foucault, *The Birth of Biopolitics* (London: Picador, 2010); Giorgio Agamben, *Homo Sacer: Sovereign Power and Bare Life*, trans. Daniel Heller-Roazen (Stanford: Stanford University Press, 1998); Jacques Derrida, *The Animal That Therefore I Am*, trans. David Wills (New York: Fordham University Press, 2008). On these critical genealogies, see Povinelli on *bios* in *Geontologies*, 1–29; Kohn on philosophical distinctions between human and animal in *How Forests Think*, 1–13; and Donna J. Haraway on Derrida's cat in *When Species Meet* (Minneapolis: Minnesota University Press, 2007), 19–23.

43. Robyn Maynard and Leanne Betasamosake Simpson, *Rehearsals for Living* (Chicago: Haymarket Press, 2022), 44.

44. On counter-worlds, see Haraway, *When Species Meet*, 92–93; and Anna Lowenhaupt Tsing, *The Mushroom at the End of the World: On the Possibility of Life in Capitalist Ruins* (Princeton, NJ: Princeton University Press, 2017), 22–27.

45. See Sylvia Wynter, "Unsettling the Coloniality of Being/Power/Truth/Freedom: Towards the Human, After Man, Its Overrepresentation—An Argument," *CR: The New Centennial Review* 3, no. 3 (Fall 2003): 257–337; 257.

46. Katherine McKittrick, *Dear Science and Other Stories* (Durham: Duke University Press, 2020), 6–7.

47. For Black animal studies and alternative humanisms, see Alexander Weheliye, *Habeas Viscus: Racializing Assemblages, Biopolitics, and Black Feminist Theories of the Human* (Durham: Duke University Press, 2014), 21–30; Bénédicte Boisseron, *Afro-Dog: Blackness and the Animal Question* (New York: Columbia University Press, 2018); King, *The Black Shoals*, 12–24; Joshua Bennett, *Being Property Once Myself: Blackness and the End of Man* (Cambridge, MA: Harvard University Press, 2020), 12–13; Jackson, *Becoming Human*, 5–21.

48. For African American science traditions, see Britt Rusert, *Fugitive Science: Empiricism and Freedom in Early African American Culture* (New York: New York University Press, 2017).

49. Marisa J. Fuentes, *Dispossessed Lives: Enslaved Women, Violence, and the Archive* (Philadelphia: University of Pennsylvania Press, 2018), 75.

50. Saidiya Hartman, "Venus in Two Acts," *Small Axe* 12, no. 2 (June 2008): 1–14; 12, 13.

51. "The king ag[ainst] Robert Wedderburn for Blasphemy, Brief for the Crown," *The Kings Bench Sittings after Hilary Term Middlesex*, in *The Horrors of Slavery and Other Writings*, ed. Iain McCalman (Princeton, NJ: Princeton University Press, 1991), 123–25; 125.

52. Wedderburn, *The Axe Laid to the Root*, no. 6, 105–10; 109.

53. Frank B. Wilderson argues that for Black writers, "freedom is an ontological, rather than an experiential question," given that liberation is only conceivable for those afforded being under colonial modernity. See Frank B. Wilderson, *Red, White, & Black: Cinema and the Structure of U.S. Antagonisms* (Durham: Duke University Press, 2010), 23.

54. Christina Sharpe, *In the Wake: On Blackness and Being* (Durham: Duke University Press, 2016), 76.

55. On sororal relations and Caribbean literature, see Elizabeth Maddock Dillon, "Reassembling the Novel: Kinlessness and the Novels of the Haitian Revolution," *Novel* 47, no. 1 (Spring 2014): 167–85.

56. Kevin Quashie, *Black Aliveness, or a Poetics of Being* (Durham: Duke University Press, 2021), 2.

57. For Caribbean testimony on slavery and British literature, see Keith Sandiford, *Measuring the Moment: Strategies of Protest in Eighteenth-Century Afro-British Writing* (Selinsgrove, PA: Susquehanna University Press, 1995); Helena Woodard, *African-British Writings in the Eighteenth Century: The Politics of Race and Rason* (Westport, CT: Praeger, 1999); Helen Thomas, *Romanticism and Slave Narratives: Transatlantic Testimonies* (Cambridge: Cambridge University Press, 2000); C. L. Innes, *A History of Black and Asian Writing in Britain* (Cambridge: Cambridge University Press, 2008); Nicole Aljoe, *Creole Testimonies: Slave Narratives from the British West Indies, 1709–1838* (New York: Palgrave Macmillan, 2012); and Sue Thomas, *Telling West Indian Lives: Life Narrative and the Reform of Plantation Slavery Cultures, 1804–1834* (New York: Palgrave Macmillan, 2015).

58. For "unwitnessed," see Drew Lopenzina, *Red Ink: Native Americans Picking up the Pen in the Colonial Period* (Albany: State University of New York Press, 2012), 5. For "disavowed," see Sibylle Fischer, *Modernity Disavowed: Haiti and the Cultures of Slavery in the Age of Revolution* (Durham: Duke University Press, 2004), x–xi.

59. Wedderburn, *The Axe Laid to the Root*, no 1, 82.

60. On theorizations of social death, see Orlando Patterson, *Slavery and Social Death* (Cambridge: Harvard University Press, 1985), 35–37; and Vincent Brown, "Social Death and Political Life in the Study of Slavery," *American Historical Review* 114, no. 5 (2009): 1231–49.

61. For queer embodiments and intimacies and early African American literature, see C. Riley Snorton, *Black on Both Sides: A Racial History of Trans Identity* (Minneapolis: University of Minnesota Press, 2017); Brigitte Fielder, *Relative Races: Genealogies of Interracial Kinship in Nineteenth-Century America* (Durham: Duke University Press,

2020); and Elahe Haschemi Yekani, *Familial Feeling: Entangled Tonalities in Early Black Atlantic Writing and the Rise of the British Novel* (London: Palgrave Macmillan, 2021). For Indigenous Two-Spirit embodiments and relations, see Deborah Miranda, "Extermination of the *Joyas*: Gendercide in Spanish California," Special Issue: "Sexuality, Nationality, Indigeneity," eds. Mark Rifkin, Daniel Heath Justice, and Bethany Schneider, *GLQ* 16, no. 1–2 (April 2010): 253–84; Kai Pyle, "Naming and Claiming: Recovering Ojibwe and Plains Cree Two-Spirit Language," *TSQ: Transgender Quarterly* 5, no. 4 (November 2018): 574–88; Leanne Betasamosake Simpson, *As We Have Always Done: Indigenous Freedom through Radical Resistance* (Minneapolis: University of Minnesota Press, 2017), chapter 8; Mark Rifkin, *When Did Indians Become Straight?: Kinship, the History of Sexuality, and Native Sovereignty* (Oxford: Oxford University Press, 2011); and Qwo-Li Driskill, *Asegi Stories: Cherokee Queer and Two-Spirit Memory* (Tuscan: University of Arizona Press, 2016). For a theorization of colonial gender, see María Lugones, "The Coloniality of Gender," in *The Palgrave Handbook of Gender and Development*, ed. W. Harcourt (London: Palgrave Macmillan 2016), 13–33.

62. Elizabeth Povinelli, *Empire of Love: Toward a Theory of Intimacy, Genealogy and Carnality* (Durham: Duke University Press, 2006).

63. See Lisa Lowe, *The Intimacies of Four Continents* (Durham: Duke University Press, 2015), 17–18, and "Response: Intimacies as Method," *Eighteenth-Century Fiction* 34, no. 2 (Winter 2022): 207–13.

64. Jonathan Goldberg in *Sodometries: Renaissance Texts, Modern Sexualities* (Stanford: Stanford University Press, 1992) calls this incident an "originary moment" in the history of settler colonialism and sexuality (179). See also Pietro Martire d'Anghiera, *De Orbe Novo*, trans. Francis Augustus MacNutt (New York: Putnam, 1912), vol. 1, 284.

65. See Jessica Hernandez, *Fresh Banana Leaves: Healing Indigenous Landscapes through Indigenous Science* (Berkeley: North Atlantic Books, 2022), 146–50.

66. For scholarship on Theodore de Bry, see Bernadette Bucher, *Icon and Conquest* (Chicago: University of Chicago Press, 1981); Michael van Groesen, *Representations of the Overseas World in the de Bry Collection of Voyages* (Leiden: Brill Academic Publishing, 2008); and Michael Gaudio, *Engraving the Savage: The New World and Techniques of Civilization* (Minneapolis: University of Minnesota Press, 2008), 45–86.

67. D'Anghiera, *De Orbe Novo*, 1:284.

68. D'Anghiera, *De Orbe Novo*, 1:284.

69. On Balboa, see Goldberg, *Sodometries*, chapter 6; Miranda, "Extermination of the *Joyas*," 256–60; and Driskill, *Asegi Stories*, 51–55.

70. Miranda, "Extermination of the *Joyas*," 256.

71. See Greta LaFleur, *The Natural History of Sexuality in Early America* (Baltimore: Johns Hopkins University Press, 2018); and Jeremy Chow, *The Queerness of Water: Troubled Ecologies in the Eighteenth Century* (Charlottesville: University of Virginia Press, 2023).

72. For Native ecologies, see Robin Wall Kimmerer, *Braiding Sweetgrass: Indigenous Wisdom, Scientific Knowledge and the Teaching of Plants* (Minneapolis: University of Minnesota Press, 2013), 3–10; Leanne Betasamosake Simpson, *As We Have Always Done: Indigenous Freedom through Radical Resistance* (Minneapolis: University of

Minnesota Press, 2017), chapter 9; Melissa K. Nelson, "Getting Dirty: The Eco-Eroticism of Women in Indigenous Oral Literatures," in *Critically Sovereign*, ed. Joanne Barker (Durham: Duke University Press, 2017), 229–60; and Hernandez, *Fresh Banana Leaves*. For African American ecologies, see Kimberly N. Ruffin, *Black on Earth: African American Ecoliterary Traditions* (Athens: University of Georgia Press, 2010); Dianne Glave, *Rooted in the Earth: Reclaiming the African American Environmental Heritage* (Chicago: Chicago Review Press, 2010); Sonya Posmentier, *Cultivation and Catastrophe: The Lyric Ecology of Modern Black Literature* (Baltimore: Johns Hopkins University Press, 2017); and Sarah Jane Cervenak, *Black Gathering: Art, Ecology, Ungiven Life* (Durham: Duke University Press, 2021).

73. Megan Peiser, "Citing Seeds, Citing People: Bibliography and Indigenous Memory, Relations, and Living Knowledge Keepers," Special Issue: "New Approaches to Critical Bibliography and Material Texts," eds. Lisa Maruca and Kate Ozment, *Criticism* 64, no. 3–4 (Summer/Fall 2022): 523–31. See also Megan Peiser, "We Have Always Been Here: Indigenous Scholars in/and Eighteenth-Century Studies," *Eighteenth-Century Fiction* 33, no. 2 (Winter 2020–21): 181–88; and Simpson, *As We Have Always Done*, 151.

74. Samson Occom, "Montaukett Tribe to the State of New York (1785/8?)," in *The Collected Writings of Samson Occom, Mohegan*, ed. Joanna Brooks (Oxford: Oxford University Press, 2006), 150–52; 151.

75. Occom, "Montaukett Tribe to the State of New York," 151. Jordy Rosenberg and Chi-ming Yang contend, "'(D)ispossession' signals above all a process of critical undoing. To be possessed is at once to hold oneself together, and to be utterly undone, occupied by another" (139). See Jordy Rosenberg and Chi-ming Yang, "The Dispossessed Eighteenth Century," *The Eighteenth Century: Theory and Interpretation* 55, no. 2–3 (Summer/Fall 2014): 137–52.

76. See Jodi Byrd, "What's Normative Got to Do with It?: Toward Indigenous Queer Relationality," *Social Text* 38, no. 4 (December 2020): 105–23, especially 105.

77. See Mark Rifkin, *Beyond Settler Time: Temporal Sovereignty and Indigenous Self-Determination* (Durham: Duke University Press, 2017), x–xi.

78. On Blackness as a "where and when" or "elsewhere and elsewhen," see Michelle M. Wright, *The Physics of Blackness: Beyond the Middle Passage Epistemology* (Minneapolis: University of Minnesota, 2015), 1–3; and Moten, "Blackness and Nothingness," 746.

79. Ana Schwartz, "We used to be friends: Brothertown and Sister Fowler," Conference Presentation, Society of Early Americanists Biennial Conference (March 5, 2021).

80. See Michel Foucault, *The History of Sexuality: Vol. I* (New York: Vintage, 1990), 5–12; and *The Order of Things: An Archeology of the Human Sciences* (New York: Vintage, 1994), 19–20, 30–38. For a response to Foucault, whose work in these texts evades imperial settings, see Ann Laura Stoler, *Race and the Education of Desire: Foucault's History of Sexuality and the Colonial Order of Things* (Durham: Duke University Press 1995).

81. Madhavi Menon, *Indifference to Difference: On Queer Universalism* (Minneapolis: University of Minnesota Press, 2015), 16.

82. Byrd, *The Transit of Empire*, xv–xvi.

83. Audre Lorde, "If You Come Softly," in *The Collected Poems of Audre Lorde* (New York: W. W. Norton, 1997), 21. I am grateful to Kate Ozment for first sharing this poem with me—and shaping the arc of this book.

84. On sensation and early American and Indigenous studies, see Peter Charles Hoffer, *Sensory Worlds in Early America* (Baltimore: Johns Hopkins University Press, 2003); Elizabeth Freeman, *Beside You in Time: Sense Methods and Queer Sociabilities in the American Nineteenth Century* (Durham: Duke University Press, 2019); and Dylan Robinson, *Hungry Listening: Resonant Theory for Indigenous Sound Studies* (Minneapolis: University of Minnesota Press, 2020).

85. Occom, *Sermon on the Execution of Moses Paul*, 188.

86. Scott Lauria Morgensen, "Theorizing Gender, Sexuality and Settler Colonialism: An Introduction," *Settler Colonial Studies* 2, no. 2 (Fall 2012): 2–22; 2.

87. Édouard Glissant, *Poetics of Relation*, trans. Betsy Wing (Ann Arbor: University of Michigan Press, 1997), 189.

88. Prince, *The History*, 74; 94.

89. See Barry O'Connell's *On Our Own Ground: The Complete Writings of William Apess, a Pequot* (Amherst: University of Massachusetts Press, 1992) for the 1831 *A Son of the Forest* (1–97) and the 1829 variants (311–24). See pages 33 and 318–19.

90. Apess, *Indian Nullification*, 168.

91. Robert Wedderburn, *The Axe Laid to the Root* (1817), in *The Horrors of Slavery and Other Writings*, ed. Iain McCalman (Princeton, NJ: Princeton University Press, 1991), No. 1, 81–88; 86.

92. Lowe, *Intimacies of Four Continents*, 175.

93. Jared Sexton, "The *Vel* of Slavery: Tracking the Figure of the Unsovereign," *Critical Sociology* 42, no. 4–5 (Fall 2016): 583–97; 593. I am grateful to Joseph Albernaz for pushing me to interpret Wedderburn in this way.

94. Mario Blaser argues "political ontology" refers to "the power-laden negotiations involved in bringing into being entities that make up a particular world or ontology" and "to a field of study that focuses on these negotiations." See *Storytelling Globalization from the Chaco and Beyond* (Durham: Duke University Press, 2010), 23.

95. On Indigenous studies and refusal, see Audra Simpson, *Mohawk Interruptus: Political Life across the Borders of the Settler States* (Durham: Duke University Press, 2014), 1–3.

96. See David Scott, *Conscripts of Modernity: The Tragedy of Colonial Enlightenment* (Durham: Duke University Press, 2004), 210; Stephen Best, *None Like Us: Blackness, Belonging, Aesthetic Life* (Durham: Duke University Press, 2018), 65–70. For an important counter to Scott, see Aaron Kamugisha, *Beyond Coloniality: Citizenship and Freedom in the Caribbean Intellectual Tradition* (Bloomington: University of Indiana Press, 2019), 63.

Chapter One

1. Samson Occom, *Sermon on the Execution of Moses Paul* (1772), *The Collected Writings of Samson Occom, Mohegan*, ed. Joanna Brooks (Oxford: Oxford University Press, 2006), 176–96; 188. On *Sermon on the Execution of Moses Paul*, see LaVonne Brown Ruoff,

"Samson Occom's *Sermon Preached by Samson Occom*," *Studies in American Indian Literature* 4, no. 2/3 (Summer/Fall 1992): 75–81; Laura Stevens, *The Poor Indians: British Missionaries, Native Americans, and Colonial Sensibility* (Philadelphia: University of Pennsylvania Press, 2004), 173–78; Philip Round, "Samson Occom and Native Print Literacy," in *Early Native Literacies in New England*, eds. Kristina Bross and Hilary Wyss (Amherst: University of Massachusetts Press, 2008), 72–83; and Christopher Bracken, "The Deaths of Moses: The Death Penalty and the Division of Sovereignty," *Critical Research on Religion* 6, no. 2 (June 2018): 168–83. On other texts where Occom takes up alcohol and addiction, see also Heather Bouwman, "Samson Occom and the Sermonic Tradition," in *Early Native Literacies in New England*, eds. Kristina Bross and Hilary Wyss (Amherst: University of Massachusetts Press, 2008), 57–71; and Kelly Wisecup, *Medical Encounters: Knowledge and Identity in Early American Literatures* (Amherst: University of Massachusetts Press, 2013), 160–68.

2. Bracken, "The Deaths of Moses," 70.

3. For execution narratives and Indigenous persons, see Jodi Schorb, "Seeing Other Wise: Reading a Pequot Execution Narrative," in *Early Native Literacies in New England*, eds. Kristina Bross and Hilary Wyss (Amherst: University of Massachusetts Press, 2008), 148–61; Jeannine DeLombard, *In the Shadow of the Gallows: Race, Crime, and American Civic Identity* (Philadelphia: University of Pennsylvania Press, 2012); Wisecup, *Medical Encounters*, 160–68; and Greta LaFleur, *The Natural History of Sexuality in Early America* (Baltimore: Johns Hopkins University Press, 2018), 103–36.

4. Occom, *Sermon on the Execution of Moses Paul*, 178.

5. Occom, *Sermon on the Execution of Moses Paul*, 192.

6. Occom, *Sermon on the Execution of Moses Paul*, 183, 189.

7. Wisecup, *Medical Encounters*, 186.

8. Peter L. Bayers, "'We Unman Ourselves': Colonial and Mohegan Manhood in the Writings of Samson Occom," *MELUS* 39, no. 1 (Spring 2014): 173–91; 173.

9. Eleazar Wheelock to George Whitefield, July 4, 1761, in *The Occom Circle Archives*, Dartmouth College. https://collections.dartmouth.edu/occom/html/validation/761404-validation.html.

10. In his claim of shared flesh, Occom challenges colonial regulations of Native speech, including the 1708 Defamation Act (extended in 1730), which made it illegal for Black or Indigenous persons to speak "actional" words against settlers, leaving few recourses for self-defense against white abuse. See John Treadwell, Enoch Perkins, and Thomas Day, *The Public Statute Laws of the State of Connecticut*, Vol. 1 (Hartford: Hudson and Goodwin, 1808), 229–30.

11. Occom, *Sermon on the Execution of Moses Paul*, 193.

12. Drawing from Elizabeth Povinelli's discussion in *Economies of Abandonment: Social Belonging and Endurance in Late Liberalism* (Durham: Duke University Press, 2011), I use "cosubstantial," rather than consubstantial, transubstantial, or trans-corporeal, because consubstantial is implicated in Christian theology as a term that portrays the essence shared by the persons of the Trinity and the Aristotelian physics for the material "substance" of Christ in the Eucharist. Coined by Stacy Alaimo in *Bodily Natures: Science, Environment, and the Materials Self* (Bloomington: Indiana University Press, 2010), "trans-corporeal" depicts the ways "the human is always intermeshed

with the more-than-human world" (2–3), but I wish to emphasize figurations of kinship and genealogy across time and space, rather than a solely *present* entanglement of human selves and ecologies.

13. Daniel Heath Justice, *Why Indigenous Literatures Matter* (Waterloo: Wilfred Laurier University Press, 2018), 104.

14. Povinelli, *Economies of Abandonment*, 155.

15. Povinelli, *Economies of Abandonment*, 155. See also Adele E. Clarke and Donna Haraway's point in *Making Kin Not Population* (Chicago: University of Chicago Press, 2018): "We live each other's lives and die each other's deaths" (3).

16. C.B. Macpherson in *The Political Theory of Possessive Individualism* (Oxford: Oxford University Press, 2011) argues that the "conception of the individual as essentially the proprietor of his own person or capacities" originated in the Enlightenment (3). Yet any single body houses multiple organisms, as scientists and scholars have also been contending. See, for instance, Scott F. Gilbert, Jan Sapp, and Alfred I. Tauber's point as such in "A Symbiotic View of Life: We Have Never Been Individuals," *Quarterly Review of Biology* 87, no. 4 (December 2012): 325–41.

17. For a reading of a contemporaneous execution sermon, see Ajay Kumar Batra, "Reading with Conviction: Abraham Johnstone and the Poetics of the Dead End," Special Issue: "Beyond Recovery, eds. Lauren Coats and Steffi Dippold, *Early American Literature* 55, no. 2 (Winter 2020): 331–54.

18. Occom is unusual in using "bone of my bone" to refer to another Indigenous man who was a member of a different nation and not his spouse or child. As Tiya Miles notes in *The Ties that Bind* (Berkeley: University of California Press, 2015), a Cherokee father named Tarsekayahke calls his children by their enslaved mother Doll "bone of my bone and flesh of my flesh" in an 1824 petition of manumission (1). Miles argues that the phrase resonated with Cherokee conceptions of procreation, where mothers offer blood and fathers bone to the fetus (121). "Bone of my bone" likewise appears as a notice of parental relation in Lydia Maria Child's *Hobomok* (1824) and Frances Watkins Harper's *Iola Leroy* (1892). In *The Savage and the Modern Self: North American Indians in Eighteenth-Century British Literature and Culture* (Toronto: University of Toronto Press, 2018), moreover, Robbie Richardson discusses James Smith, who was adopted by the Lenape in the 1750s and wrote that the "tribe proclaimed him 'flesh of our flesh, and bone of our bone,'" to denote his transculturation within a Lenape community (94). Smith's use of the phrase probably comes closest to Occom's in its evocation of adoptive kinship, but Smith eventually left the Lenape nation, while Occom's claim of shared flesh with Paul endures even beyond Paul's execution. On the phrase "flesh of my flesh" in early modern to contemporary art and philosophy, see also Kaja Silverman, *Flesh of My Flesh* (Berkeley: University of California Press, 2009).

19. On Occom and Christianity, see David Murray, *Forked Tongues: Speech, Writing, and Representation in North American Indian Texts* (Bloomington: University of Indiana Press, 1991), 49–56; Michael Elliot, "'This Indian Bait': Samson Occom and the Voice of Liminality," *Early American Literature* 29, no. 3 (Spring 1994): 233–53; Bernd Peyer, *The Tutor'd Mind: Indian Missionary Writing in Antebellum America* (Amherst: University of Massachusetts Press, 1997); Keely McCarthy, "Conversion, Identity, and the Indian Missionary," *Early American Literature* 36, no. 3 (Spring 2001): 353–69; Joanna

Brooks, *American Lazarus: Religion and the Rise of African-American and Native American Literature* (Oxford: Oxford University Press, 2003), 51–86; Stevens, *The Poor Indians*, 11–26; Michael Leblanc, "Putting on the 'Helmut of Salvation' and Wielding 'the Sword of the Spirit': Joseph Johnson, Moses Paul, and the Word of God," *Studies in American Indian Literature* 24, no. 3 (Fall 2012): 26–52; and Linford Fisher, *The Indian Great Awakening: Religion and the Shaping of Native Cultures in Early America* (Oxford: Oxford University Press, 2012), 56–76.

20. Stuart Hall with Kuan-Hsing Chen, "The Formation of a Diasporic Intellectual: An Interview with Stuart Hall," in *Stuart Hall: Critical Dialogues in Cultural Studies*, eds. David Morley and Kuan-Hsing Chen (New York: Routledge, 1996), 486–505; 488. Glen Sean Coulthard in *Red Skin, White Masks: Rejecting the Colonial Politics of Recognition* (Minneapolis: University of Minnesota Press, 2014) also traces the psychic condition of colonialism as an "internalization" whereby "social relations . . . come to seem as 'true' or 'natural' to the colonized themselves" (13).

21. By turning to sensation, I also am influenced by Dian Million, who argues that sensory protocols indicate how Indigenous persons "*feel* . . . histories as well as think them" (54). See Dian Million, "Felt Theory: An Indigenous Feminist Approach to Affect and History," *Wicazo Sa Review* 24, no. 2 (Fall 2009): 53–76; 54.

22. For Brothertown's planning, see Hilary Wyss, *Writing Indians: Literacy, Christianity, and Native Community in Early America* (Amherst: University of Massachusetts Press, 2003), chapter 4; David J. Silverman, *Red Brethren: The Brothertown and Stockbridge Indians and the Problem of Race in Early America* (Ithaca: Cornell University Press, 2016), chapter 5; and Drew Lopenzina, *Red Ink: Native Americans Picking up the Pen in the Colonial Period* (Albany: State University of New York Press, 2012), chapter 5.

23. Samson Occom, "Mohegan Tribe to Sir William Johnson" (1764), *The Collected Writings of Samson Occom, Mohegan*, ed. Joanna Brooks (Oxford: Oxford University Press, 2006), 144–45; 145.

24. On Occom's petitions, see Brooks, *The Common Pot*, 110–11; and Caroline Wiginton, "Extending Root and Branch: Community Regeneration in the Petitions of Samson Occom," *Studies in American Indian Literatures* 20, no. 4 (Winter 2008): 24–55; 34–35.

25. Bones are important materials and images across colonial Indigenous and settler archives. For settlers, reanimated life begins with conversion, with John Winthrop imagining it as a conjoined skeleton *in* Christ: "[It] gathers together the scattered bones of perfect old man Adam and knits them into one body againe in Christ whereby a man is become againe a living soul" (186). Puritan discourses would come to represent the conversion of *both* Native peoples and landscapes as central to their "errand in the wilderness" by drawing on Biblical images, such as the valley of dry bones animated by God's breath in Ezekiel 37, to represent a new world in need of Christian cultivation. Yet in new materialist scholarship, bones suggest different genealogies of relation, which Occom may anticipate in his grammar for kinship. Biologist Samuel DeLanda argues, for instance, that soft tissues dominated for millennia, but when bone evolved, it made new locomotion "possible among animals" (qtd. Bennett 11). Jane Bennett builds on DeLanda's point to suggest that "all bodies are kin in the sense of inextricably enmeshed in a dense network of

relations" (13). See John Winthrop, "A Modell of Christian Charity," in *The Norton Anthology of American Literature: Beginnings to 1820*, eds. Robert S. Levine, et al., 8th ed. (New York: W. W. Norton, 2017), 178–89; and Jane Bennett, *Vibrant Matter: A Political Ecology of Things* (Durham: Duke University Press, 2010).

26. Samson Occom, "To All the Indians in this Boundless Continent" (1784), 196–98; 196.

27. On Occom's visit to the Oneida, see Angela Calcaterra, *Literary Indians: Aesthetics and Encounter in American Literature to 1920* (Chapel Hill: University of North Carolina Press, 2018), 49–50.

28. Hendrick Aupaumut, "Narrative of an Embassy to the Western Indians," *Collections of the Massachusetts Historical Society*, 1st ser., 9: 61–131; 88. Qtd. by Lisa Brooks, *The Common Pot: The Recovery of Native Space in the Northeast* (Minneapolis: University of Minnesota Press, 2010), 158.

29. See especially Peter Hoffer's discussion of sensation in "Brave New Worlds: The First Century of Indian-English Encounters," in *Colonial Mediascapes: Sensory Worlds in Early America*, eds. Matt Cohen and Jeffrey Glover, (Lincoln: University of Nebraska Press, 2014), 233–65.

30. See Jodi Byrd, "What's Normative Got to Do with It?: Toward Indigenous Queer Relationality," *Social Text* 38, no. 4 (December 2020): 105–23; 107.

31. On sovereign erotics, see Qwo-Li Driskill, "Call Me Brother: Two-Spiritedness, the Erotic, and Mixed-Blood Identity as Sites of Sovereignty and Resistance in Gregory Scofield's Poetry," in *Speak to Me Words*, eds. Janice Gould and Dean Rader (Tucson: University of Arizona Press, 2003), 223–34; Justice, *Why Indigenous Literatures Matter*, 96–110; Robert Warrior, "Your Skin Is a Map: The Theoretical Challenges of Joy Harjo's Erotic Poetics," in *Reasoning Together: The Native Critics Collective*, eds. Craig S. Womack, Daniel Heath Justice, and Christopher B. Teuton (Norman: University of Oklahoma Press, 2008), 340–52; Lisa Tatonetti, *Written on the Body: Gender Expansiveness and Indigenous Non-Cis Masculinity* (Minneapolis: University of Minnesota Press, 2021), 110–12; Mark Rifkin, *Erotics of Sovereignty: Queer Native Writing in the Era of Self-Determination* (Minneapolis: University of Minnesota Press, 2012); and the anthology *Sovereign Erotics*, eds. Daniel Heath Justice, Deborah Miranda, Qwo-Li Driskill, and Lisa Tatonetti (Tuscan: University of Arizona Press, 2011).

32. Richardson, *The Savage and the Modern Self*, 7.

33. I draw from Catriona Mortimer-Sandilands and Bruce Erickson's definition of a queer ecology as "an important point of conversation between queer and ecological politics because they reveal the powerful ways in which understandings of nature inform discourses of sexuality" (2–3). See Catriona Mortimer-Sandilands and Bruce Erickson, "Introduction: A Genealogy of Queer Ecologies," in *Queer Ecologies*, ed. Catriona Mortimer-Sandilands and Bruce Erickson (Bloomington: Indiana University Press, 2010), 1–41.

34. William Hubbard, *A History of the Indian Wars in New England* (Stockbridge: Heman Willard 1803), 251–52.

35. Hubbard, *A History of the Indian Wars*, 252. See also Fisher, *Indian Great Awakening*, 13–14.

36. Melissa Tantaquidgeon Zobel (formerly Melissa Jayne Fawcett) and Gladys Tantaquidgeon, *Medicine Trail: The Life and Lessons of Gladys Tantaquidgeon* (Tuscan: University of Arizona Press, 2000), 53.

37. Fisher, *Indian Great Awakening*, 13.

38. Samson Occom, "To Eleazar Wheelock (1765)," *The Collected Writings of Samson Occom, Mohegan*, ed. Joanna Brooks (Oxford: Oxford University Press, 2006), 74–75; 74.

39. Mary Favret, *War at a Distance: Romanticism and the Making of Modern Wartime* (Princeton: Princeton University Press, 2009), 129; 137.

40. Occom, "Short Narrative (First Draft)," *The Collected Writings of Samson Occom, Mohegan*, ed. Joanna Brooks (Oxford: Oxford University Press, 2006), 51–52. The imbrication of race and environment demonstrates Katy Chiles's point: "Early Americans largely considered race . . . to be potentially mutable: it was thought to be an exterior bodily trait, incrementally produced by environmental factors (such as climate, food, and mode of living) and subject to change" (2). See Katy Chiles, *Transformable Race: Surprising Metamorphoses in the Literature of Early America* (Oxford: Oxford University Press, 2014); and Roxann Wheeler, *The Complexion of Race: Categories of Difference in Eighteenth-Century British Culture* (Philadelphia: University of Pennsylvania Press, 2000), 1–48.

41. Robert Warrior, *The People and the Word: Reading Native Nonfiction* (Minneapolis: University of Minnesota Press, 2005), xxix.

42. For Occom in England, see Brooks, "This Indian World," 24–26; Coll Thrush, *Indigenous London: Native Travelers at the Heart of Empire* (New Haven: Yale University Press, 2016), 108–13; and Hilary Wyss, *English Letters and Indian Literacies: Reading, Writing, and New England Missionary Schools, 1750–1830* (Philadelphia: University of Pennsylvania Press, 2012), 56–72.

43. For Occom's relationship with Wheelock, see Wyss, *Writing Indians*, 124–31; Brooks, "This Indian World," 21–23; Brooks, *The Common Pot*, 84–86; and Bayers, "We Unman Ourselves," 176–79.

44. Stevens, *The Poor Indians*, 14–17.

45. Occom, "Letter to Eleazar Wheelock (1772)," *The Collected Writings of Samson Occom, Mohegan*, ed. Joanna Brooks (Oxford: Oxford University Press, 2006), 98–100; 99.

46. For the Mohegan land case, see Mark D. Walters, "Mohegan Indians v. Connecticut (1705–1773) and the Legal Status of Aboriginal Customary Laws and Government in British North America," *Osgood Hall Law Journal* 33, no. 4 (Winter 1995): 785–829; Amy Den Ouden, *Beyond Conquest: Native Peoples and the Struggle for History in New England* (Lincoln: University of Nebraska Press, 2005), 1–3; 68–99; Brooks, "This Indian World," 10–11; Brooks, *The Common Pot*, 53–80; 83–100; Jean M. O'Brien, *Firsting and Lasting: Writing Indians Out of Existence in New England* (Minneapolis: University of Minnesota Press, 2010), 159–70; Silverman, *Red Brethren*, 46–51; and Craig Bryan Yirush, "Claiming the New World: Empire, Law, and Indigenous Rights in the Mohegan Case, 1704–1743," *Law and History Review* 29, no. 2 (May 2011): 333–73.

47. Brooks, "This Indian World," 12.

48. Occom, "Mohegan Tribe to Sir William Johnson," 145.

49. Brooks, "Chronology," xxii–xxiii.

50. Samson Occom, "Short Narrative of My Life (First Draft) (1761)," 51–52; 51.

51. Occom, "Short Narrative (Second Draft)," 52.

52. Occom, "Short Narrative (Second Draft)," 52. For Indigenous perspectives on colonial economies, see Joshua David Bellin, *The Demon of the Continent: Indians and the Shaping of American Literature* (Philadelphia: University of Pennsylvania Press, 2000), 42–43; and Stevens, *The Poor Indians*, 38–43.

53. Occom, "Short Narrative (Second Draft)," 53.

54. Lisa Brooks, *Our Beloved Kin: A New History of King Philip's War* (New Haven: Yale University Press, 2018), 175.

55. For many Algonquian communities, "a dog howling is a sign of death," as noted by William Simmons, "The Mystic Voice: Pequot Folklore from the Seventeenth Century to the Present," in *The Pequots in Southern New England*, eds. Laurence Hauptman and James D. Wherry (Norman: University of Oklahoma Press, 1990), 141–76; 154. Narragansett belief suggested that the "souls of the dead were guarded by a great dog," as Simmons further explains in *Cautantowwit's House* (Providence: University of Rhode Island Press, 1970), 55. For dogs within Indigenous cultures in the Native Northeast, see also Marion Schwartz, *A History of Dogs in the Early Americas* (New Haven: Yale University Press, 1997), 93–103; and Matt Cohen, *The Networked Wilderness: Communicating in Early New England* (Minneapolis: University of Minnesota Press, 2010), 142–43.

56. Elizabeth Freeman, *Beside You in Time: Sense Methods and Queer Sociabilities in the American Nineteenth Century* (Durham: Duke University Press, 2019), 14.

57. Rifkin, *Erotics of Sovereignty*, 33.

58. Occom, "Short Narrative (Second Draft)," 58.

59. Occom, "Short Narrative (Second Draft)," 53.

60. Fisher, *Indian Great Awakening*, 63; 75. See also Brooks, "This Indian World," 13.

61. Fisher, *Indian Great Awakening*, 67–71; and Joanna Brooks, *American Lazarus*, 46–49.

62. Occom, "Letter to Eleazar Wheelock," 74.

63. Misty G. Anderson, *Imagining Methodism in Eighteenth-Century Britain: Enthusiasm, Belief, and the Borders of the Self* (Baltimore: Johns Hopkins University Press, 2012), 2–3. On Occom's conversion, see also Stevens, *The Poor Indians*, 141–42.

64. Jonathan Edwards, "Personal Narrative," in *The Norton Anthology of American Literature: Beginnings to 1820*, eds. Robert S. Levine, et al., 8th ed. (New York: W. W. Norton, 2017), 358–68; 360.

65. Edwards, "Personal Narrative," 360.

66. Occom, "Letter to Eleazar Wheelock," 74. On American "wilderness," see Timothy Sweet, *American Georgics: Economy and Environment in Early American Literature* (Philadelphia: University of Pennsylvania Press, 2002), 3–10; and William Cronon, *Changes in the Land: Indians, Colonists, and the Ecology of New England* (New York: Hill and Wang, 2003), 3–6.

67. Occom, "Letter to Eleazar Wheelock," 74.

68. Kimberly Takahata reads the letter as an instance of Occom recuperating Native care practices, as she elaborated in "'Where my Bones must be Buried': Indig-

enous Care in Settler Narratives," Conference Presentation. Society of Early Americanists (March 5, 2021). I am also indebted to Ana Schwartz for her remarks on this passage in Occom.

69. Samson Occom, "The Most Remarkable and Strange State Situation and Appearance of Indian Tribes in this Great Continent" (1783), *The Collected Writings of Samson Occom, Mohegan*, ed. Joanna Brooks (Oxford: Oxford University Press, 2006), 58–59; 58. See also his sermon, "Thou Shalt Love Thy Neighbor as Thyself" (1787), *The Collected Writings of Samson Occom, Mohegan*, ed. Joanna Brooks (Oxford: Oxford University Press, 2006), 198–207.

70. See Jean M. O'Brien, *Dispossession by Degrees: Indian Land and Identity in Natick, Massachusetts, 1650–1790* (Lincoln: University of Nebraska Press, 2003), 210–11.

71. See Elizabeth Povinelli, *Empire of Love: Toward a Theory of Intimacy, Genealogy and Carnality* (Durham: Duke University Press, 2006), 16–21; and Mark Rifkin, *When Did Indians Become Straight?: Kinship, the History of Sexuality, and Native Sovereignty* (Oxford: Oxford University Press, 2011), 36–38.

72. See, for instance, Brooks's discussion on Indigenous containment in *Our Beloved Kin*, 65–66.

73. Sharon Holland, *The Erotic Life of Racism* (Durham: Duke University Press, 2012), 9.

74. See Qwo-Li Driskill, *Asegi Stories: Cherokee Queer and Two-Spirit Memory* (Tuscan: University of Arizona Press, 2016), 41. Michael Warner argues that settlers not only projected a perverse and queer mortality onto Indigenous populations but also turned to anti-queer rhetoric to distinguish American settlements from England: by comparing Britain to Sodom, for instance, Puritans iterated norms of sober polities. See "New English Sodom," *American Literature* 64, no. 1 (1992): 19–47. For colonial histories of gender and sexuality, see also Jonathan Goldberg, *Sodometries: Renaissance Texts, Modern Sexualities* (Stanford: Stanford University Press, 1992), chapters 6–7.

75. Melissa K. Nelson, "Getting Dirty: The Eco-Eroticism of Women in Indigenous Oral Literatures," in *Critically Sovereign*, ed. Joanne Barker (Durham: Duke University Press, 2017), 229–60.

76. Nelson, "Getting Dirty," 236–40.

77. Nelson, "Getting Dirty," 232.

78. On "Herbs & Roots," see Kelly Wisecup, "Medicine, Communication, and Authority in Samson Occom's Herbal," *Early American Studies* 10, no. 3 (Fall 2012): 540–65; and *Assembled for Use: Indigenous Compilation and the Archives of Early Native American Literatures* (New Haven: Yale University Press, 2021), 23–59.

79. On Indigenous extended kinships and relational networks in the Northeast, see also Cohen, *Networked Wilderness*, 71–72, 103–4; Brooks, *The Common Pot*, 84–90; and Wyss, *Writing Indians*, 123–31.

80. Samson Occom, "Herbs & Roots" (1754), *The Collected Writings of Samson Occom, Mohegan*, ed. Joanna Brooks (Oxford: Oxford University Press, 2006), 44–47; 45.

81. Wisecup, "Medicine," 565. I am also grateful to Kelly for sharing her chapter on Occom in *Assembled for Use* prior to its publication. Her point that Occom's medicinal knowledge embedded him within Algonquian seasonal routines and relations deeply shaped my own sense of the queer survivance that his botanic knowledge sustained.

82. Siobhan Senier, "Commentary: Sovereignty and Sustainability in Mohegan Ethnobotanical Literature," *The Journal of Ecocriticism* 6, no. 1 (Spring 2014): 1–15; 6–7.

83. LaFleur, *Natural History of Sexuality*, 6.

84. Wisecup, "Medicine," 554.

85. Occom, "Herbs & Roots," 46–47.

86. For a prescient discussion of dominionism and Genesis in the context of our contemporary climate crisis, see Lynn White Jr., "The Historical Roots of Our Ecologic Crisis," *Science* 155, no. 3767 (March 1967): 1203–07.

87. Brooks, "This Indian World," 15.

88. John Strong, *The Montaukett Indians of Eastern Long Island* (Syracuse: Syracuse University Press, 2006), 60–87.

89. Fisher, *Indian Great Awakening*, 168.

90. Rifkin, *When Did Indians Become Straight?*, 33.

91. Occom, "Short Narrative (Second Draft)," 58. See also Povinelli, *Empire of Love*, 7.

92. Samson Occom, "Mohegan Tribe on Rents" (1778), *The Collected Writings of Samson Occom, Mohegan*, ed. Joanna Brooks (Oxford: Oxford University Press, 2006), 147.

93. Occom, "Mohegan Tribe on Rents," 147.

94. Lisa Brooks, "Digging at the Roots: Locating an Ethical, Native Criticism," in *Reasoning Together: The Native Critics Collective*, eds. Daniel Heath Justice, Christopher B. Teuton, and Craig S. Womack (Norman: University of Oklahoma Press, 2008), 234–64; 247.

95. Samson Occom, "Account of the Montauk Indians, on Long Island" (1761), *The Collected Writings of Samson Occom, Mohegan*, ed. Joanna Brooks (Oxford: Oxford University Press, 2006), 47–51; 47.

96. Occom, "Account of the Montauk Indians," 48.

97. Brooks, *The Common Pot*, 3–8; See also Brooks, *Collected Writings*, 48n24.

98. Ann Marie Plane, *Colonial Intimacies: Indian Marriage in New England* (Ithaca: Cornell University Press, 2002), 24.

99. Occom, "Short Narrative (First Draft)," 51–2. For Occom's itinerancy, see Eve Tavor Bannet, *Transatlantic Stories and the History of Reading* (Cambridge: Cambridge University Press, 2011), 158–86.

100. Samson Occom, *Journal 3* (1757–1760), *The Collected Writings of Samson Occom, Mohegan*, ed. Joanna Brooks (Oxford: Oxford University Press, 2006), 252–59; 254. I am grateful to Ana Schwartz for reminding me of this passage.

101. Brooks, *Our Beloved Kin*, 29; See also Kathleen Bragdon, *Native People of Southern New England* (Norman: University of Oklahoma Press, 1996), 156–68; and Andrew Lipman, *The Saltwater Frontier: Indians and the Contest for the American Coast* (New Haven: Yale University Press, 2015), 35–36.

102. Samson Occom, *Journal 12* (1785), *The Collected Writings of Samson Occom, Mohegan*, ed. Joanna Brooks (Oxford: Oxford University Press, 2006), 301–13; 307.

103. On the Green Corn ceremony, see also Craig S. Womack, *Red on Red: Native American Literary Separatism* (Minneapolis: University of Minnesota Press, 1999), 44–49.

104. Zobel and Tantaquidgeon, *Medicine Trail*, 53–59.

105. Occom, *Journal 12*, 306.

106. Anthony Wonderley, "Brothertown, New York, 1785–1796," *New York History* 81, no. 4 (October 2000): 457–92; 470–74.

107. Samson Occom, "Hymns" (1774), *The Collected Writings of Samson Occom, Mohegan*, ed. Joanna Brooks (Oxford: Oxford University Press, 2006), 233–39; 235. Joanna Brooks argues in *American Lazarus* that *A Choice Collection of Hymns and Spiritual Songs* (1774) renders "hymn texts as instruments of personal and communal renewal" (70).

108. Marisol de la Cadena and Mario Blaser, "Pluriverse: Proposals for a World of Many Worlds," in *A World of Many Worlds*, eds. Marisol de la Cadena and Mario Blaser (Durham: Duke University Press, 2018), 1–22; 3.

109. Occom, "Mohegan Tribe to Sir William Johnson," 145. On Indigenous cosmologies of animate matter, see Marisol de la Cadena, *Earth Beings: Ecologies of Practice across Andean Worlds* (Durham: Duke University Press, 2015); and Elizabeth Povinelli, *Geontologies: A Requiem to Late Liberalism* (Durham: Duke University Press, 2016).

110. On Algonquian conceptions of Manitou, see Calvin Martin, *Keepers of the Game: Indian-Animal Relationships and the Fur Trade* (Berkeley: University of California Press, 1982), 34; and Daniel K. Richter, *Facing East from Indian Country: A Native History of Early America* (Cambridge: Harvard University Press, 2001), 14–15.

111. Neal Salisbury, *Manitou and Providence: Indians, Europeans, and the Making of New England* (Oxford: Oxford University Press, 1982), 10.

112. On critical ocean studies and Indigenous scholarship, see Karin Amimoto Ingersoll, *Waves of Knowing: A Seascape Epistemology* (Durham: Duke University Press, 2016); Elizabeth DeLoughrey, *Allegories of the Anthropocene* (Durham: Duke University Press, 2019), chapters 4–5, and "Submarine Futures of the Anthropocene," *Comparative Literature Journal* 69, no. 1 (2017): 32–44. See also the special issues on "Oceanic Studies," ed. Margaret Cohen, *PMLA* no. 125, vol. 3 (May 2010), and on "Hydro-Criticism," ed. Laura Winkiel, *English Language Notes*, 57, no. 1 (April 2019).

113. On grounded normativity, see Coulthard, *Red Skin, White Masks*, 60; Leanne Betasamosake Simpson, *As We Have Always Done: Indigenous Freedom through Radical Resistance* (Minneapolis: University of Minnesota Press, 2017), 22–24; and Byrd, "What's Normative Got to Do With It?", 115–18.

114. Astrida Neimanis, *Bodies of Water: Posthuman Feminist Phenomenology* (London: Bloomsbury, 2017), 2.

115. Lipman, *Saltwater Frontier*, 3–5.

116. Linda Hogan, *Solar Storms* (New York: Scribner, 1995), 350. See also Emanuele Coccia's argument that "life has never abandoned fluid space," in *The Life of Plants*, trans. Dylan J. Montanari (Cambridge: Polity, 2017), 35–53.

117. Samson Occom, "Montaukett Tribe to the State of New York" (1785/8?), *The Collected Writings of Samson Occom, Mohegan*, ed. Joanna Brooks (Oxford: Oxford University Press, 2006), 150–52; 151. On Algonquian knowledge of waterways, see also Stephanie Fitzgerald, "'I Wunnatuckquannum, This Is My Hand': Native Performance in Massachusetts Language Indian Deeds," in *Native Acts: Indian*

Performance, 1603–1832, eds. Joshua David Bellin and Laura L. Mielke (Lincoln: University of Nebraska Press, 2011), 145–68; 154.

118. Cronon, *Changes in the Land*, 31.

119. Strother E. Roberts, *Colonial Ecology, Atlantic Economy: Transforming Nature in Early New England* (Philadelphia: University of Pennsylvania Press, 2018), 25–30. In *Skunny Wundy: Seneca Indian Tales* (Syracuse: Syracuse University Press, 1994), Arthur C. Parker relates a tale where Beaver says, "I am worker, builder, channel maker. Where I go, there the ponds grow larger and life is more [abundant]" (170).

120. On settler cultivation practices and efforts towards sustainable husbandry, see Brian Donahue, *The Great Meadow: Farmers and Land in Colonial Concord* (New Haven: Yale University Press, 2004), 23; and Abby L. Goode, *Agrotopias: An American Literary History of Sustainability* (Chapel Hill: University of North Carolina, 2023). On Indigenous agriculture, see also Jane Mt. Pleasant, "A New Paradigm for Pre-Columbian Agriculture in North America," *Early American Studies* 13, no. 2 (Spring 2015): 374–412.

121. Roberts, *Colonial Ecology, Atlantic Economy*, 49–50; Wonderley, "Brothertown," 472.

122. For the Great Beaver, see Brooks, *The Common Pot*, 14–23; and Cheryl Savageau, *Mother/land* (Cambridge: Folio Publications, 2006), 15. Savageau is also quoted in Brooks, *The Common Pot*, 20–21.

123. Gerald Horne, *The Apocalypse of Settler Colonialism: The Roots of Slavery, White Supremacy, and Capitalism in Seventeenth-Century North America and the Caribbean* (New York: Monthly Review Press, 2017), 9.

124. Cadwallader Colden, *The history of the five Indian nations of Canada* (London, 1755), 13.

125. John Locke, *Second Treatise on Government*, ed. Ian Shapiro (New Haven: Yale University Press, 2003), 117; and William Wood, *New England's Prospect* (1634), ed. Alden T. Vaughan (Amherst: University of Massachusetts Press, 1977), 96.

126. Qtd. Allan Greer, *Property and Dispossession: Natives, Empires, and Land in Early Modern North America* (Cambridge: Cambridge University Press, 2018), 213.

127. Samuel Kirkland, *The Journals of Samuel Kirkland*, ed. W. Pilkington (Clinton: Hamilton College, 1980), 162.

128. Brooks, "This Indian World," 24.

129. Joseph Johnson, "Speech to the Oneidas, January 20, 1774," in *To Do Good to My Indian Brethren: The Writings of Joseph Johnson, 1751–1776*, ed. Laura Murray (Amherst: University of Minnesota Press, 1998), 206–11; 206.

130. On Johnson's diplomatic trip to the Oneida, see also Wonderley, "Brothertown," 464; Wyss, *Writing Indians*, 126–27; and Calcaterra, *Literary Indians*, 73–82.

131. For the American Revolution and the Mohegan Nation, see Silverman, *Red Brethren*, 102–6; 109–17.

132. W. DeLoss Love, *Samson Occom and the Christian Indians of New England* (Syracuse: Syracuse University Press, 2000), 225. See also Wonderley, "Brothertown," 465–67.

133. Samson Occom, "Mohegan and Niantic Tribes to the Connecticut Assembly" (1785), *The Collected Writings of Samson Occom, Mohegan*, ed. Joanna Brooks (Oxford: Oxford University Press, 2006), 147–48; 148.

134. Occom, "Mohegan and Niantic Tribes to the Connecticut Assembly," 148.

135. Occom, "Mohegan and Niantic Tribes to the Connecticut Assembly," 148.

136. Kimberly Roppolo Wieser, "Samson Occom as Writing Instructor: The Search for an Intertribal Rhetoric," in *Reasoning Together: The Native Critics Collective*, Daniel Heath Justice, Christopher B. Teuton, and Craig S. Womack (Norman: University of Oklahoma Press, 2008), 303–24; 307.

137. Scott Richard Lyons, "Rhetorical Sovereignty: What Do American Indians Want from Writing?," *College Composition and Communication* 51, no. 3 (February 2000): 447–68; 449.

138. Samson Occom, "Letter to John Bailey" (1783), *The Collected Writings of Samson Occom, Mohegan*, ed. Joanna Brooks (Oxford: Oxford University Press, 2006), 118–20; 119.

139. Occom, *Journal* 12, 308–9.

140. Drew Lopenzina, "'The Whole Wilderness Shall Blossom as the Rose': Samson Occom, Joseph Johnson, and the Question of Native Settlement on Cooper's Frontier," *American Quarterly* 58, no. 4 (December 2006): 1119–45; 1120; 1122.

141. On Brothertown's land title, see Brooks, "This Indian World," 26–27; and Silverman, *Red Brethren*, 196–97.

142. Samson Occom, "Indians Must Have Teachers of Their Own Coular or Nation" (1791), *The Collected Writings of Samson Occom, Mohegan*, ed. Joanna Brooks (Oxford: Oxford University Press, 2006), 133–35; 133.

143. Samson Occom, "Brotherton Tribe to the United States Congress," *The Collected Writings of Samson Occom, Mohegan*, ed. Joanna Brooks (Oxford: Oxford University Press, 2006), 148–50; 150.

144. Occom, "Brotherton Tribe to the United States Congress," 150.

145. On Algonquian diplomacy, see David Murray, *Indian Giving: Economies of Power in Indian-White Exchanges* (Amherst: University of Massachusetts Press, 2000), 28–29; and Brooks, *The Common Pot*, 225–26.

146. Occom, "Brotherton Tribe to the United States Congress," 149.

147. For Haudenosaunee creation stories of Skywoman, see David Cusick, *Sketches of the Ancient History of the Six Nations* (Lewiston: Tuscarora Village Press, 1828); Thomas King, *The Truth About Stories* (Minneapolis: University of Minnesota Press, 2008), 1–30; Brooks, "Digging," 235–36; and Robin Wall Kimmerer, *Braiding Sweetgrass: Indigenous Wisdom, Scientific Knowledge and the Teaching of Plants* (Minneapolis: University of Minnesota Press, 2013), 3–10. For European encounters with Native creation stories, see Lopenzina, *Red Ink*, 29–40.

148. Occom, "Brothertown Tribe to the United States Congress," 149.

149. Locke, *Second Treatise of Government*, 111.

150. Locke, *Second Treatise of Government*, 113. See also Paul Corcoran, "John Locke on Native Right, Colonial Possession, and the Concept of *Vacuum Domicilium*," *The European Legacy* 23, no. 3 (December 2017): 225–50.

151. Hannah Arendt, *The Origins of Totalitarianism* (New York: Harcourt, Brace, Jovanovich, 1973), 145.

152. I am indebted to Carrie Shanafelt for her incisive comments on this chapter and for her reading of Locke in *Uncommon Sense: Jeremy Bentham, Queer Aesthetics, and the Politics of Taste* (Charlottesville: University of Virginia Press, 2022), 8–10.

153. Raymond Williams, *The Long Revolution* (Peterborough: Pelican, 2011), 64–66.

154. For queer ecologies and water, see Jeremy Chow and Brandi Bushman, "Hydro-Eroticism," special issue: "Hydro-Criticism," ed. Laura Winkiel, *English Language Notes* 57, no. 1 (April 2019): 96–115; and Jeremy Chow, *The Queerness of Water: Troubled Ecologies in the Eighteenth Century* (Charlottesville: University of Virginia Press, 2023).

155. On beavers as a keystone species and their decline, see Roberts, *Colonial Ecology, Atlantic Economy*, 43–51. On animal declines and extinctions in the wake of colonial expansion, see Lipman's discussion of the right whale in *Saltwater Frontier*, 222–35; and Elizabeth Kolbert on the great auk in *The Sixth Extinction: An Unnatural History* (New York: Picador, 2014), 47–69.

156. For Occom and fishing, see Joanna Brooks's introduction to his journals, "Journals," *The Collected Writings of Samson Occom, Mohegan*, ed. Joanna Brooks (Oxford: Oxford University Press, 2006), 241. See also examples in Occom's *Journals*, 276–77; 374.

157. Even Carl Schmitt, whose thoughts on the state of exception have haunted accounts of modern sovereignty, argued that a "primeval act" of "land-appropriation" originated international law and treated Native territories as ontologically blank spaces into which settlers moved. See Carl Schmitt, *The Nomos of the Earth in the International Law of the* Jus Publicum Europaeum, trans. G. L. Ulmen (New York: Telos Press Publishing, 2006), 45. On international law, sovereignty, and land theft, see also Jonathan Elmer, *On Lingering and Being Last: Race and Sovereignty in the New World* (New York: Fordham University Press, 2008), 12–13; and Robert Nichols, *Theft Is Property!* (Durham: Duke University Press, 2020), 53.

158. Phillis Wheatley Peters, "On Imagination," in *Poems on Various Subjects*, ed. Vincent Carretta (London: Penguin Books, 2001), 36–37; 36.

159. Isabelle Stengers, "The Challenge of Ontological Politics," in *A World of Many Worlds*, eds. Marisol de la Cadena and Mario Blaser (Durham: Duke University Press, 2018), 83–111; 86.

160. José Esteban Muñoz, *Cruising Utopia: The Then and There of Queer Futurity* (New York: New York University Press, 2009), 189.

161. Occom, "To All the Indians in This Boundless Continent," 196–97; 197.

162. Wigginton, "Extending Root and Branch," 49.

163. Occom, "Teachers of their Own Coular," 133.

164. Occom, "Teachers of their Own Coular," 134.

165. On the Brothertown move to Wisconsin, see Silverman, *Red Brethren*, 184–90.

166. Occom's works offer an approach for "completing the turn" in early American studies, as Alyssa MT. Pleasant, Caroline Wigginton, and Kelly Wisecup put it, by revealing Native sensory traditions archived in material objects. See "Materials and Methods in Native American and Indigenous Studies: Completing the Turn," *Early American Literature* 53, no. 2 (April 2018): 407–44. For the Occom archives, see Ivy Schweitzer, "Native Sovereignty and the Archive: Samson Occom and Digital Humanities," *American Literary Study* 38 (June 2015): 21–52. For Native medias, see Joshua David Bellin and Laura L. Mielke, eds., *Native Acts*; Matt Cohen and Jeffrey Glover, eds., *Colonial Mediascapes*; and Kristina Bross and Hilary Wyss, *Early Native Literacies*

in New England. For scholarship that revises conceptions of American literature through Indigenous textualities, see Cohen, *Networked Wilderness*; Birgit Brander Rasmussen, *Queequeg's Coffin: Indigenous Literacies and Early American Literature* (Durham: Duke University Press, 2012); and Calcaterra, *Literary Indians*. The Occom Papers housed at Dartmouth College were recently rematriated to the Mohegan Nation in 2022.

167. Donna J. Haraway, *When Species Meet* (Minneapolis: Minnesota University Press, 2007), 36. See also Peter Charles Hoffer, *Sensory Worlds in Early America* (Baltimore: Johns Hopkins University Press, 2003), 10–11.

168. Occom, "Account of the Montauk Indians," 49.

169. Occom, "Account of the Montauk Indians," 49.

170. Occom, "Account of the Montauk Indians," 49.

171. For discussions of the box Occom created and sent to Lucy, see Brooks, "This Indian World," 1–2; Zobel and Tantaquidgeon, *Medicine Trail*, 135–36; and Calcaterra, *Literary Indians*, 83–88.

172. Zobel and Tantaquidgeon, *Medicine Trail*, 135.

173. Zobel and Tantaquidgeon, *Medicine Trail*, 135.

174. Kimmerer, *Braiding Sweetgrass*, 153. The basket also, as Kimmerer suggests, "knows the dual powers of destruction and creation" (256). In this way, Occom's small carved box refuses the ruinous momentum of settler consumption, where resources are used until destroyed, as Hannah Arendt wrote of Lockean formations of property. On baskets as carriers of history, see also Drew Lopenzina, *Through an Indian's Looking-Glass: A Cultural Biography of William Apess* (Amherst: University of Massachusetts Press, 2018), 26.

175. Stephanie Fitzgerald, "The Cultural Work of a Mohegan Painted Basket," in *Early Native Literacies in New England*, eds. Kristina Bross and Hilary E. Wyss (Amherst: University of Massachusetts Press, 2008), 52–56. Tantaquidgeon's practice as curator of the Tantaquidgeon Museum also emphasized touch: she encouraged visitors to handle objects on display, as discussed by Tantaquidgeon and Zobel in *Medicine Trail*, 152–53. On touch and Indigenous archives, see also Wisecup, *Assembled for Use*, 56–59.

176. For Algonquian practices of dream interpretation, see William S. Simmons, *The Spirit of the New England Tribes* (Hanover: Dartmouth University Press, 1986), 49–55. For colonial practices of dream interpretation, see also Ann Marie Plane, *Dreams and the Invisible World in Colonial New England* (Philadelphia: University of Pennsylvania Press, 2014); and Ann Marie Plane and Leslie Tuttle, eds., *Dreams, Dreamers, and Visions* (Philadelphia: University of Pennsylvania Press, 2013).

177. Samson Occom, *Journal 15* (1786), *The Collected Writings of Samson Occom, Mohegan*, ed. Joanna Brooks (Oxford: Oxford University Press, 2006), 325–36; 334.

178. Occom, *Journal 15*, 334; Peyer, *Tutor'd Mind*, 97.

179. On Occom's dream of Whitefield, see Peyer, *Tutor'd Mind*, 97–98; Brooks, *American Lazarus*, 84–86; McCarthy, "Conversion, Identity, and the Indian Missionary," 356–58; and Jessica M. Parr, *Inventing George Whitefield: Race, Revivalism, and the Making of a Religious Icon* (Oxford: University of Mississippi Press, 2015), 103–4.

180. For dogs and racialized flesh, see Donna J. Haraway, *The Companion Species Manifesto* (Chicago: University of Chicago Press, 2003); Colin Dayan, *The Law Is a White Dog* (Princeton: Princeton University Press, 2013), and *With Dogs at the Edge of*

Life (New York: Columbia University Press, 2016); Deborah Bird Rose, *Wild Dog Dreaming: Love and Extinction* (Charlottesville: University of Virginia Press, 2012); Bénédicte Boisseron, *Afro-Dog: Blackness and the Animal Question* (New York: Columbia University Press, 2018); Joshua Bennett, *Being Property Once Myself: Blackness and the End of Man* (Cambridge: Harvard University Press, 2020), chapter 4.

181. William Sprague, *Annals of the American Pulpit*, 3 vols. (New York: R. Carter and Brothers, 1859), 2: 40.

182. The Mohegan Vision Statement proclaims, "We are the Wolf People, children of Mundo," as foregrounded by Tantaquidgeon and Zobel in *Medicine Trail*, 3. For dogs who guard the path to the afterlife, see also Wood, *New England's Prospect*, 111; and Brooks, *American Lazarus*, 85.

183. Dayan, *With Dogs at the Edge of Life*, xiii.

184. Joanna Brooks, "This Indian World," 152n10; See also Fisher, *Indian Great Awakening*, 168.

185. Occom, "Montaukett Tribe to the State of New York," 151.

186. Occom's vision of Whitefield parallels an encounter that Eduardo Kohn, in his consideration of Quechua perspectives on dogs and dreaming, calls a way "to enter intimate (significant) relations with [others] who are radically not us" (134). See Eduardo Kohn, *How Forests Think: Toward an Anthropology Beyond the Human* (Berkeley: University of California Press, 2013).

187. Jodi Byrd, *The Transit of Empire: Indigenous Critiques of Colonialism* (Minneapolis: University of Minnesota Press, 2011), xv.

188. Occom, *Sermon on the Execution of Moses Paul*, 192.

189. Thomas Hobbes, *Leviathan*, ed. Ian Shapiro (New Haven: Yale University Press, 2010), 78.

190. Amanda Cobb, Unpublished Manuscript. Qtd. Daniel Heath Justice, "'Go Away Water!': Kinship Criticism and the Decolonizing Imperative," in *Reasoning Together: The Native Critics Collective*, eds. Daniel Heath Justice, Christopher B. Teuton, and Craig S. Womack (Norman: University of Oklahoma Press, 2008), 147–68; 152.

191. Bracken, "The Deaths of Moses," 181–83.

192. Kristina Bross, *Dry Bones and Indian Sermons: Praying Indians in Colonial America* (Ithaca: Cornell University Press, 2004), 34–39; and Stevens, *The Poor Indians*, 43–49.

193. Occom, *Sermon on the Execution of Moses Paul*, 186.

194. Occom, *Sermon on the Execution of Moses Paul*, 186. For respiration and expiration, I am paraphrasing Beth H. Piatote's analysis of E. Pauline Johnson's "A Red Girl's Reasoning" in *Domestic Subjects: Gender, Citizenship, and Law in Native American Literature* (New Haven: Yale University Press, 2013), 33.

195. Deborah Miranda, *The Zen of La Llorona* (Cromer: Salt Publishing, 2005), 4.

Chapter Two

1. Margot Maddison-MacFayden, "Mary Prince and the Grand Turk," *Bermuda Journal of Archeology and Maritime History* 19 (2009): 102–23; 111–12. Pringle likely concealed Darrell's identity with the pseudonym "Mr. D—" to prevent being sued for libel. Members of Prince's extended family may have also still been enslaved by the Darrells.

2. Mary Prince, *The History of Mary Prince, a West Indian Slave, Related by Herself*, ed. Moira Ferguson (Ann Arbor: University of Michigan Press, 1997), 72.

3. Prince, *The History*, 72.

4. Prince, *The History*, 74. See also Mark Kurlansky, *Salt: A World History* (London: Penguin Books, 2003), 1–5.

5. Prince, *The History*, 73.

6. *A Collection of hymns of the children of God* (London, 1754), 336. The hymn reads: "I, who in tend'rest union am to all thy Cross's air-doves bound, smell to and kiss each Corpse's wound; yet at the *Pleura's* smart, there pants and throbs my Heart. I see still, how the soldier fierce did thy most lovely *Pleura* pierce, that dearest Side-whole! . . . I've lick'd this Rock's salt round and round. Where can such relish else be found!"

7. See Matthew Rowney, "Preserver and Destroyer: Salt and *The History of Mary Prince*," *European Romantic Review* 29, no. 3 (June 2018): 357–63; 357–58; and Michele Speitz, "Blood Sugar and Salt Licks: Corroding Bodies and Preserving Nations in *The History of Mary Prince, a West Indian Slave, Related by Herself*," *Circulations: Romanticism and the Black Atlantic*, eds. Paul Youngquist and Fran Botkin. *Romantic Circles*. 18 Dec. 2016. https://romantic-circles.org/praxis/circulations/HTML/praxis.2011.speitz.

8. On eighteenth-century sympathy and sentimentality, see Markman Ellis, *The Politics of Sensibility: Race, Gender, and Commerce in the Sentimental Novel* (Cambridge: Cambridge University Press, 1996); Marcus Wood, *Slavery, Empathy, and Pornography* (Oxford: Oxford University Press, 2003); Brycchan Carey, *British Abolition and the Rhetoric of Sensibility* (New York: Palgrave Macmillan, 2005); Lynn Festa, *Sentimental Figures of Empire in Eighteenth-Century Britain and France* (Baltimore: Johns Hopkins University Press, 2006); Christine Levecq, *Slavery and Sentiment: The Politics of Feeling in Black Atlantic Antislavery Writing* (Durham, NH: University of New Hampshire Press, 2008); Ramesh Mallipeddi, *Spectacular Suffering: Witnessing Culture in the Eighteenth-Century British Atlantic* (Charlottesville: University of Virginia Press, 2016); Stefan M. Wheelock, *Barbaric Culture and Black Critique* (Charlottesville: University of Virginia Press, 2016); and Stephen Ahern's edited collection, *Affect and Abolition in the Anglo-Atlantic World, 1770–1830* (New York: Routledge, 2016).

9. Lynn Festa in *Fiction Without Humanity: Person, Animal, Thing in Early Enlightenment Literature and Culture* (Philadelphia: University of Pennsylvania Press, 2021) argues that "sympathy and benevolence become entrenched as the privileged signifiers of human nature" (7). For Prince's dissent to this, see Charlotte Sussman, *Consuming Anxieties: Consumer Protest, Gender, and British Slavery* (Stanford: Stanford University Press, 2000), 130–35.

10. Saidiya Hartman, *Scenes of Subjection: Terror, Slavery, and Self-Making in Nineteenth-Century America* (Oxford: Oxford University Press, 1997), 18.

11. Craig Atwood, trans., *Litany of Wounds of the Husband* (State College, PA: Pennsylvania State University Press, 2012), 233–56; 235–36. Misty G. Anderson in *Imagining Methodism in Eighteenth-Century Britain: Enthusiasm, Belief, and the Borders of the Self* (Baltimore: Johns Hopkins University Press, 2012) argues that a "penetrable self" defined evangelical narratives of conversion—and registered significant differences to Lockean subjectivity (7).

12. Kathryn Yusoff, *A Billion Black Anthropocenes or None* (Minneapolis: University of Minnesota, 2018), 5; 11.

13. Tiffany Lethabo King, *The Black Shoals: Offshore Formations in Black and Native Studies* (Durham; Duke University Press, 2019), 114; 78. See also Zakiyyah Iman Jackson, *Becoming Human: Matter and Meaning in an Antiblack World* (New York: New York University Press, 2020), 1–8.

14. Prince, *The History*, 64.

15. Roland Barthes, *A Lover's Discourse: Fragments*, trans. Richard Howard (New York: Hill and Wang, 2010), 180.

16. Christina Sharpe, *In the Wake: On Blackness and Being* (Durham: Duke University Press, 2016), 19.

17. For Pringle's editorship, see Gillian Whitlock, *The Intimate Empire: Reading Women's Autobiography* (London: Continuum, 2000), 8–37; Sara Salih, "*The History of Mary Prince*, the Black Subject, and the Black Canon," in *Discourses of Abolition and Slavery: Britain and its Colonies, 1760–1838*, eds. Brycchan Carey, Markman Ellis, and Sara Salih (London: Palgrave Macmillan, 2004), 123–38; Jessica Allen, "Pringle's Pruning of Prince: *The History of Mary Prince* and the Question of Repetition," *Callaloo* 35, no. 2 (Spring 2012): 509–19; and Rachel Banner, "Surface and Stasis: Re-Reading Slave Narratives vis *The History of Mary Prince*," *Callaloo* 36, no. 2 (Spring 2013): 298–311.

18. Mary Jeanne Larrabee, "'I know what a slave knows': Mary Prince's Epistemology of Resistance," *Women's Studies* vol. 35, no. 5 (August 2006): 453–73; 453. See also Kerry Sinanan, "The 'Slave' as Cultural Artifact: The Case of Mary Prince," *Studies in Eighteenth-Century Culture* vol. 49, no. 1 (Spring 2020): 69–87; 74.

19. Édouard Glissant, *Poetics of Relation*, trans. Betsy Wing (Ann Arbor: University of Michigan Press, 1997), 189.

20. Prince, *The History*, 74; cf. 94.

21. Hazel Carby, *Imperial Intimacies: A Tale of Two Islands* (New York: Verso, 2019), 178.

22. Ereck Jarvis names these discourses an instance of "Enwhitenmen'" rationality, a "pun [that] marks the maintenance of patriarchy and the development of white supremacy. See Ereck Jarvis, "'Enwhitenmen' and the *Woman of Colour*—A Roundtable on the *Woman of Colour* (1808): Pedagogic and Critical Approaches," *Studies in Religion and Enlightenment* 2, no. 2 (Fall 2021), 45–47; 45. I am also grateful to Ereck for his thoughtful comments on this chapter.

23. Prince, *The History*, 74. Anglo-American evangelical cultures broadly emphasized that "[ecstasy] came when saints . . . escaped their bodies and entered into the realm" of sympathetic vision, as Susan Juster has put it. See Susan Juster, *Doomsayers: Anglo-American Prophecy in the Age of Revolutions* (Philadelphia: University of Pennsylvania Press, 2003), 113–14.

24. Alexis Pauline Gumbs, "The Age of Stolen Salt," *Orien: People and Nature* (Summer 2022): https://orionmagazine.org/article/the-age-of-stolen-salt/.

25. Michel-Rolph Trouillot, *Silencing the Past: Power and the Production of History* (Boston: Beacon Books, 1995), xix; and Prince, *The History*, 93.

26. Saidiya Hartman, "Venus in Two Acts," *Small Axe* 12, no. 2 (June 2008): 1–14; 12.

27. Hartman, "Venus in Two Acts," 11.

28. Nalo Hopkinson, *The Salt Roads* (New York: Warner Books, 2003), 9–10.

29. Prince *The History*, 64–71.

30. Prince, *The History*, 70.

31. Prince, *The History*, 70.

32. Adam Smith, *Theory of Moral Sentiments*, ed. Ryan Hanley (London: Penguin Books, 2009), 13–14.

33. Jean-Jacques Rousseau, "Essay on the Origin of Languages," in *The Discourses and Other Early Political Writings*, ed. Victor Gourevitch (Cambridge: Cambridge University Press, 1997), 247–99; 267–68.

34. Thomas Clarkson, *The History of the Rise, Progress, and Accomplishment of the Abolition of the African Slave-Trade by the British Parliament* (London: R. Taylor and Company, 1808), 395–96.

35. Avery Gordon, *Ghostly Matters: Haunting and the Sociological Imagination* (Minneapolis: University of Minnesota Press, 2008), 177. For the *Brookes*, see also Jennifer L. Morgan, *Reckoning with Slavery: Gender, Kinship, and Capitalism in the Early Black Atlantic* (Durham: Duke University Press, 2021), 151–69.

36. Ian Baucom, *Specters of the Atlantic: Finance Capital, Slavery, and the Philosophy of History* (Durham: Duke University Press, 2005), 250.

37. Smith, *Theory of Moral Sentiments*, 14–15.

38. William Wilberforce, "To Lord Holland" (1823), in *The Correspondence of William Wilberforce*, 1. (London: John Murray, 1840), 326–27; 326.

39. Prince, *The History*, 129.

40. For "seasoning" in the context of slavery as consumption of Black labor and flesh, see Vincent Woodard, *The Delectable Negro: Human Consumption and Homoeroticism within U.S. Culture*, ed. Dwight McBride and Justin A. Joyce (New York: New York University Press, 2014), 30–31; and Kyla Wazana Tompkins, *Racial Indigestion: Eating Bodies in the Nineteenth Century* (New York: New York University Press, 2012), 44–45.

41. Sean Gaston, "The Impossibility of Sympathy," *The Eighteenth Century: Theory and Interpretation* 51, no. 1–2 (Spring/Summer 2010): 129–51; 132.

42. David Hume, *A Treatise of Human Nature*, eds. David Fate Norton and Mary J. Norton (Oxford: Oxford University Press, 2007), 369–70; and Lynn Festa, "Humanity Without Feathers," *Humanity: An International Journal of Human Rights, Humanitarianism, and Development* 1, no. 1 (Fall 2010): 3–27; 2.

43. As Margaret Pringle (Thomas Pringle's wife) relates in a letter that was appended to the third edition of *The History*: "The whole of the back part of her body is distinctly scarred, and, as it were, *chequered*, with the vestiges of severe floggings" (130). The letter was also signed and corroborated by Susanna Strickland, Susan Brown, and Martha A. Browne, white women active in the abolition movement. On Prince's scars, see also Kerry Sinanan, "Mary Prince's Back and Her Critique of Anti-Slavery Sympathy," *Studies in Romanticism* 61, no. 1 (Spring 2022): 67–78. I am grateful to Kerry for sharing this work with me prior to its publication.

44. Samantha Pinto, "On the Skin: Mary Prince and the Narration of Black Feeling in the Early Nineteenth Century," *Early American Literature* 56, no. 2 (Summer 2021): 499–529; 500.

45. Prince, *The History*, 61.

46. Orlando Patterson, *Slavery and Social Death* (Cambridge: Harvard University Press, 1985), 60.

47. Prince, *The History*, 71.

48. Prince, *The History*, 61.

49. Morgan, *Reckoning with Slavery*, 160.

50. Prince, *The History*, 74.

51. Prince, *The History*, 94.

52. Mallipeddi, *Spectacular Suffering*, 6.

53. Mallipeddi, *Spectacular Suffering*, 78.

54. Rob Nixon, *Slow Violence and the Environmentalism of the Poor* (Cambridge: Harvard University Press 2013), 3.

55. On ecocriticism and scale, see Anna Lowenhaupt Tsing, "On Nonscalability: The Living World Is Not Amenable to Precision-Nested Scales," *Common Knowledge* 18, no. 3 (Fall 2012): 505–24.

56. Prince, *The History*, 75.

57. Prince, *The History*, 75.

58. Prince, *The History*, 74.

59. Sue Tait, "Bearing Witness, Journalism and Moral Responsibility," *Media, Culture, and Society* 33, no. 8 (November 2011): 1120–35; 1121–22, emphasis original. On visuality and witnessing, see also Kelly Oliver, *Witnessing: Beyond Recognition* (Minneapolis: University of Minnesota Press, 2001), 85–106. On witnessing racial violence in *The History*, see Jenny Sharpe, *Ghosts of Slavery: A Literary Archive of Black Women's Lives* (Minneapolis: University of Minnesota Press, 2003), 140–51

60. Prince, *The History*, 75.

61. An early Victoria historian of German Moravian history, J.E. Hutton, scathingly argues that "blood and wounds theology" severed the connection between rationality and spiritual contemplation. Meditating on Christ's bodily wounds instead encouraged Moravian believers to "lay all the stress on physical details": "As long as Zinzendorf used his own mental powers, he was able to make his 'Blood and Wounds Theology' a power for good; but as soon as he bade goodbye to his intellect he made his doctrine a laughing-stock and a scandal" (274). See J.E. Hutton, *A History of the Moravian Church* (London: Moravian Publication Office, 1909). For more on Moravian "blood and wounds" theology, see Atwood, *Community of the Cross*, 96–111; 195–237; and "Deep in the Side of Jesus: The Persistence of Zinzendorfian Piety in Colonial America," *Pious Pursuits: German Moravians in the Atlantic World*, eds. Michele Gillespie and Robert Beachy (New York: Berghahn Books, 2007), 50–64.

62. *A Collection of Hymns*, 336.

63. *A Collection of Hymns*, 336, emphasis original.

64. *A Collection of Hymns*, 336.

65. Anderson, *Imagining Methodism*, 119. On the Moravian "time of sifting," see also Atwood, *Community of the Cross*, 97–107; 141–48; 161–96; Aaron Fogelman, *Jesus is Female: Moravians and Radical Religion in Early America* (Philadelphia: University of Pennsylvania Press, 2007), 13; 73–93; 141–51; and Paul Peucker, *A Time of Sifting:*

Mystical Marriage and the Crisis of Moravian Piety in the Eighteenth Century (State College, PA: Pennsylvania State University Press, 2015), 64–74, 93–103.

66. Stephanie E. Smallwood, *Saltwater Slavery: A Middle Passage from Africa to the American Diaspora* (Cambridge: Harvard University Press, 2007), 8.

67. Natasha Lightfoot, *Troubling Freedom: Antigua and the Aftermath of British Emancipation* (Durham: Duke University Press, 2015), 60.

68. Sue Thomas, *Telling West Indians Lives: Life Narrative and the Reform of Plantation Slavery Cultures, 1804–1834* (New York: Palgrave Macmillan, 2015), 124.

69. Thomas, *Telling West Indian Lives*, 125.

70. Prince, *The History*, 83.

71. See Lightfoot, *Troubling Freedom*, chapter 3.

72. Prince, *The History*, 83, emphasis original.

73. Caribbean periodicals argued about whether evangelical missionary activity inflamed or quieted enslaved populations, as in the Jamaican *Royal Gazette*: "Adverting to the subject of Missionaries, he distinguished between the Methodist and Moravian missionaries. The former, he contended, did great mischief . . . The latter were eminent for their zeal and purity. A slave, who was known to be a Moravian convert, sold for a larger price on that account" (4; August 10, 1816). Moravian missionaries still came under suspicion for having a hand in unrest in Jamaica in 1832 (see the article series on "The Disturbance" in *The Watchman* between January 11–February 22, 1832). For enslaved unrest on Antigua, see David Barry Gaspar, *Bondmen and Rebels: A Study of Master-Slave Relations in Antigua* (Durham: Duke University Press, 1989), chapters 8–9; and Michael Craton, *Testing the Chains: Resistance to Slavery in the British West Indies* (Ithaca: Cornell University Press, 2009), 115–24.

74. Ifeoma Nwankwo, *Black Cosmopolitanism: Racial Consciousness and Transnational Identity in the Nineteenth-Century Americas* (Philadelphia: University of Pennsylvania Press, 2005), 176.

75. In 1828, when the Woods traveled to London with Prince, her position became legally precarious. The 1772 *Somerset v. Stewart* case found that slavery was unlawful in England, a ruling based on Chief Justice Mansfield's interpretation of William Blackstone: "this spirit of liberty is . . . rooted even in our very soil" (92). Peter Linebaugh observes that the case was rooted in an ecological argument: "The peculiar notion that ground confers freedom . . . was being introduced precisely at the moment when the ground—fenced, divided, hedged, enclosed—was less free than ever" (115). Prince could leave the Woods' household but risked re-enslavement if she returned to Antigua. On Mansfield, see William Blackstone, *Commentaries on the Laws of England*, Vol. 1 (Philadelphia, 1900); and Peter Linebaugh, *The Magna Carta Manifesto: Liberties and Commons for All* (Berkeley: University of California Press, 2009). For the Mansfield Decision and its many (mis)interpretations, see Cheryl Harris, "'Too Pure an Air': Somerset's Legacy from Anti-Slavery to Colorblindness," *Texas Wesleyan Law Review* 439, no. 2 (October 2007): 440–58.

76. Prince, *The History*, 86.

77. Prince, *The History*, 90.

78. Katharine Gerbner, *Christian Slavery: Conversion and Race in the Protestant Atlantic World* (Philadelphia: University of Pennsylvania Press, 2018), 9–10.

79. Thomas, *Telling West Indian Lives*, 123. See also Diana Paton, *No Bond but the Law: Punishment, Race, and Gender in Jamaican State Formation* (Durham: Duke University Press, 2004), 7.

80. Gershen Kaufman, *Shame: The Power of Caring* (Rochester: Schnekman Books, 1985), x.

81. Prince, *The History*, 82–83.

82. Prince, *The History*, 83.

83. Prince, *The History*, 82. Methodist gatherings may have been in Creole vernacular. See Thomas, *Telling West Indian Lives*, 124–25.

84. Prince, *The History*, 82–83.

85. Prince *The History*, 93.

86. Prince *The History*, 83.

87. *A Collection of Hymns* (Manchester, 1809), xxiv. Qtd. Thomas, *Telling West Indian Lives*, 126.

88. Prince, *The History*, 77–78.

89. Lindon Barrett, "African-American Slave Narratives: Literacy, the Body, Authority," in *Conditions of the Present: Selected Essays*, ed. Janet Neary (Durham: Duke University Press, 2018), 92–118; 112–13.

90. For white consumption of *The History*, see Sussman, *Consuming Anxieties*, 130–58; and Moira Ferguson, *Subject to Others: British Women Writers and Colonial Slavery, 1670–1834* (New York: Routledge, 1992), 282–98.

91. James Macqueen, "The Colonial Empire of Great Britain," *Blackwood's Magazine* 30 (November 1831): 744–64.

92. "Court Case Involving Mary Prince: *Pringle v. Cadell*" (February 21, 1833), Appendix 5 in Moira Ferguson's edition of *The History*, 136–39. See also Barbara Baumgartner, "The Body as Evidence: Resistance, Collaboration, and Appropriation in *The History of Mary Prince*," *Callaloo* 24, no. 1: (Winter 2001): 253–75; Janice Schroeder, "'Narrat[ing] Some Poor Little Fable': Evidence of Bodily Pain in 'The History of Mary Prince' and 'Wife-Torture in England'," *Tulsa Studies in Women's Literature* 23, no. 2 (Summer 2004): 261–81; Sue Thomas, "Pringle v. Cadell and Wood v. Pringle: The Libel Cases over the History of Mary Prince," *Journal of Commonwealth Literature* 40, no. 1 (Spring 2005): 113–35; and Nicole Aljoe, *Creole Testimonies: Slave Narratives from the British West Indies, 1709–1838* (New York: Palgrave Macmillan, 2012), 93–118.

93. "Court Case Involving Mary Prince: *Wood v. Pringle*" (March 1, 1833), Appendix 6 in Moira Ferguson's edition of *The History*, 140–49.

94. Prince, *The History*, 98.

95. Thomas Pringle, "Preface," in *The History*, 55–56; 55.

96. Aljoe, *Creole Testimonies*, 14. See also Baumgartner, "The Body as Evidence," 261.

97. For Black social life in *The History*, see Sharpe, *Ghosts of Slavery*, 138–51; Sandra Pouchet Paquet, "The Heartbeat of a West Indian Slave: *The History of Mary Prince*," *African American Review* 26, no. 1 (Spring 1992): 131–46; Thomas, *Telling West Indian Lives*, 119–66; and Elizabeth Bohls, *Slavery and the Politics of Place* (Cambridge: Cambridge University Press, 2014), 165–83. For a literary re-imagining of Black Caribbean sociality, see Gale Jackson's poem, "mary prince. bermuda. turks island.

antigua, 1787," *The Kenyan Review* 14, no. 1 (Winter 1992): 6–8. On engaging with questions of Black social life, I am also indebted to Kristina Huang's conference presentation at the American Society of Eighteenth-Century Studies on March 22, 2019: "The Unfinished Poetics of a Rival Geography and *The History of Mary Prince*," as well as her roundtable presentation with Kerry Sinanan at the British Association for Romanticism Studies (July 29, 2019) on "Seeing Through Whiteness: Mary Prince and the Challenge to Romanticism."

98. "Court Case Involving Mary Prince: *Wood v. Pringle*," 146; 147.

99. Early anti-Moravian "tell all" narratives, such as Andrew Frey's *A True and Authentic Account of Andrew Frey* (1753) and Henry Rimius's *A Candid Narrative of the Rise and Progress of the Herrnhuters* (1753), offered exposés of the Moravians' supposed sexual license, exemplified in love feasts and hymnody. Yet by the end of the century, Moravians were often noted for their sexual purity, with the *Antigua Weekly Register* facetiously noting: "With respect to the habits of the Moravian females, they may be described by negatives; they neither read novels (those effusions of disordered imagination), nor scribble poetry; they neither paint fire screens nor their faces; instead of Moore's amatory and inflammatory songs, they chaunt hymns" (4; September 9, 1828). See also Fogelman, *Jesus is Female*, 91–95.

100. "Court Case Involving Mary Prince: *Wood v. Pringle*," 147.

101. Prince, *The History*, 80–81.

102. Prince, *The History*, 81–82.

103. Prince, *The History*, 79; 81.

104. Prince, *The History*, 81.

105. Erysipelas, according to Mallipeddi in *Spectacular Suffering*, can "[cause] the skin to turn dark and culminates in death and insanity [and] is a deficiency disorder, occasioned by a diet heavily centered on corn (the slaves' staple food on Turk's Island)" (79).

106. Sue Thomas, "New Information on Mary Prince in London," *Notes and Queries* 58, no. 1 (March 2011): 82–85.

107. Lightfoot, *Troubling Freedom*, 161.

108. Lightfoot, *Troubling Freedom*, 161–62.

109. Prince, *The History*, 85.

110. Marisa J. Fuentes, *Dispossessed Lives: Enslaved Women, Violence, and the Archive* (Philadelphia: University of Pennsylvania Press, 2018), 75; 16.

111. Caroline Walker Bynum, for instance, explores the somatic feminizing of Christ in *Jesus as Mother: Studies in the Spirituality of the High Middle Ages* (Berkley: University of California Press, 1982), 120–23. Richard Rambuss, however, argues that Bynum's turn to feminization occludes other possibilities for reading queer representations of Christ's gender. See Richard Rambus, *Closet Devotions* (Durham: Duke University Press, 1998), chapter 2.

112. Elaine Scarry, *The Body in Pain* (Oxford: Oxford University Press, 1985), 250.

113. Atwood, *Community of the Cross*, 335–36.

114. Prince, *The History*, 72.

115. Carolyn Dinshaw, *Getting Medieval: Sexualities and Communities Pre- and Postmodern* (Durham: Duke University Press, 1999), 3.

116. On queer Jesus, see Graham Ward, "The Displaced Body of Jesus Christ," in *Radical Orthodoxy: A New Theology*, eds. John Milbank, Graham Ward, and Catherine Pickstock (New York: Routledge, 1999), 163–81; and Richard Rambuss, "Pleasure and Devotion: The Body of Jesus and Seventeenth-Century Religious Lyric," in *Queering the Renaissance*, ed. Jonathan Goldberg (Durham: Duke University Press, 1994), 253–79.

117. Derrick R. Miller, "Moravian Familiarities: Queer Community in the Moravian Church in Europe and North America in the Mid-Eighteenth Century," *Journal of Moravian History* 13, no. 1 (Spring 2013): 54–75; 57.

118. The *Litany* re-genders the Holy Spirit as the "mother of Christendom," the "Mother of all God's people," and the "mother of the Congregation" in the *Te Matrem*. See Atwood, *Community of the Cross*, 245–47.

119. In German, ". . . seine *Pleura* ist die *Matrix*, in der mein Geist gezeuget und getragen worden ist." See Nicholas von Zinzendorf, "Ein und zwanzig Discurse über die Augsburgische Confession, gehalten vom 15. Dec. 1747. bis zum 3. Mart. 1748" (1748). This hymn is reprinted in *Nikolaus Ludwig von Zinzendorf: Ergänzungsbände zu den Hauptschriften*, eds. Erich Beyruther and Gerhard Meyer (Hildesheim, 1966–1985, 14 volumes), 6: 101–6; and quoted by Fogelman, *Jesus is Female*, 77.

120. Atwood, *Community of the Cross*, 233–56; 238.

121. In *Telling West Indian Lives*, Thomas writes: "The 'devotional vocabulary' of the so-called 'sifting period' . . . was notably and controversially sensual . . . and its excesses were subsequently repressed within the church, although traces of it are found in later life narratives" (127). For discussions of the time of sifting, see also Katherine M. Faull, *Moravian Women's Memoirs: Related Lives, 1750–1820* (Syracuse: Syracuse University Press, 1997), *passim*; and Peucker, *A Time of Sifting*, 135–46.

122. Hortense Spillers, "Mama's Baby, Papa's Maybe: An American Grammar," in *Black, White, and in Color* (Chicago: University of Chicago Press, 2003), 203–29; 206.

123. To offer a historical example, Esteban Montejo, formerly enslaved, recalls queer partnerships cultivated on sugar plantations on Cuba: "Others had sex with each other and didn't want to have anything to do with women. Sodomy, that was their life . . . It never mattered to me, sincerely" (40–41). See Miguel Barnet (ed.), *Biography of a Runaway Slave*, trans. W. Nick Hill (Willimantic, CT, 1994). For queer Caribbean and Black kinships, see also Omise'eke Natasha Tinsley, "Black Atlantic, Queer Atlantic," *GLQ* vol. 14, no. 2-3 (June 2008): 191–215; 198. Siobhan Somerville, *Queering the Color Line: Race and the Invention of Homosexuality in American Culture* (Durham: Duke University Press, 2000), 81-84; Omise'eke Tinsley, *Thiefing Sugar: Eroticism between Caribbean Women* (Durham: Duke University Press, 2010); Keja Valens, *Desire Between Women in Caribbean Literature* (London: Palgrave Macmillan, 2013); and Zoran Pecic, *Queer Narratives of the Caribbean Diaspora: Exploring Tactics* (London: Palgrave Macmillan, 2013).

124. See Sylvia Wynter, "Unsettling the Coloniality of Being/Power/Truth/Freedom: Towards the Human, After Man, Its Overrepresentation—An Argument," *CR: The New Centennial Review* 3, no. 3 (Fall 2003): 257–337; 257.

125. Prince, *The History*, 68.

126. Prince, *The History*, 67.

127. Thomas, *Telling West Indian Lives*, 127.

128. Prince, *The History*, 67.

129. Speitz, "Blood Sugar and Salt Licks," 3, emphasis original.

130. Omise'eke Natasha Tinsley, "Black Atlantic, Queer Atlantic," *GLQ* 14, no. 2–3 (June 2008): 191–215; 198.

131. Bruce D. Hindmarsh argues in *The Evangelical Conversion Narrative: Spiritual Autobiography in Early Modern England* (Oxford: Oxford University Press, 2005) that providentialist tropes emerged out of Calvinist traditions, whereas early "Moravian narratives influenced by Zinzendorf were, by contrast, self-abasing and quietist, upholding an ideal of exquisite contemplation of the wounded Saviour" (324).

132. Sharpe, *In the Wake*, 106.

133. Louis P. Nelson, "The Jamaican Plantation: Industrial, Global, Contested," in *The Eighteenth Centuries*, eds. Cynthia Wall and David T. Gies (Charlottesville: University of Virginia Press, 2018), 120–43; 132–36.

134. Karen Barad, *Meeting the Universe Halfway: Quantum Physics and the Entanglement of Matter and Meaning* (Durham: Duke University Press, 2007), 33.

135. Monique Allewaert, *Ariel's Ecology: Plantations, Personhood, and Colonialism in the American Tropics* (Minneapolis: University of Minnesota Press, 2013), 87; see especially the discussion from 87–99.

136. For queer ecology and contingency, see Timothy Morton, *Ecology Without Nature: Rethinking Environmental Aesthetics* (Cambridge: Harvard University Press, 2007), 160–69.

137. Prince, *The History*, 68.

138. Prince, *The History*, 68–69.

139. Prince, *The History*, 69.

140. Prince, *The History*, 68.

141. Phillis Wheatley Peters, "On Being Brought from Africa to America," in *Poems on Various Subjects*, ed. Vincent Carretta (London: Penguin Books, 2001), 13; and Honorée Fanonne Jeffers, "An Issue of Mercy #1," in *The Age of Phillis* (Middletown: Wesleyan University Press, 2020), 3–4; 4.

142. Paul Gilroy, *The Black Atlantic: Modernity and Double Consciousness* (Cambridge, MA: Harvard University Press, 1993), 37–38.

143. Prince, *The History*, 76–77.

144. For West African spirituality, see Natalie Zacek, *Settler Society in the English Leeward Islands* (Cambridge: Cambridge University Press, 2010), chapter 3; and Babacar M'Baye, *The Trickster Comes West: Pan-African Influence in Early Black Diasporan Narratives* (Jackson, MS: University of Mississippi Press, 2011), 178–205.

145. Prince, *The History*, 77.

146. Prince, *The History*, 72.

147. Anna Lowenhaupt Tsing, *The Mushroom at the End of the World: On the Possibility of Life in Capitalist Ruins* (Princeton, NJ: Princeton University Press, 2017), 6; 131.

148. Elizabeth Povinelli, *Geontologies: A Requiem to Late Liberalism* (Durham: Duke University Press, 2016), 58.

149. Povinelli, *Geontologies*, 58.

150. Katherine McKittrick, *Demonic Grounds: Black Women and the Cartographies of Struggle* (Minneapolis: University of Minnesota, 2006), xii.

151. Walter Johnson, *River of Dark Dreams: Slavery and Empire in the Cotton Kingdom* (Cambridge, MA: Harvard University Press, 2013), 207–8.

152. Prince, *The History*, 94.

153. Camille Dungy, "Introduction: The Nature of African American Poetry," in *Black Nature*, ed. Camille Dungy (Athens: University of Georgia Press, 2009), xix–xxxv. Debapriya Sarkar, Jennifer Park, Hillary Eklund, and Ayanna Thompson's panel at the Shakespeare Association of American 2021 conference, "Shakespeare Futures Panel: Critical Futures of Modern Eco-Studies and Race Studies," argued that the turn to nonhuman agency is still fraught from the perspective of Black studies, given the constitutive violences of racial capitalism on Black bodies.

154. King, *The Black Shoals*, 3.

155. For Salone Cuthbert, see Aljoe, *Creole Testimonies*, 127–29, 144; and Thomas, *Telling West Indian Lives*, 129–32. For Archibald Monteath, see Angelo Constanzo, "The Narrative of Archibald Monteith, A Jamaican Slave," *Callaloo* 13, no. 1 (Spring 1990): 115–30; and Maureen Warner-Lewis, *Archibald Monteath: Igbo, Jamaican, Moravian* (Mona: University Press of the West Indies, 2007). For Afro-Moravians, see Katherine Faull Eze, "Self-Encounters: Two Eighteenth-Century African Memoirs from Bethlehem," in *Beyond Douglass: New Perspectives on Early African American Literature*, eds. Michael Drexler and Ed White (Lewisburg: Bucknell University Press, 2008), 21–53; and Jon Sensbach, *A Separate Canaan: The Making of an Afro-Moravian World in North Carolina, 1763–1840* (Chapel Hill: University of North Carolina Press, 1998), 109–15; and *Rebecca's Revival: Creating Black Christianity in the Atlantic World* (Cambridge: Harvard University Press, 2006), 43–64.

156. Sensbach, *Separate Canaan*, 111.

157. Hartman, "Venus in Two Acts," 12.

158. Prince, *The History*, 76.

159. Prince, *The History*, 76.

160. Prince, *The History*, 76; and Sharpe, *In the Wake*, 2–3.

161. Dionne Brand, *A Map to the Door of No Return* (New York: Vintage, 2002), 43. See also Cedric Robinson, *Black Marxism: The Making of the Black Radical Tradition* (Chapel Hill: University of North Carolina Press, 1983), 169.

162. Pascale-Anne Brault and Michael Naas, "Introduction," for Jacques Derrida, *The Work of Mourning*, trans. Pascale-Anne Brault (Chicago: University of Chicago Press, 2003), 1–30; 25, emphasis added.

163. Marcus Rediker, *The Slave Ship: A Human History* (London: Penguin Books, 2007), 5.

164. For more on the *Zong* and the court cases, see Baucom, *Specters of the Atlantic*, 32–33; 162–68.

165. Hartman, "Venus in Two Acts," 12.

166. M. NourbeSe Philip, *Zong!* (Fishers: Wesleyan University Press, 2011), 201.

167. Philip, *Zong!*, 201.

168. Sharpe, *In the Wake*, 37.

169. Zora Neale Hurston, *Tell My Horse: Voodoo and Life in Haiti and Jamaica* (New York: Amistad, 2008), 183–84.

170. Prince's witness echoes a mode of memory that Toni Morrison has described: "All water has a perfect memory and is forever trying to get back to where it was." See Toni Morrison, "The Site of Memory," in *Inventing the Truth: The Art and Craft of Memoir*, ed. William Zinsser (New York: Houghton Mifflin Company, 1995), 83–102; 99.

171. Derek Walcott, "The Sea is History," in *Selected Poems*, ed. Edward Baugh (New York: Farrar, Straus, and Giroux, 2007), 137–39; line 27.

172. Giorgio Agamben, *Remnants of Auschwitz: The Witness and the Archive*, trans. Daniel Heller-Roazen (New York: Zone Books, 1999), 17–18, 34–35; and Primo Levi, *The Drowned and the Saved*, trans. Raymond Rosenthal (New York: Simon and Schuster, 2017), 70–71.

173. Prince, *The History*, 76.

174. Prince, *The History*, 76.

175. Saidiya Hartman, *Lose Your Mother: A Journey Along the Atlantic Slave Route* (New York: Farrer, Straus and Giroux, 2007), 6; and Sharpe, *In the Wake*, 15.

176. Prince, *The History*, 76.

177. Jacques Derrida, "This Is Not an Oral Footnote," in *Annotation and Its Texts*, ed. Stephen A. Barney (Oxford: Oxford University Press, 1991), 192–206; 193.

178. Simon Gikandi, *Slavery and the Culture of Taste* (Princeton: Princeton University Press, 2011), 39.

179. Banner, "Surface and Stasis," 302.

Chapter Three

1. Drew Lopenzina, *Through an Indian's Looking-Glass: A Cultural Biography of William Apess* (Amherst: University of Massachusetts Press, 2018), 102–9.

2. Lopenzina, *Looking-Glass*, 84.

3. See Barry O'Connell's *On Our Own Ground: The Complete Writings of William Apess, a Pequot* (Amherst: University of Massachusetts Press, 1992) for the 1831 *A Son of the Forest* (1–97) and the 1829 variants (311–24). See pages 33 and 318–19.

4. Lopenzina, *Looking-Glass*, 115–34.

5. Lopenzina, *Looking-Glass*, 132.

6. For Haudenosaunee diplomacy, see Lisa Brooks, *The Common Pot: The Recovery of Native Space in the Northeast* (Minneapolis: University of Minnesota Press, 2008), 157–58; and Angela Calcaterra, *Literary Indians: Aesthetics and Encounter in American Literature to 1920* (Chapel Hill: University of North Carolina Press, 2018), 52–59.

7. Arthur C. Parker, *The Constitution of the Five Nations*, in *Parker on the Iroquois*, ed. William N. Fenton (Syracuse: Syracuse University Press, 1968), 112. See also Lopenzina, *Looking-Glass*, 119.

8. Parker, *Constitution*, 110.

9. Parker, *Constitution*, 103.

10. Brooks, *The Common Pot*, 3–8.

11. Indian Papers 2: 230, Connecticut State Library, Hartford, Connecticut. Qtd. Brooks, *The Common Pot*, 52. In *Constitution*, Parker also writes that Haudenosaunee practices acknowledged: "We shall only have one dish (or bowl) . . . and we should

all have coequal right to it. . . . This one dish or bowl signifies that they will make their hunting grounds one common tract and all have a coequal right to hunt within it" (103).

12. Elizabeth Maddock Dillon, *New World Drama: The Performative Commons in the Atlantic World* (Durham: Duke University Press, 2014), 3–5.

13. O'Connell, "Textual Afterword," 318–19.

14. As Peter Linebaugh argues in *The Magna Carta Manifesto: Liberties and Commons for All* (Berkeley: University of California Press, 2009): "The expansion of the British empire was by means of wood products and it was to the end of acquiring wood products" (90).

15. Roger Williams, *A Key into the Language of America* (Bedford: Applewood Books, 1936), 135.

16. Linda Tuhiwai Smith, *Decolonizing Methodologies*, 2nd ed. (London: Zed Books, 2012), 12–13.

17. Mark Rifkin, *Speaking for the People: Native Writing and the Question of Political Form* (Durham: Duke University Press, 2021), 86.

18. On decolonial ecocriticism, see Kim Tallbear, "Why Interspecies Thinking Needs Indigenous Studies," *Fieldsights* (November 18, 2011). I am also guided by the collection *Ecocriticism and Indigenous Studies*, eds. Salma Monani and Joni Adamson (New York: Routledge, 2020), which maps local Native knowledges in global networks.

19. See Michel Foucault, *The Order of Things: An Archeology of the Human Sciences* (New York: Vintage, 1994), xx–xxiii. Denise Ferreira da Silva argues that this onto-epistemic regime is anchored in racial difference, while the West's "rational" institutions (law, capitalism, liberalism) reifies Black obliteration—a structure she calls globality. See Denise Ferreira da Silva, *Toward a Global Idea of Race* (Minneapolis: University of Minnesota Press, 2007, xi–xiv, 177–79.

20. On edge ecologies, see William Cronon, *Changes in the Land: Indians, Colonists, and the Ecology of New England* (New York: Hill and Wang, 2003), 51; Brooks, *The Common Pot*, 168; and Strother E. Roberts, *Colonial Ecology, Atlantic Economy: Transforming Nature in Early New England* (Philadelphia: University of Pennsylvania Press, 2018), 101–2. See also E. Pauline Johnson's poem, "Fire Flowers," in *Tekahionwake: Collected Poems and Selected Prose*, eds. Carole Gerson and Veronica Strong-Boag (Toronto: University of Toronto Press, 2002), 100.

21. Cronon, *Changes in the Land*, 56–57. See also Andrew Lipman, *The Saltwater Frontier: Indians and the Contest for the American Coast* (New Haven: Yale University Press, 2015), 32–35.

22. Drew Lopenzina, *Red Ink: Native Americans Picking up the Pen in the Colonial Period* (Albany: State University of New York Press, 2012), 5. In James Fenimore Cooper's *The Last of the Mohicans* (London: Penguin Books, 1986), for instance, one footnote describes a forest cleared of underbrush, without recognizing Native labor: "The American forests admit the passage of horse, there being little underbrush, and few tangled brakes" (331).

23. Roger Williams, *The Complete Writings of Roger Williams* (New York: Russell & Russell, 1963), 46–47. On Williams and edge ecologies, see Cronon, *Changes in the Land*, 57–58; and Allan Greer, *Property and Dispossession: Natives, Empires, and Land in Early Modern North America* (Cambridge: Cambridge University Press, 2018), 85.

24. For Apess and Indigenous historiography, see Cheryl Walker, *Indian Nation: Native American Literature and Nineteenth-Century Nationalisms* (Durham: Duke University Press, 1997), 41–59, 164–81; Andy Doolen, *Fugitive Empire: Locating Early American Imperialisms* (Minneapolis: University of Minnesota Press, 2005), 147–74; Arnold Krupat, *All That Remains: Varieties of Indigenous Expression* (Lincoln: University of Nebraska Press, 2009), 74–99; Maureen Konkle, *Writing Indian Nations: Native Intellectuals and the Problem of Historiography, 1827–1863* (Chapel Hill: University of North Carolina Press, 2004), 114–68; Jean M. O'Brien, *Firsting and Lasting: Writing Indians Out of Existence in New England* (Minneapolis: University of Minnesota Press, 2010), 178–91; Brooks, *The Common Pot*, 198–208; and Mark Rifkin, *Settler Common Sense: Queerness and Everyday Colonialism in the American Renaissance* (Minneapolis: University of Minnesota Press, 2014), 14–17, 127–30.

25. Robert Nichols, *Theft is Property!* (Durham: Duke University Press, 2020), 6.

26. Nichols, *Theft is Property!*, 103–6. For Apess's relations to Methodism and Christianity, see Bernd Peyer, *The Tutor'd Mind: Indian Missionary Writing in Antebellum America* (Amherst: University of Massachusetts Press, 1997), 117–65; Robert Warrior, "William Apess: A Pequot and a Methodist Under the Sign of Modernity," in *Liberation Theologies, Postmodernity, and the Americas*, eds. David Batstone, Eduardo Mendieta, Lois Ann Lorentzen, and Dwight N. Hopkins (New York: Routledge, 1997), 188–202; Laura Donaldson, "Making a Joyful Noise: William Apess and the Search for Postcolonial Method(ism)," in *Messy Beginnings: Postcoloniality and Early American Studies*, eds. Malini Johar Schueller and Edward Watts (New Brunswick: New Jersey University Press, 2003), 29–44; Eileen Razzari Elrod, *Piety and Dissent: Race, Gender, and Biblical Rhetoric in Early American Autobiography* (Amherst: University of Massachusetts Press, 2008), 146–70; and Mark J. Miller, "'Mouth for God': Temperate Labor, Race, and Methodist Reform in William Apess's *A Son of the Forest*," *Journal of the Early Republic* 30, no. 2 (Summer 2010): 225–51; and Mark Miller, *Cast Down: Abjection in Early America, 1700–1850* (Philadelphia: University of Pennsylvania Press, 2016), 55–83.

27. Robyn Maynard and Leanne Betasamosake Simpson, *Rehearsals for Living* (Chicago: Haymarket Books, 2022), 216. I am grateful to Kerry Sinanan for bringing me to this point and for her generous engagement with this chapter.

28. Audra Simpson, *Mohawk Interruptus: Political Life across the Borders of the Settler States* (Durham: Duke University Press, 2014), 2, emphasis original.

29. On tracing early modern climate change, see Mark A. Maslin and Simon L. Lewis, "A Transparent Framework for Defining the Anthropocene Epoch," *The Anthropocene Review* 2, no. 2 (Summer 2015): 128–46; Richard J. Nevle and Dennis K. Bird, "Effects of Syn-Pandemic Fire Reduction and Reforestation in the Tropical Americas on Atmospheric CO^2, During European Conquest," *Palaeogeography, Palaeoclimatology, Paleoecology* 264, no. 1–2 (Spring/Summer 2008): 25–38.

30. Paul J. Crutzen and Eugene F. Stoermer first elaborated the term "Anthropocene" to define our current geologic epoch in "The 'Anthropocene'," *Global Change Newsletter* 41 (May 2000): 17–18. However, Crutzen came to recognize the limitations of Anthropocene as a term because it suggests an undifferentiated and abstract "humanity" as the source for climate change—see "Geology of Mankind," *Nature* 415

(January 2002): 23. Françoise Vergés does similar work from the standpoint of Black studies in "Racial Capitalocene," in *Futures of Black Radicalism*, eds. Gaye Theresa Johnson and Alex Lubin (New York: Verso, 2017), 72–82. See also Steve Mentz, *Break Up the Anthropocene* (Minneapolis: University of Minnesota Press, 2019), 2–5; and Stacy Alaimo, *Exposed: Environmental Politics and Pleasures in Posthuman Times* (Minneapolis: University of Minnesota Press, 2016), 1–3.

31. Kathryn Yusoff, *A Billion Black Anthropocenes or None* (Minneapolis, 2018), 32.

32. Greer reminds us of the stakes of treating land hunger and Indigenous decline as a simple historical arc: "Across the Americas, colonial regimes came to dominate peoples and spaces through a complex set of practices and relationships, some of them violent and lethal, others not directly so. To treat all this as if it were a simple matter of transferring an object—land—from one group to another is to slip into reification" (192). Geoffrey Parker's *Global Crisis: War, Catastrophe, and Climate Change in the Seventeenth Century* (New Haven: Yale University Press, 2013) offers a particularly egregious example of a sole focus on Indigenous population decline, 445–56.

33. Dian Million, "'We are the land, and the land is us': Indigenous Land, Lives, and Embodied Ecologies in the Twenty-First Century," in *Racial Ecologies*, eds. Leilani Nishime and Kim D. Hester Williams (Seattle: University of Washington Press, 2018), 19–33; 21.

34. Patrick Wolfe claims that "invasion is a structure, not an event" in *Settler Colonialism and the Transformation of Anthropology: The Politics and Poetics of an Ethnographic Event* (New York: Continuum, 1999), 2.

35. For Apess and Indigenous historiography, see Cheryl Walker, *Indian Nation: Native American Literature and Nineteenth-Century Nationalisms* (Durham: Duke University Press, 1997), 41–59, 164–81; Andy Doolen, *Fugitive Empire: Locating Early American Imperialisms* (Minneapolis: University of Minnesota Press, 2005), 147–74; Arnold Krupat, *All That Remains: Varieties of Indigenous Expression* (Lincoln: University of Nebraska Press, 2009), 74–99; Maureen Konkle, *Writing Indian Nations: Native Intellectuals and the Problem of Historiography, 1827–1863* (Chapel Hill: University of North Carolina Press, 2004), 114–68; Jean M. O'Brien, *Firsting and Lasting: Writing Indians Out of Existence in New England* (Minneapolis: University of Minnesota Press, 2010), 178–91; Brooks, *The Common Pot*, 198–208; and Mark Rifkin, *Settler Common Sense: Queerness and Everyday Colonialism in the American Renaissance* (Minneapolis: University of Minnesota Press, 2014), 14–17, 127–30.

36. On tribal-national criticism, see Simon Ortiz, "Towards a National Indian Literature: Cultural Authenticity in Nationalism," *MELUS* 8, no. 2 (Summer 1981): 7–12; Jace Weaver, Craig Womack, and Robert Warrior, *American Indian Literary Nationalism* (Albuquerque: University of New Mexico Press, 2006); Daniel Heath Justice, *Our Fire Survives the Storm: A Cherokee Literary History* (Minneapolis: University of Minnesota Press, 2006); and Craig Womack, *Red on Red: Native American Literary Separatism* (Minneapolis: University of Minnesota Press, 1999).

37. Different scholars have elaborated alternatives to Anthropocene, including Capitalocene, Chthulucene, White Supremacy Scene, and Plantationocene. For Capitalocene, see Jason W. Moore, *Capitalism in the Web of Life: Ecology and the Accumulation of Capital* (New York: Verso, 2015). For Chthulucene, see Donna Haraway, *Staying*

with the Trouble: Making Kin in the Chthulucene (Durham: Duke University Press, 2016). For White Supremacy Scene, see Nicholas Mirzoeff, "It's Not the Anthropocene, It's the White Supremacy Scene; or, The Geological Color Line," in *After Extinction*, ed. Richard Grusin (Minneapolis: University of Minnesota Press, 2016), 123–50. And for Plantationocene, see Sophie Sapp Moore, Monique Allewaert, Gregg Mitman, and Pablo F. Gómez, "Plantation Legacies," *Edge Effect* (January 22, 2019) at https://edgeeffects.net/plantation-legacies-plantationocene/.

38. Katherine Grandjean, "New World Tempests: Environment, Scarcity, and the Coming of the Pequot War," *The William and Mary Quarterly* 68, no. 1 (January 2018): 75–100; 80n.11.

39. Grandjean, "New World Tempests," 81–82.

40. Grandjean, "New World Tempests," 80.

41. Grandjean, "New World Tempests," 83. For hunger, see also Carla Cevasco, "Hunger Knowledges and Cultures in New England's Borderlands, 1675–1770," *Early American Studies* 16, no. 2 (Spring 2019): 255–81; Heidi Oberholtzer Lee, "'The Hungry Soul': Sacramental Appetite and the Transformation of Taste in Early American Travel Writing," *Early American Studies* 3, no. 1 (Spring 2005): 65–93; and Rachel Herrmann, *No Useless Mouth: Waging War and Fighting Hunger in the American Revolution* (Ithaca: Cornell University Press, 2019).

42. Grandjean, "New World Tempests," 75.

43. William Bradford, *History of Plymouth Plantation, 1604–1646*, ed. William Thomas Davis (New York: C. Scribner's Sons, 1920), 323. See also Grandjean, "New World Tempests," 80; and Lipman, *Saltwater Frontier*, 39.

44. *The Winthrop Papers, 1498–1645*, ed. Allyn B. Forbes et al. (Boston: Massachusetts Historical Society, 1929–92), 6 volumes; 3: 167. On providentialist rhetoric, see also Greer, *Property and Dispossession*, 197–98.

45. Rob Nixon, *Slow Violence and the Environmentalism of the Poor* (Cambridge: Harvard University Press, 2013), 3.

46. Kyle Powys Whyte, "Indigenous Science (Fiction) for the Anthropocene: Ancestral Dystopias and Fantasies of Climate Change Crisis," *Environment and Planning E: Nature and Space* 1, no. 1–2 (Spring/Summer 2018): 224–42; 225.

47. Cronon's *Changes in the Land* relies primarily on colonial perspectives, and the question of Indigenous archives does not come up in an otherwise detailed discussion of the kinds of evidence he coordinated in his research (5–9). Susan Sleeper-Smith's *Indigenous Prosperity and American: Indian Women of the Ohio River Valley, 1690–1792 Conquest* (Chapel Hill: University of North Carolina Press, 2018), however, exemplifies new efforts to foreground Native textualities in environmental studies. She centers Native women as major facilitators of agricultural bounty in the Ohio River valley and turns to Native women's crafts, as well as environmental data, as alternative archives.

48. David J. Carlson, *Sovereign Selves: Native American Autobiography and the Law* (Chicago: University of Chicago Press, 2005), 72–73.

49. Cronon, *Changes in the Land*, 122–26, 147–49.

50. Cronon, *Changes in the Land*, 136–37; and Lipman, *Saltwater Frontier*, 147–48.

51. Virginia DeJohn Anderson, *Creatures of Empire: How Domestic Animals Transformed Early America* (Oxford: Oxford University Press, 2004), 171.

52. Greer, *Property and Dispossession*, 263, 268–69.

53. English land hunger was one cause of the conflict, as Francis Jennings argues in *The Invasion of America: Indians, Colonists, and the Cant of Conquest* (Chapel Hill: University of North Carolina Press, 1975), 178–79. Neal Salisbury in *Manitou and Providence: Indians, Europeans, and the Making of New England* (Oxford: Oxford University Press, 1982) also cites English "hunger for land," although he identifies Puritan theology as an impetus, namely their view of Indigenous peoples "as instruments of Satan's purposes" (225). Alfred Cave in *The Pequot War* (Amherst: University of Massachusetts Press, 1996) concurs, arguing that "English greed" and the "desire to annex land and seize fur, slaves, and wampum" were compounded by Puritans' "suspicion that the history of God's people in the wilderness would be marked by recurrent conflicts with the Devil's minions" (9–11 and 121). For Puritan views on the Pequot War, see also Susan Juster, *Sacred Violence in Early America* (Philadelphia: University of Pennsylvania Press, 2016), 53–54. For food scarcity and the war, see Grandjean, "New World Tempests," 80–84; Lipman, *Saltwater Frontier*, 127–42; and Roberts, *Colonial Ecology, Atlantic Economy*, 63–64.

54. For the Pequot War, see Cave, *The Pequot War*, passim; Alden T. Vaughan, "Pequots and Puritans: The Causes of the War of 1637," *William and Mary Quarterly* 21, no. 2 (April 1964): 256–69; Alden T. Vaughan, *New England Frontier: Puritans and Indians, 1620–1675* (Norman: University of Oklahoma Press, 1995), 93–154; Jennings, *The Invasion of America*, 177–227; Salisbury, *Manitou and Providence*, 203–24; and Laurence M. Hauptman, "The Pequot War and its Legacies," in *The Pequots in Southern New England*, eds. Laurence M. Hauptman and James D. Wherry (Norman: University of Oklahoma Press, 1990), 69–80. For semiotic controversies regarding the war and body parts, see Andrew Lipman, "'A Meanes to Knitt Them Together': The Exchange of Body Parts in the Pequot War," *The William and Mary Quarterly* 65, no. 1 (January 2008): 3–28.

55. *The Winthrop Papers*, 6: 63. See also Lipman, *Saltwater Frontier*, 217.

56. John Mason, *A Brief History of the Pequot War* (Boston: Thomas Prince, 1736), 14. See also Juster, *Sacred Violence*, 53–54.

57. For the Treaty of Hartford, see Vaughn, *New England Frontier*, 340–41, and Cave, *The Pequot War*, 161–63.

58. Apess added the "s" to the family's last name to make "Apess." See O'Connell, "Introduction," xxvii–xxviii.

59. Lopenzina, *Looking Glass*, 46–47.

60. Lopenzina, *Looking-Glass*, 50.

61. Lopenzina, *Looking-Glass*, 51–55.

62. For Apess's early life, see O'Connell, "Introduction," xxvii–xxxiii; Konkle, *Writing Indian Nations*, 106–11; and Lopenzina, *Looking Glass*, 45–76.

63. Apess, *A Son of the Forest*, 6. See also Lopenzina, *Looking-Glass*, 14–16.

64. Apess, *A Son of the Forest*, 7.

65. Miller, *Cast Down*, 55–58.

66. Lopenzina, *Looking-Glass*, 69. Hillhouse and his brother likely presided over and prosecuted Moses Paul's trial.

67. Rifkin, *Speaking for the People*, 89–90.

68. Lopenzina, *Looking-Glass*, 20.

69. Apess, *A Son of the Forest*, 12.

70. Apess, *A Son of the Forest*, 14.

71. Apess, *A Son of the Forest*, 15, emphasis original; and Joshua Bennett, *Being Property Once Myself: Blackness and the End of Man* (Cambridge: Harvard University Press, 2020), 141, emphasis original.

72. Apess, *A Son of the Forest*, 10.

73. Apess, *A Son of the Forest*, 10–11.

74. For the "tale of blood" scene, see O'Connell, "Introduction," xlix–l; Peyer, *Tutor'd Mind*, 130–31; Konkle, *Writing Indian Nations*, 110–14; Doolen, *Fugitive Empire*, 152–53; and Lopenzina, *Looking-Glass*, 64–66.

75. Frantz Fanon, *Black Skin, White Masks*, trans. Charles Lam Markmann (New York: Grove Press, 1967), 112–13. As Fanon puts it, "My body was given back to me sprawled out, distorted, recolored, clad in mourning" (112). See also Glen Sean Coulthard's discussion of Fanon and double alienation in *Red Skin, White Masks: Rejecting the Colonial Politics of Recognition* (Minneapolis: University of Minnesota Press, 2014), 23–34.

76. Brooks, *The Common Pot*, 20.

77. Jennifer Fay, *Inhospitable World: Cinema in the Time of the Anthropocene* (Oxford: Oxford University Press, 2018), 2.

78. On the Carlisle Indian School and coerced assimilation, see Hayes Peter Mauro, *The Art of Americanization at the Carlisle Indian School* (Albuquerque: University of New Mexico Press, 2011).

79. Anna Lowenhaupt Tsing, "Feral Biologies," presented at the "Anthropological Visions of Sustainable Futures" Conference, University College London, February 12–14, 2015, and quoted by Donna Haraway in *Staying with the Trouble*, 100–101. See also the digital project, *Feral Atlas: The More-than-Human Anthropocene*, eds. Anna Lowenhaupt Tsing, Jennifer Deger, Alder Saxena Keleman, and Feifei Zhou, and hosted by Stanford University at www.feralatlas.org.

80. Apess, *A Son of the Forest*, 32–33.

81. Lopenzina, *Looking Glass*, 129.

82. Brooks, *The Common Pot*, 174–76.

83. Brooks, *The Common Pot*, 175.

84. Apess, *A Son of the Forest*, 40.

85. O'Connell, "Introduction," lxi. See also Lopenzina, *Looking-Glass*, 147–48.

86. Haraway, *Staying with the Trouble*, 2; 1.

87. See Cheryl Harris, "Whiteness as Property," *Harvard Law Review* 106, no. 8 (June 1993): 1707–91.

88. Apess, *A Son of the Forest*, 31; emphasis added.

89. Apess, *A Son of the Forest*, 25.

90. Apess, *A Son of the Forest*, 46. See also Rifkin, *Speaking for the People*, 93–5.

91. Jack Campisi, "The Emergence of the Mashantucket Pequot Tribe, 1637–1975," in *The Pequots in Southern New England*, eds. Laurence M. Hauptman and James D. Wherry (Norman: University of Oklahoma Press, 1990), 117–40; 127.

92. Fanon, *Black Skin, White Masks*, 112.

93. On Indigenous studies and the politics of recognition, see Coulthard, *Red Skin, White Masks*, 1–3, 42–43; and Audra Simpson, *Mohawk Interruptus*, 34–38, 134–52.

94. Fanon, *Black Skin, White Masks*, 257–58.

95. Apess, *Indian's Looking-Glass*, 157.

96. See Francis Paul Prucha, *The Great Father: The United States Government and the American Indians* (Lincoln: University of Nebraska Press, 1984), for Jacksonian policies and paternalism.

97. For American cotton empires, see Sven Beckert, *Empire of Cotton: A Global History* (London: Vintage, 2014); Walter Johnson, *River of Dark Dreams: Slavery and Empire in the Cotton Kingdom* (Cambridge: Harvard University Press, 2013); Edward E. Baptist, *The Half that Has Never Been Told: Slavery and the Making of American Capitalism* (New York: Basic Books, 2016); and Sven Beckert and Seth Rockman, eds., *Slavery's Capitalism: A New History of American Economic Development* (Philadelphia: University of Pennsylvania Press, 2018).

98. Apess, *Indian's Looking-Glass*, 160; and John Kucich, "William Apess's Nullifications: Sovereignty, Identity, and the Mashpee Revolt," in *Sovereignty, Separatism, and Survivance: Ideological Encounters in the Literature of Native North America*, ed. Benjamin D. Carson (Newcastle: Cambridge Scholars, 2009), 1–16; 11.

99. Apess, *Indian's Looking-Glass*, 157. Ronald N. Satz in *American Indian Policy in the Jacksonian Era* (Norman: University of Oklahoma Press, 2002) notes that the status of Black and Native witnesses was so fraught during the age of Indian Removal because debates over displacement quickly became entangled with questions of the expansion of slavery west (10–30, 218–30).

100. Andrea Hairston, *Redwood and Wildfire* (Seattle: Aqueduct Press, 2011), 87.

101. Apess, *Indian's Looking-Glass*, 157.

102. For readings of scars as evidence, see William Andrews, *To Tell a Free Story: The First Century of Afro-American Autobiography* (Champaign: University of Illinois Press 1986), 77–87; Dwight McBride, *Impossible Witnesses: Truth, Abolitionism, and Slave Testimony* (New York: New York University Press, 2002), 88–99; Carol E. Henderson, *Scarring the Black Body: Race and Representation in African American Literature* (Columbia: University of Missouri Press, 2002), 1–10, 23–34; and Jennifer Putzi, *Identifying Marks: Race, Gender, and the Marked Body in Nineteenth-Century America* (Athens: University of Georgia Press, 2006), 99–120, 130–53.

103. Apess, *A Son of the Forest*, 68, emphasis original.

104. Lindon Barrett, "African-American Slave Narratives: Literacy, the Body, Authority," *Conditions of the Present: Selected Essays*, ed. Janet Neary (Durham: Duke University Press, 2018), 92–118; 111–12.

105. Avery Gordon, *Ghostly Matters: Haunting and the Sociological Imagination* (Minneapolis: University of Minnesota Press, 2008), xii. For criticism on Native peoples and hauntings, see Renée L. Bergland, *The National Uncanny: Indian Ghosts and American Subjects* (Hanover: University of New Hampshire Press, 2000); Ann Laura Stoler, ed., *Haunted by Empire: Geographies of Intimacy in North American History* (Durham: Duke University Press, 2006); and Colleen E. Boyd and Coll Thrush, eds., *Phantom Past, Indigenous Presence: Native Ghosts in North American Culture and History* (Lincoln: University of Nebraska Press, 2011).

106. See Tiffany Lethabo King's discussion of formations of Indigenous and Black flesh in *The Black Shoals: Offshore Formations in Black and Native Studies* (Durham: Duke University Press, 2019), chapter 3.

107. Apess, *Indian's Looking-Glass*, 158. Apess's *The Indians: The Ten Lost Tribes* (1831) deploys narratives claiming that Native peoples descended from the ten Hebrew tribes carried into Assyrian captivity, reflected in texts like Elias Boudinot's *A Star in the West* (1816). On this theory of Indigenous descent, see also Sandra Gustafson, "Nations of Israelites: Prophecy and Cultural Autonomy in the Writings of William Apess," *Religion and Literature* 26, no. 1 (Spring 1994): 31–53; Stuart Kirsch, "Lost Tribes: Indigenous People and the Social Imaginary," *Anthropological Quarterly* 70, no. 2 (Summer 1997): 58–67; Meghan C. L. Howey, "The Question Which Has Puzzled, and Still Puzzles': How American Indian Authors Challenged Dominant Discourse about Native American Origins in the Nineteenth Century," *American Indian Quarterly* 34, no. 4 (Winter 2010): 453–74; William H. Stiebing, *Uncovering the Past: A History of Archeology* (Oxford: Oxford University Press, 1994), 174–76; Colin Kidd, *The Forging of Races: Race and Scripture in the Protestant Atlantic World, 1600–2000* (Cambridge: Cambridge University Press, 2006) 205–210; and Kristina Bross, *Dry Bones and Indian Sermons: Praying Indians in Colonial America* (Ithaca: Cornell University Press, 2004), 12–13, 28–39.

108. Apess, *Indian's Looking-Glass*, 158. See also Edward J. Blum and Paul Harvey, *The Color of Christ: The Son of God and the Saga of Race in America* (Chapel Hill: University of North Carolina Press, 2012), 105–6.

109. Phillis Wheatley Peters reverses this theology in her poem "On Being Brought from Africa to America" (1772): "Some view our sable race with a scornful eye,/'Their colour is a diabolic die.'/Remember, *Christians, Negros*, black as *Cain*,/May be refin'd and join the angelic train." See Phillis Wheatley Peters, "On Being Brought from Africa to America," *Poems on Various Subjects*, ed. Vincent Carretta (London: Penguin Books, 2001), 13.

110. Hannah Arendt, *Love and Saint Augustine*, eds. Joanna Vecchiarelli Scott and Judith Chelius Stark (Chicago: University of Chicago Press, 1998), 301. On Arendt, Augustine, and witnessing, see also Kelly Oliver, *Witnessing: Beyond Recognition* (Minneapolis: University of Minnesota Press, 2001), chapter 1.

111. Apess, *Indian's Looking-Glass*, 157.

112. Rifkin, *Settler Common Sense*, 122–39.

113. Samson Occom, *Sermon on the Execution of Moses Paul* (1772), *The Collected Writings of Samson Occom, Mohegan*, ed. Joanna Brooks (Oxford: Oxford University Press, 2006), 176–96; 192.

114. See Beth Piatote, *Domestic Subjects: Gender, Citizenship, and Law in Native American Literature* (New Haven: Yale University Press, 2013), 1–9.

115. Apess, *Indian's Looking-Glass*, 159.

116. Aileen Moreton-Robinson, *The White Possessive: Property, Power, and Indigenous Sovereignty* (Minneapolis: University of Minnesota Press, 2015), 81.

117. Apess, *Indian's Looking-Glass*, 157; Fanon, *Black Skin, White Masks*, 41–42.

118. Richard Iton, *In Search of the Black Fantastic: Politics and Popular Culture in the Post-Civil Rights Era* (Oxford: Oxford University Press, 2008), 8.

119. Apess, *Indian's Looking-Glass*, 160. In *Economies of Abandonment: Social Belonging and Endurance in Late Liberalism* (Durham: Duke University Press, 2011), Elizabeth Povinelli argues: "What we witness in all these alternative social projects . . . is an entwinement of endurance and exhaustion" (125).

120. Andreas Hejnol argues that when tree metaphors came to prominence in nineteenth-century biological sciences they served a regressive, racist "tree thinking": "In their shape, biological trees retained the sense of movement through time from a simple world to a more complex one—from a single trunk toward countless branches" (90). See "Ladders, Trees, Complexity, and Other Metaphors," in *Arts of Living on a Damaged Planet*, eds. Anna Tsing, Heather Anne Swanson, Elaine Gan, and Nils Bubandt (Minneapolis: University of Minnesota, 2017), 87–102.

121. Lopenzina, *Looking-Glass*, 241–42.

122. Deborah Miranda, "Extermination of the *Joyas*: Gendercide in Spanish California," Special Issue: "Sexuality, Nationality, Indigeneity," eds. Mark Rifkin, Daniel Heath Justice, and Bethany Schneider, *GLQ* 16, no. 1–2 (April 2010): 253–84; 256.

123. Keith Basso, *Wisdom Sits in Places: Landscape and Language among the Western Apache* (Albuquerque: University of New Mexico Press, 1996), 6, emphasis original.

124. On settler enclosures and Indigenous commons, see Thomas Flanagan, "The Agricultural Argument and Original Appropriation: Indian Lands and Political Philosophy," *Canadian Journal of Political Science* 22, no. 3 (September 1989): 589–602; Patricia Seed, *American Pentimento: The Invention of Indians and the Pursuit of Riches* (Minneapolis: University of Minnesota Press, 2001), 32–34; Nancy Shoemaker, *A Strange Likeness: Becoming Red and White in Eighteenth-Century North America* (Oxford: Oxford University Press, 2004), 20–22; and Stuart Banner, *How the Indians Lost Their Land* (Cambridge: Harvard University Press, 2005), 37–39.

125. Dana D. Nelson, *Commons Democracy: Reading the Politics of Participation in the Early United States* (New York: Fordham University Press, 2016), 7.

126. Greer, *Property and Dispossession*, 242. For his full discussion, see 241–54.

127. In the nineteenth century, Mashpee was often spelled "Marshpee," which is Apess's general practice.

128. On *Indian Nullification*'s plural audiences, see Theresa Strouth Gaul, "Dialogue and Public Discourse in William Apess's *Indian Nullification*," *American Transcendental Quarterly* 15, no. 4 (December 2001): 275–92.

129. Hannah Manshel, "William Apess and the Nullification of Settler Law," *Early American Literature* 55, no. 3 (Fall 2020): 753–79; 755. See also Adam Dahl, "Nullifying Settler Democracy: William Apess and the Paradox of Settler Sovereignty," *Polity* 48, no. 2 (Summer 2016): 279–304; and Neil Meyer, "'To Preserve this Remnant': William Apess, the Mashpee Indians, and the Politics of Nullification," *European Journal of American Studies* 13, no. 2 (Summer 2018): 1–16. I am deeply grateful to Hannah for her generous comments on this chapter.

130. Lopenzina, *Looking-Glass*, 194–95.

131. Apess, *Indian Nullification*, 169–73.

132. Apess, *Indian Nullification*, 170.

133. Apess, *Indian Nullification*, 171.

134. Kevin Bruyneel, *The Third Space of Sovereignty: The Postcolonial Politics of U.S.-Indigenous Relations* (Minneapolis: University of Minnesota Press, 2007), xvii.

135. Apess, *Indian Nullification*, 168.

136. Apess, *Indian Nullification*, 264.

137. Black Hawk, *The Life of Black Hawk*, ed. J. Gerald Kennedy (London: Penguin Books, 2008), 56, emphasis original.

138. Apess, *Indian Nullification*, 179, emphasis original.

139. See Herman Melville's "The Maids of Tartarus" (1855) for a depiction of the production of paper from cotton.

140. Apess, *A Son of the Forest*, 68. I am deeply grateful to Sam Plasencia for suggesting this reading and for her generous insights on this chapter.

141. Apess, *Indian Nullification*, 175; and Lopenzina, *Looking-Glass*, 202.

142. Apess, *Indian Nullification*, 181.

143. Apess, *Indian Nullification*, 181.

144. Apess, *Indian Nullification*, 187.

145. Apess, *Indian Nullification*, 185.

146. Lopenzina, *Looking-Glass*, 198.

147. Apess, *Indian Nullification*, 226, emphasis original.

148. Moore, *Capitalism in the Web of Life*, 181–89.

149. Cronon, *Changes in the Land*, 120–21.

150. Roberts, *Colonial Ecology, Atlantic Economy*, 120.

151. Roberts, *Colonial Ecology, Atlantic Economy*, 120–21.

152. William Howard Tucker, *History of Hartford, Vermont* (Burlington: Free Press Association, 1889), 14–15.

153. On the history of American deforestation, see Cronon, *Changes in the Land*, 108–21; Michael Williams, *Americans and Their Forests: A Historical Geography* (Cambridge: Cambridge University Press, 1989), 149–57; and Roberts, *Colonial Ecology, Atlantic Economy*, 154–63.

154. Andrew Jackson, *State of the Union Address* (December 6, 1830), in *The Cherokee Removal: A Brief History with Documents*, ed. Theda Perdue (New York: Bedford/St. Martin's, 2016), 120–21; 120.

155. Nick Estes, *Our History is the Future: Standing Rock Versus the Dakota Access Pipeline, and the Long Tradition of Indigenous Resistance* (New York: Verso, 2019), 22.

156. Apess, *Indian Nullification*, 175. For Mashpee resistance to timber theft, see also Konkle, *Writing Indian Nations*, 119–31; O'Brien, *Firsting and Lasting*, 201–5; and Lopenzina, *Looking Glass*, 195–209.

157. O'Brien, *Firsting and Lasting*, 183. For rights discourses in Apess's work more broadly, see also Carlson, *Sovereign Selves*, 91–120; and Konkle, *Writing Indian Nations*, 119–31.

158. Nichols, *Theft is Property!*, 29.

159. Nandita Sharma and Cynthia Wright, "Decolonizing Resistance, Challenging Colonial States," *Social Justice* 35, no. 3 (2008–2009): 120–38; 121. See also Nichols, *Theft is Property!*, 6–7.

160. Nichols, *Theft is Property!*, 130–31.

161. Eduardo Kohn, *How Forests Think: Toward an Anthropology Beyond the Human* (Berkeley: University of California Press, 2013), 16. See also Peter Wohlleben, *The Hidden Life of Trees*, trans. Jane Billinghurst (Vancouver: Graystone Books, 2016); and Suzanne Simard, *Finding the Mother Tree* (New York: Knopf, 2021).

162. Donna Haraway, *The Companion Species Manifesto* (Chicago: University of Chicago Press, 2003), 5.

163. Kim Tallbear, "Caretaking Relations, Not American Dreaming," *Kalfou: A Journal of Comparative and Relational Ethnic Studies* 6, no. 1 (Spring 2019): 24–41; 25; and Robin Wall Kimmerer, "Learning the Grammar of Animacy," *Anthropology of Consciousness* 28, no. 2 (2017): 128–34; 131. On Anishinaabemowin and animacy, see also Louise Erdrich, *Books and Islands in Ojibwe Country: Traveling through the Land of My Ancestors* (New York: Harper Perennial, 2014), 69–70.

164. Apess, *A Son of the Forest*, 33.

165. Brooks, *The Common Pot*, 175.

166. Apess, *Indian Nullification*, 168.

167. Jack Campisi, *The Mashpee Indians: Tribe on Trial* (Syracuse: Syracuse University Press, 1991), 60–61.

168. On the Mashpee trials, see James Clifford, "Identity at Mashpee," in *The Predicament of Culture: Twentieth-Century Ethnography, Literature, and Art* (Cambridge: Harvard University Press, 1988), 277–348; Paul Brodeur, *Restitution: The Land Claims of the Mashpee, Passamaquoddy, and Penobscot Indians of New England* (Boston: Northeastern University Press, 1985), 25–67; Russell M. Peters, *The Wampanoags of Mashpee: An Indian Perspective on American History* (Jamaica Plain, MA: RM Peters, 1987), 49–57; Jack Campisi, "The Trade and Intercourse Acts: Land Claims on the Eastern Seaboard," in *Irredeemable America: The Indians' Estate and Land Claims*, ed. Imre Sutton (Albuquerque: University of New Mexico Press, 1985), 337–62, and *The Mashpee Indians*, 9–58. For the trials in relationship to Apess, see Donaldson, "Making a Joyful Noise," 29–30; Carlson, *Sovereign Selves*, 120–21; and Shelby Johnson, "Histories Made Flesh: William Apess's Juridical Theologies," *MELUS* 42, no. 3 (Fall 2017): 6–25; 6; 9–11.

169. For Mashpee sovereignty and the Trump administration, see Ali Tal-Mason, "Will a Trump Tweet Sabotage a Popular Bipartisan Bill to Restore Tribal Lands?," *Slate* (July 5, 2019) at https://slate.com/news-and-politics/2019/07/indian-reoarga nization-act-anniversary-congress-native-land-bill.html. For the status of the land trust as of 2021, see Morgan C. Mullings, "Cape Cod's Mashpee Tribe Reclaims Land Trust," *Bay State Banner* (February 25, 2021) at https://www.baystatebanner .com/2021/02/25/cape-cods-mashpee-tribe-reclaims-land-trust/.

170. Apess, *Eulogy*, 306. See also Greer, *Property and Dispossession*, 227–37.

171. Daniel Hartley, "Anthropocene, Capitalocene, and the Problem of Culture," in *Anthropocene or Capitalocene?: Nature, History, and the Crisis of Capitalism*, ed. Jason W. Moore (Oakland: PM Press, 2016), 154–65; 155–56.

172. Robert Warrior, "William Apess," 201.

173. Apess, *Eulogy*, 279.

174. For historical scholarship on King Philip's War, see Jill Lepore, *The Name of War: King Philip's War and the Origins of American Identity* (New York: Vintage, 1999); Eric B. Schultz and Michael J. Tougias, *King Philip's War: The History and Legacy of*

America's Forgotten Conflict (Woodstock: Countrymen Press, 2000); and James D. Drake, *King Philip's War: Civil War in New England, 1675–1676* (Amherst: University of Massachusetts Press, 2000). For Indigenous and land-centered perspectives, see Lisa Brooks, *Our Beloved Kin: A New History of King Philip's War* (New Haven: Yale University Press, 2018); and Christine Delucia, *Memory Lands: King Philip's War and the Place of Violence in the Northeast* (New Haven: Yale University Press, 2019).

175. Lepore, *Name of War*, xiii.

176. Lepore, *Name of War*, 52.

177. Brooks, *Our Beloved Kin*, 4.

178. For the *Eulogy*, see Walker, *Indian Nation*, 164–81; Konkle, *Writing Indian Nations*, 131–56; Doolen, *Fugitive Empire*, 168–75; Carlson, *Sovereign Selves*, 93–96; Deborah Gussman, "'O savage where art thou': Rhetorics of Reform in William Apess's *Eulogy on King Philip*, *New England Quarterly* 77, no. 3 (Fall 2004): 451–77; Dana Luciano, *Arranging Grief: Sacred Time and the Body in Nineteenth-Century America* (New York: New York University Press, 2007), 53–56; O'Brien, *Firsting and Lasting*, 183–86; Eric A. Wolfe, "Mourning, Melancholia, and Rhetorical Sovereignty in William Apess's *Eulogy on King Philip*," *Studies in American Indian Literatures* 20, no. 4 (Winter 2008): 1–23; Desirée Henderson, *Grief and Genre in American Literature, 1790–1870* (New York: Routledge, 2011), 47–50; Clayton Zuba, "William Apess's *Eulogy on King Philip* and the Politics of Native Visualcy," *Early American Literature* 52, no. 3 (Fall 2017): 651–77; and Lopenzina, *Looking-Glass*, 221–40.

179. Delucia, *Memory Lands*, 2, 3, emphasis original. For Delucia's discussion of Apess, see 76–77.

180. Apess, *Eulogy*, 277. On Apess's performances of the *Eulogy*, see also Daniel Radus, "Apess's *Eulogy* on Tour: Kinship and the Transnational History of Native New England," *Studies in American Indian Literatures* 28, no. 3 (Fall 2016): 81–110; and Lopenzina, *Looking-Glass*, 227–28.

181. Thomas Church, *Entertaining Passages Relating to Philip's War* (1716), in *So Dreadfull a Judgment: Puritan Responses to King Philip's War, 1676–1677*, eds. Richard Slotkin and James K. Folsom (Middletown: Wesleyan University Press, 1978), 370–470; 451.

182. Increase Mather, "A Brief History of the Warr with the Indians in New England," in *So Dreadfull a Judgment: Puritan Responses to King Philip's War, 1676–1677*, eds. Richard Slotkin and James K. Folsom (Middletown: Wesleyan University Press, 1978), 55–206; 139.

183. Kathleen Bragdon, *Native People of Southern New England* (Norman: University of Oklahoma Press, 2009), 50.

184. Apess, *Eulogy*, 302–3.

185. On "re-memberment/re-membrance," see Brooks, *The Common Pot*, 65–67.

186. Ariella Aïsha Azoulay, *Potential History: Unlearning Imperialism* (New York: Verso 2019), 148.

187. Apess, *Eulogy*, 289.

188. Apess, *A Son of the Forest*, 7.

189. Jacques Derrida, *The Beast and the Sovereign II*, trans. Geoffrey Bennington, eds. Michel Lisse, Marie-Louise Mallet, and Ginette Michaud (Chicago: University of Chicago Press, 2010), 32.

190. Jacques Derrida, *Sovereignties in Question: The Poetics of Paul Celan*, eds. Thomas Dutoit and Outi Pasanen (New York: Fordham University Press, 2005), 140.

191. Derrida, *The Beast and the Sovereign*, 358, emphasis original.

192. Kelly Oliver, *Earth and World: Philosophy after the Apollo Missions* (New York: Columbia University Press, 2015), 206. See also Michael Naas, *The End of the World and Other Teachable Moments: Jacques Derrida's Final Seminar* (New York: Fordham University Press, 2014), 68–69.

193. Jodi Byrd, *The Transit of Empire: Indigenous Critiques of Colonialism* (Minneapolis: University of Minnesota Press, 2011), xv. On grievable life, see also Judith Butler, *Frames of War: What is Grievable Life?* (New York, Verso Books, 2009).

194. Joy Harjo, "Reconciliation, a Prayer," in *How We Became Human: New and Selected Poems* (New York: W. W. Norton, 2002), 90.

195. See Daniel K. Richter, *Facing East from Indian Country: A Native History of Early America* (Cambridge: Harvard University Press, 2001), 158–59.

196. Apess, *Eulogy*, 307.

Chapter Four

1. Robert Wedderburn, *The Axe Laid to the Root* (1817), in *The Horrors of Slavery and Other Writings*, ed. Iain McCalman (Princeton: Princeton University Press, 1991), No. 1, 81–88; 86.

2. Here, I draw on Eric Foner, who calls the Reconstruction period an "unfinished revolution," and Matt Sandler, who argues that Black Romantic poets "offer some perspective on what it might look like to finish that revolution." See Eric Foner, *Reconstruction: American's Unfinished Revolution* (New York: Harper Perennial, 2001), 3–5; and Matt Sandler, *The Black Romantic Revolution: Abolitionist Poets at the End of Slavery* (New York: Verso, 2020), 22.

3. Marcus Rediker and Peter Linebaugh in *The Many-Headed Hydra: Sailors, Slaves, Commoners, and the Hidden History of the Revolutionary Atlantic* (Boston: Beacon Books, 2000) call the Haitian Revolution the "first successful workers' revolt in modern history" (319).

4. Jeremy Matthew Glick, *The Black Radical Tragic: Performance, Aesthetics, and the Unfinished Haitian Revolution* (New York: New York University Press, 2016), 6. This chapter is also indebted to queer theory on unfinished revolutionary utopias, especially Carla Freccero in *Queer/Early/Modern* (Durham: Duke University Press, 2006), 2–9; and José Esteban Muñoz, *Cruising Utopia: The Then and There of Queer Futurity* (New York: New York University Press, 2009), 97–101.

5. On Romanticism, radicalism, and prophecy, see J.F.C. Harrison, *The Second Coming: Popular Millennialism, 1780–1850* (New Brunswick: University of New Jersey Press, 1979), chapters 7–8; Jon Mee, *Dangerous Enthusiasm: William Blake and the Culture of Radicalism in the 1790s* (Oxford: Oxford University Press, 1992), 36–38; and *Romanticism, Enthusiasm, and Regulation* (Oxford: Oxford University Press, 2003), chapter 1; Saree Makdisi, *William Blake and the Impossible History of the 1790s* (Chicago: University of Chicago Press, 2002), chapters 5–6; Jeffrey Cox, *Romanticism in the*

Shadow of War (Cambridge: Cambridge University Press, 2014), 93–159; and Tim Fulford, ed., *Romanticism and Millenarianism* (London: Palgrave Macmillan, 2002), 1–22.

6. On the question of Wedderburn's literacy, see Peter Linebaugh, "A Little Jubilee? The Literacy of Robert Wedderburn in 1817," in *Protest and Survival: Essays for E. P. Thompson*, eds. John Rule and Robert Malcolmson (London, 1993), 174–220; Sue Thomas, *Telling West Indian Lives: Life Narrative and the Reform of Plantation Slavery Cultures, 1804–1834* (New York: Palgrave Macmillan, 2015), 100–105; and Eric Penceck, "Intolerable Anonymity: Robert Wedderburn and the Discourse of Ultra-Radicalism," *Nineteenth-Century Contexts* 37, no. 1 (Spring 2015): 61–77; 62–63.

7. Iain McCalman, *Radical Underworld: Prophets, Revolutionaries, and Pornographers in London, 1795–1840* (Cambridge: Cambridge University Press, 1988), 53.

8. McCalman, *Radical Underworld*, 65.

9. For the life and career of Thomas Spence, see McCalman, *Radical Underworld*, 3–25, 63–72; David Worrall, *Radical Culture: Discourse, Resistance, and Surveillance, 1790–1820* (Detroit: Wayne State University Press, 1992), 2–12; Linebaugh and Rediker, *Many-Headed Hydra*, 293–96; and John Barrell, *Imagining the King's Death: Figurative Treason, Fantasies of Regicide, 1793–1796* (Oxford: Oxford University Press, 2000), 215–26.

10. McCalman, *Radical Underworld*, 128–29. For the Hopkins Street Chapel, see also 130–51, 191–92.

11. Wedderburn, *The Horrors of Slavery*, 61.

12. While McCalman is attuned to race and colonialism, the geographical and temporal dimensions of his project do not extend to the Caribbean, given his focus on London. Worrall similarly turns to Ireland as another arena of British imperial management. See McCalman, *Radical Underworld*, 50–72; and Worrall, *Radical Culture*, 129–46.

13. For scholarship on Wedderburn and transatlantic radicalism, see Paul Gilroy, *The Black Atlantic: Modernity and Double Consciousness* (Cambridge: Cambridge University Press, 1993), 11–13; Rediker and Linebaugh, *Many-Headed-Hydra*, chapter 9; Paul Edwards, "Unreconciled Strivings and Ironic Strategies: Three Afro-British Authors of the Late Georgian Period," in *Africans in Britain*, ed. David Killingray (New York: Routledge: 1994), 28–48; Helen Thomas, *Romanticism and Slave Narratives: Transatlantic Testimonies* (Cambridge: Cambridge University Press, 2000), 255–70; Marcus Wood, *Slavery, Empathy, and Pornography* (Oxford; Oxford University Press, 2003), 141–80; Alan Rice, "Ghostly and Vernacular Presences in the Black Atlantic," in *Transatlantic Literary Studies*, eds. Susan Manning and Eve Tavor Bannet (Cambridge: Cambridge University Press, 2012), 154–68, and *Radical Narratives of the Black Atlantic* (London: Continuum, 2003), 8–17; Elizabeth Bohls, *Romantic Literature and Postcolonial Studies* (Cambridge: Cambridge University Press, 2013), 74–78; Sue Thomas, *Telling West Indian Lives*, 97–118; Ryan Hanley, *Beyond Slavery and Abolition: Black British Writing, c. 1770–1830* (Cambridge: Cambridge University Press, 2019), 203–39; and Castellano, "Provision Grounds," 17–27.

14. "Haitian Declaration of Independence," in *Slave Revolution in the Caribbean, 1789–1804: A Brief History with Documents*, Laurent Dubois and John D. Garrigus (New York: Bedford/St. Martin's Press, 2006), 179.

15. Fred Moten, "Black Op," *PMLA* 123, no. 5 (October 2008): 1743–47; 1743.

16. Michel-Rolph Trouillot, *Silencing the Past: Power and the Production of History* (Boston: Beacon Books, 1995), 70–107. For scholarship that engages with the Haitian Revolution as a radical refusal of racial capitalism and the European Enlightenment, see C. L. R. James, *The Black Jacobins: Toussaint Louverture and the San Domingo Revolution*, 2nd Ed. (New York: Vintage, 1989); Sibylle Fischer, *Modernity Disavowed: Haiti and the Cultures of Slavery in the Age of Revolution* (Durham: Duke University Press, 2004) 132–42; Nick Nesbitt, *Universal Emancipation and the Radical Enlightenment* (Charlottesville: University of Virginia Press, 2008), 2–26; Sunil M. Agnani, *Hating Empire Properly: The Two Indies and the Limits of Enlightenment Anticolonialism* (New York: Fordham University Press, 2013), 133–61; Marlene Daut, *Tropics of Haiti: Race and the Literary History of the Haitian Revolution in the Atlantic World* (Liverpool: Liverpool University Press, 2015), 3–6; Jared Hickman, *The Black Prometheus: Race and Radicalism in the Age of Atlantic Slavery* (Oxford: Oxford University Press, 2017), 253–58; and Julius Scott, *The Common Wind: Afro-American Currents in the Age of Haitian Revolution* (New York: Verso, 2018), 118–58. For the Haitian Revolution and Romantic-era writing, see Paul Youngquist, "Introduction," in *Race, Romanticism, and the Atlantic*, ed. Paul Youngquist (New York: Routledge, 2013), 1–22. For Haitian nation-building after the Revolution, see Laurent Dubois, *Haiti: The Aftershocks of History* (New York: Picador, 2013), 52–88.

17. Frederick Douglass, "Emigration to Haiti," *Douglass' Monthly* (Rochester, NY: January 1861).

18. Ifeoma Nwankwo, *Black Cosmopolitanism: Racial Consciousness and Transnational Identity in the Nineteenth-Century Americas* (Philadelphia: University of Pennsylvania Press, 2005), 7.

19. Anthony Bogues, *Black Heretics, Black Prophets: Radical Political Intellectuals* (New York: Routledge, 2003), 13.

20. Wedderburn relates that his mother was purchased by the Campbell family in Kingston. See Sue Thomas, "Robert Wedderburn's Correspondent Miss Campbell," *Notes and Queries* 61, no. 4 (September 2014): 510–14.

21. I am so grateful to Kristina Huang for helping me consider Wedderburn's narrative practices as a way of writing emancipation into being, what she in our conversation called a "literary critical practice of abolition."

22. Katey Castellano, "Provision Grounds against the Plantation: Robert Wedderburn's *Axe Laid to the Root*," *Small Axe* 25, no. 1 (March 2021): 17–27; 17.

23. Lisa Lowe, *The Intimacies of Four Continents* (Durham: Duke University Press, 2015), 175.

24. See Lowe, *Intimacies of Four Continents*, 39–40; and Scott, *Conscripts of Modernity*, 90–98.

25. *The Axe Laid to the Root* echoes the probable print history of Martin Delaney's novel *Blake*, published serially in 1859 and 1861–1862, which similarly ends abruptly and without depicting the anticipated slave revolution.

26. Christina Sharpe, *In the Wake: On Blackness and Being* (Durham: Duke University Press, 2016), 14. Hartman, *Lose Your Mother*, 6. For "useable past," I am drawing from Hortense Spillers's discussion of Ralph Ellison's desire for "usable past," even if

the past is figured as non-recoverable. See "Ellison's 'Usable Past': Toward a Theory of Myth," *Black, White, and In Color* (Chicago: University of Chicago Press, 2003), 65–80.

27. Stephen Best, *None Like Us: Blackness, Belonging, Aesthetic Life* (Durham: Duke University Press, 2018), 123. See also David Scott, *Conscripts of Modernity: The Tragedy of Colonial Enlightenment* (Durham: Duke University Press, 2004), 20–23 and 206–18.

28. Jared Sexton, "The *Vel* of Slavery: Tracking the Figure of the Unsovereign," *Critical Sociology* 42, no. 4–5 (December 2016): 583–97; 593.

29. Joseph Albernaz, email to Shelby Johnson, April 9, 2021. I am deeply grateful to Joe for drawing my attention to the conceptual work offered by the title of *The Axe Laid to the Root*.

30. Walter Benjamin, "Theses on the Philosophy of History," in *Illuminations: Essays and Reflections*, eds. Hannah Arendt and trans. Harry Zohn (New York: Knopf Doubleday, 2007), 253–64; 263.

31. Jennifer L. Morgan, *Laboring Women: Reproduction and Gender in New World Slavery* (Philadelphia: University of Pennsylvania Press, 2004), 1.

32. Linebaugh and Rediker, *Many-Headed Hydra*, 288.

33. McCalman, "Introduction," in *The Horrors of Slavery and Other Writings* (Princeton: Princeton University Press, 1991), 1–40; 1–2; and Thomas, *Telling West Indian Lives*, 109–10.

34. Wedderburn, *The Horrors of Slavery*, 46–48.

35. Jessica Marie Johnson, *Wicked Flesh: Black Women, Freedom, and Intimacy in the Atlantic World* (Philadelphia: University of Pennsylvania, 2020), 173.

36. See Hanley, *Beyond Slavery and Abolition*, 204; and Nadine Hunt, "Remembering Africans in Diaspora: Robert Wedderburn's 'Freedom Narrative'," in *Slavery in Africa and the Caribbean: A History of Enslavement and Identity since the Eighteenth Century*, eds. Olatunji Ojo and Nadine Hunt (London: I.B. Taurus, 2012), 175–98.

37. Linebaugh and Rediker, *Many-Headed Hydra*, 403.

38. Rice, *Radical Narratives of the Black Atlantic*, 13.

39. Wedderburn, *The Horrors of Slavery*, 51, emphasis original.

40. Wedderburn, *The Horrors of Slavery*, 48.

41. Diana Paton, *The Cultural Politics of Obeah: Religion, Colonialism, and Modernity in the Caribbean World* (Cambridge: Cambridge University Press, 2017), 17–21.

42. Wedderburn, *The Horrors of Slavery*, 49.

43. Wedderburn, *The Horrors of Slavery*, 49.

44. Saidiya Hartman, *Scenes of Subjection: Terror, Slavery, and Self-Making in Nineteenth-Century America* (Oxford: Oxford University Press, 1997), 2–4.

45. For Jamaican Obeah, see Magarite Fernándes Olmos and Lizabeth Paravisini-Gebert's helpful introduction in *Creole Religions of the Caribbean: An Introduction from Vodou and Santeria to Obeah and Espiritismo* (New York: New York University Press, 2011), 155–82; Srinivas Aravamudan's introduction to *Obi; or, The of History Three-Fingered Jack* (Peterborough.: Broadview Press, 2005), 23–51; and Diana Paton and Maarit Forde's edited collection, *Obeah and Other Powers: The Politics of Caribbean Religion and Healing* (Durham: Duke University Press, 2012), 1–42. For historical accounts of Obeah, see Alan Richardson, "Romantic Voodoo: Obeah and British Culture, 1797–1807," in *Sacred Possessions: Vodou, Santeria, Obeah, and the Caribbean*, eds. Magarite

Fernándes Olmos and Lizabeth Paravisini-Gebert (New Brunswick: New Jersey University Press, 2000), 171–94; Toni Wall Jaudon, "Obeah Sensations: Rethinking Religion at the Transnational Turn," *American Literature* 84, no. 4 (Winter 2012): 715–41; Elizabeth Maddock Dillon, "Obi, Assemblage, Enchantment," *J19* 1, no. 1 (Spring 2013): 172–77; and the special issue of *Atlantic* Studies, eds. Kelly Wisecup and Toni Wall Jaudon, 12, no. 2 (Summer 2015).

46. Wedderburn, *The Horrors of Slavery*, 49.

47. Hartman, *Scenes of Subjection*, 4.

48. Richardson, "Romantic Voodoo," 189.

49. Richardson, "Romantic Voodoo," 173.

50. Wedderburn, *The Horrors of Slavery*, 47–48.

51. Wedderburn, *The Axe Laid to the Root*, No. 1, 86.

52. Wedderburn, *The Horrors of Slavery*, 48.

53. Daut, *Tropics of Haiti*, 4.

54. Wedderburn, *The Axe Laid to the Root*, No. 4, 96.

55. Wedderburn, *The Axe Laid to the Root*, No. 4, 96.

56. Wedderburn, *The Axe Laid to the Root*, No. 4, 96.

57. Robin D. G. Kelley, *Freedom Dreams: The Black Radical Imagination* (Boston: Beacon Press, 2003), 3–6.

58. Hanley, *Beyond Slavery and Abolition*, 223.

59. Brigitte Fielder, *Relative Races: Genealogies of Interracial Kinship in Nineteenth-Century America* (Durham: Duke University Press, 2020), 4.

60. "The king ag[ainst] Robert Wedderburn for Blasphemy, Brief for the Crown," *The Kings Bench Sittings after Hilary Term Middlesex*, in *The Horrors of Slavery and Other Writings*, ed. Iain McCalman (Princeton, NJ: Princeton University Press, 1991), 123–25; 125.

61. Wedderburn married Elizabeth Ryan in 1781 when he was around twenty years old.

62. Wedderburn, *The Horrors of Slavery*, 59.

63. Wedderburn, *The Horrors of Slavery*, 58.

64. Muñoz, *Cruising Utopia*, 16. In its orientation towards futurity, Wedderburn's matrilineal vision is not quite an evasion of "reproductive futurity," or a position that refuses sociality and politics in the mode of Lee Edelman's *No Future: Queer Theory and the Death Drive* (Durham: Duke University Press, 2004). Instead, his orientation to Black kinship seeks to recover reproductive sovereignty—the ability of Black fathers and mothers to claim their children outside the logics of heteronormative patriarchy and white supremacist denials of Black family-formation.

65. Stefano Harney and Fred Moten, *The Undercommons: Fugitive Planning and Black Study* (New York: Autonomedia, 2013), 67.

66. McCalman, *Radical Underworld*, 50.

67. In *Radical Underwood*, McCalman argues, "For Robert Wedderburn Methodism was a stepping stone to political unrespectibilty and extremism" (50). See his larger discussion on 51–66.

68. Gustavo Esteva, Unpublished manuscript; and qtd. Arturo Escobar, *Designs for the Pluriverse: Radical Interdependence, Autonomy, and the Making of Worlds* (Durham: Duke University Press, 2018), 189.

69. For Methodist quietism, see Elie Halévy, *The History of the English People in 1815*, trans. Asa Briggs (London: AKA Paperbacks, 1987), and *The Birth of Methodism in England*, trans. Bernard Semmel (Chicago: University of Chicago Press, 1971); and E. P. Thompson, *The Making of the English Working Class* (New York: Vintage, 1963, 1966), 388–97. For criticism of Elie Halévy, see Gerald Wayne Olsen, ed., *Religion and Revolution in Early Industrial England: The Halévy Thesis and Its Critics* (Boston: University Press of America, 1989). For popular Methodism, see Arnold Rattenbury, "Methodism and the Tatterdemalions," in *Popular Culture and Class Conflict, 1590–1914: Explorations in the History of Labour and Leisure*, eds. Eileen and Stephen Yao (Sussex: Harvester Press, 1981), 28–61; David Hempton, *Methodism and Politics in British Society, 1750–1850* (Stanford: Stanford University Press, 1984), *The Religion of the People: Methodism and Popular Religion, 1750–1900* (New York: Routledge, 1996), and *Methodism: Empire of the Spirit* (New Haven: Yale University Press, 2005); Phyllis K. Mack, *Heart Religion in the British Enlightenment: Gender and Emotion in Early Methodism* (Cambridge: Cambridge University Press, 2008), 3–5; 29–59; and Misty G. Anderson, *Imagining Methodism in Eighteenth-Century Britain: Enthusiasm, Belief, and the Borders of the Self* (Baltimore: Johns Hopkins University Press, 2012), 18–22.

70. Anderson, *Imagining Methodism*, 4. Here, I also take inspiration from Gauri Viswanathan's point in *Outside the Fold: Conversion, Modernity, and Belief* (Princeton: Princeton University Press, 1998): "Conversion is not limited to the function of either preserving or erasing identity but, in far more complex ways, is associated with a deconstructive activity central to modernity itself" (76).

71. Wedderburn, *Truth Self-Supported* (1802), 65–77; 66.

72. Joanna Brooks, *American Lazarus: Religion and the Rise of African-American and Native American Literature* (Oxford: Oxford University Press, 2003), 112.

73. Wedderburn, *Truth Self-Supported*, 71, emphasis original.

74. Slavoj Žižek, *First as Tragedy, Then as Farce* (New York: Verso, 2009), 102.

75. Brooks, *American Lazarus*, 8–10. Sharon Holland's *Raising the Dead: Readings of Death and (Black) Subjectivity* (Durham: Duke University Press, 2000) likewise establishes methods for regenerating subjectivities rendered dead in twentieth-century cultures. For a productive counter to Brooks, see also Elizabeth Maddock Dillon, "Zombie Biopolitics," *American Quarterly* 71, no. 3 (Fall 2019): 625–52.

76. In *The Reaper's Garden: Death and Power in the World of Atlantic Slavery* (Cambridge: Cambridge University Press, 2010), Vincent Brown argues that sites of struggle over mortuary are not merely the purview of theology, but resonate with profound material, social, and political meaning: "All during the inexorable journey to the Americas, as Africans repeatedly made and lost fragile social connections, they trailed a lengthening column of displaced souls. This was a spiritual cataclysm, perhaps the most horrifying aspect of the experience of enslavement. Embarking for America, enslaved Africans had entered into a theater of ghosts" (43). I am especially drawn to Brown's image of a "theater of ghosts" because it opens a reading of Wedderburn's "City of Refuge"—a city of the dead that maintains connections to haunted landscapes and genealogies across the African diaspora.

77. Brown, *The Reaper's Garden*, 203, 255.

78. Joseph Roach, *Cities of the Dead: Circum-Atlantic Performances* (New York: Columbia University Press, 1996), 7–10.

79. For plural futures in Romantic writing, see Ian Balfour, *The Rhetoric of Romantic Prophecy* (Stanford: Stanford University Press), 1–19; and Anahid Nersessian, *Utopia, Limited: Romanticism and Adjustment* (Cambridge: Harvard University Press, 2015), 6–23.

80. On *hōs mē*, see also Jacques Derrida, *The Beast and the Sovereign II*, trans. Geoffrey Bennington (Chicago: University of Chicago Press, 2011), 148–50.

81. Benjamin, "Theses on the Philosophy of History," 263.

82. Benjamin, "Theses on the Philosophy of History," 257.

83. Benjamin, "Theses on the Philosophy of History," 257–58.

84. See Paul de Man, "Shelley Disfigured," in *The Rhetoric of Romanticism* (New York: Columbia University Press, 1984), 93–123; 122. For Black archives as incomplete, see Saidiya Hartman, *Lose Your Mother: A Journey Along the Atlantic Slave Route* (New York: Farrer, Straus and Giroux, 2007), 136–53; Imtiaz Habib, *Black Lives in the English Archives, 1500–1677: Imprints of the Invisible* (New York: Routledge, 2017), 1–17; and Marisa J. Fuentes, *Dispossessed Lives: Enslaved Women, Violence, and the Archive* (Philadelphia: University of Pennsylvania Press, 2018), 6–12.

85. Katherine McKittrick, "Plantation Futures," *Small Axe* 17, no. 3 (November 2013): 1–15; 12.

86. See Orlando Patterson, *Slavery and Social Death* (Cambridge: Harvard University Press, 1982), 38; and Achille Mbembe, "Necropolitics," trans. Libby Meintjes, *Public Culture* 15, no. 1 (Spring 2003): 11–40; 21.

87. See Hartman, *Lose Your Mother*, 87; and Frank B. Wilderson III, *Red, White, & Black: Cinema and the Structure of U.S. Antagonisms* (Durham: Duke University Press, 2010), 17–18. On kinlessness, see also Hortense Spillers, "Mama's Baby, Papa's Maybe: An American Grammar," in *Black, White, and in Color* (Chicago: University of Chicago Press, 2003), 203–29; and Elizabeth Freeman, *Beside You in Time: Sense Methods and Queer Sociabilities in the American Nineteenth Century* (Durham: Duke University Press, 2019), 53–55.

88. Isabelle Stengers, "The Cosmopolitical Proposal," in *Making Things Public: Atmospheres of Democracy*, eds. Bruno Latour and Peter Weibel (Boston: MIT Press, 2005), 994–1003; 995. See also *Cosmopolitics I*, trans. Robert Bononno (Minneapolis: University of Minnesota Press, 2010), chapter 3.

89. Cedric Robinson, *Black Marxism: The Making of the Black Radical Tradition* (Chapel Hill: University of North Carolina Press, 1983), 72–73.

90. In some ways, Wedderburn's position on finitude contrasts with Olaudah Equiano's *Interesting Narrative* (1789), which represents the African continent as "an inexhaustible source of wealth to the manufacturing interests of Great Britain" (234). See *The Interesting Narrative and Other Writings*, ed. Vincent Carretta (London, Penguin: 2003).

91. Eduardo Kohn, *How Forests Think: Toward an Anthropology Beyond the Human* (Berkeley: University of California Press, 2013), 6.

92. Elizabeth Povinelli, *The Cunning of Recognition: Indigenous Alterities and the Making of Australian Multiculturalisms* (Durham: Duke University Press, 2013), 17–39.

93. McCalman, *Radical Underworld*, 1–8; and Worrall, *Radical Culture*, 1–3.

94. Wedderburn, *The Axe Laid to the Root*, no. 1, 84.

95. John Locke, *Second Treatise on Government*, ed. Ian Shapiro (New Haven: Yale University Press, 2003), 111.

96. In *Radical Culture*, Worrall argues that even possession of Leviticus 25 could be construed by a paranoid state as evidence of Jacobin tendencies. When Thomas Spence was arrested in December of 1792 for selling Thomas Paine's *The Rights of Man* (Part II), the Bow Street runners searched his pockets and found "'the 25th chapter of the book of Leviticus . . . which may, according to the present system of proceedings, be equally termed libelous'" (10).

97. Wedderburn, *The Axe Laid to the Root*, no. 1, 85. See also Linebaugh and Rediker, *Many-Headed Hydra*, 292; and Worrall, *Radical Culture*, 10.

98. One spy report reproduces one of Wedderburn's speeches at the Hopkins Street Chapel where he invokes "the earth was given to the children of men": "There were but two classes of people in England very Rich and very Poor how did this happen? . . . but who gave them this Land? God gave the World to the Children of Men as their Inheritance and they have been fleeced out of it" (*Horrors of Slavery*, 120).

99. Wedderburn, *The Axe Laid to the Root*, No. 1, 83.

100. Michel Serres, *Malfeasance*, trans. Anne-Marie Feenberg Dibon (Stanford: Stanford University Press, 2010), 73.

101. Serres, *Malfeasance*, 20.

102. Serres, *Malfeasance*, 19, emphasis original.

103. Nersessian, *Utopia, Limited*, 80.

104. Robinson, *Black Marxism*, 168.

105. Thomas Spence, *The Reign of Felicity* (London: Little Turnstile, 1796), 1–2.

106. Linebaugh and Rediker, *Many-Headed Hydra*, 294–96.

107. Wedderburn, *The Axe Laid to the Root*, No. 4, 99.

108. Elizabeth Maddock Dillon, *New World Drama: The Performative Commons in the Atlantic World* (Durham: Duke University Press, 2014), 3.

109. Silvia Federici, "Commons Against and Beyond Capitalism," in *Re-Enchanting the World* (Oakland: PM Books, 2019), 85–98; 94. See also Peter Linebaugh, *Red Round Globe Hot Burning* (Berkeley: University of California Press, 2021), 13–15.

110. Matilde Cazzola, "'All shall be happy by land and sea': Thomas Spence as Atlantic Thinker," *Atlantic Studies* 15, no. 4 (Winter 2017): 431–50.

111. Penceck, "Intolerable Anonymity," 61.

112. Thomas Spence, *A Supplement to the History of Robinson Crusoe* (London: T. Saint, 1782), 32.

113. Daniel Defoe, *Robinson Crusoe*, ed. Michael Shinagel (New York: W. W. Norton, 1994), 149, emphasis original.

114. Julia Prewett Brown, *The Bourgeois Interior: How the Middle Class Imagines Itself in Literature and Film* (Charlottesville: University of Virginia Press, 2008), 36.

115. Spence, *Supplement*, 30.

116. Wedderburn, *The Axe Laid to the Root*, No. 1, 82.

117. Worrall, *Radical Culture*, 7.

118. McCalman, "Introduction," 8–9.

119. McCalman, "Introduction," 1.

120. Wedderburn responded to the topic, "Whether the refusal of Chief-Justice Abbott to allow Mr. Carlile to read the Bible in his defense was to be attributed to the sincere belief he had for the sacred writings, or to a fear lest the absurdities it contained should be exposed." Carlile had been imprisoned for seditious libel earlier that year. On Wedderburn's trial, see Thomas, *Telling West Indian Lives*, 98; and Hanley, *Beyond Slavery and Abolition*, 217–20.

121. Thomas, *Telling West Indian Lives*, 99.

122. McCalman, "Introduction," 1; and Worrall, *Radical Culture*, 135.

123. Linebaugh and Rediker, *Many-Headed Hydra*, 320–22.

124. Worrall, *Radical Culture*, 178–90.

125. Worrall, *Radical Culture*, 12.

126. Thomas, *Telling West Indian Lives*, 99.

127. 29 November 1819, HO 42/198, 490; and qtd. Worrall, *Radical Culture*, 180–81.

128. For Jewish communities in the Caribbean, see Sarah Philips Casteel, *Calypso Jews: Jewishness in the Caribbean Literary Imagination* (New York: Columbia University Press, 2016); Mordechai Arbell, *The Jewish Nation of the Caribbean: The Spanish-Portuguese Jewish Settlements in the Caribbean and Guianas* (Jerusalem: Gefen Publishing House, 2002), and *The Portuguese Jews of Jamaica* (Mona: University Press of the West Indies, 2000); Alan F. Benjamin, *Jews of the Dutch Caribbean: Exploring Ethnic Identity on Curacao* (New York: Routledge, 2002); Richard L. Kagan and Philip D. Morgan, eds., *Atlantic Diasporas: Jews, Conversos, and Crypto-Jews in the Age of Mercantilism, 1500–1800* (Baltimore: Johns Hopkins University Press, 2008), especially essays by Jonathan Israel, "Jews and Crypto-Jews in the Atlantic World Systems," 3–17, and Holly Snyder, "English Markets, Jewish Merchants, and Atlantic Endeavors: Jews and the Making of British Transatlantic Commercial Culture," 50–74; and Kristin Ruggiero, ed., *The Jewish Diaspora in Latin America and the Caribbean: Fragments of Memory* (Eastbourne, UK: Sussex Academic Press, 2005), especially the essays on the British West Indies.

129. Richard Brothers, *Revealed Knowledge of the Prophecies and Times* (London: Edward Gray, 1794), 88. For Brothers, see Mee, *Dangerous Enthusiasm*, 29–35; Makdisi, *William Blake*, 59–70; Barrell, *Imagining the King's Death*, 504–43; Susan Juster, *Doomsayers: Anglo-American Prophecy in the Age of Revolutions* (Philadelphia: University of Pennsylvania Press, 2003), 178–215; Deborah Madden, *The Paddington Prophet: Richard Brothers's Journey to Jerusalem* (Manchester: Manchester University Press, 2010), 2–20; and Mary Favret, *War at a Distance: Romanticism and the Making of Modern Wartime* (Princeton: Princeton University Press, 2009), 81–97.

130. Brothers, *Revealed Knowledge*, 22, emphasis original.

131. Favret, *War at a Distance*, 88.

132. Wedderburn, *The Axe Laid to the Root*, no. 1, 87.

133. On Wedderburn and Wilberforce, see Rice, "Ghostly Consolation," 166–67.

134. Wood, *Blind Memory*, 167.

135. On *The New Union Club* print, see Wood, *Blind Memory*, 165–71; Jenna Gibbs, *Performing the Temple of Liberty: Slavery, Theater, and Popular Culture in London and Philadelphia, 1760–1850* (Baltimore: Johns Hopkins University Press, 2014), 123–24; and Hanley, *Beyond Slavery and Abolition*, 228–32.

136. Tina Campt, *Listening to Images* (Durham: Duke University Press, 2017), 3–5.

137. McCalman, *Radical Underworld*, 116.

138. McCalman, "Introduction," 18.

139. McCalman, "Introduction," 16–19.

140. Wedderburn, *The Axe Laid to the Root*, No. 4, 96.

141. Wedderburn, *The Axe Laid to the Root*, No. 6, 108.

142. Scott, *Common Wind*, 1–2.

143. David Kazanjian, *The Brink of Freedom: Improvising Life in the Nineteenth-Century Atlantic World* (Durham: Duke University Press, 2016), 13.

144. Wedderburn, *The Axe Laid to the Root*, No. 2, 89–95; 90.

145. For Jamaican marronage and Atlantic performance cultures, see Michael Warner, *Publics and Counterpublics* (New York: Zone Books, 2005), 225–68; Kathleen Wilson, "The Performance of Freedom: Maroons and the Colonial Order in Eighteenth-Century Jamaica and the Atlantic Sound," *William and Mary Quarterly* 56, no. 3 (Fall 2009): 45–86; and Dillon, *New World Drama*, 241–46.

146. Wedderburn, *The Axe Laid to the Root*, No. 6, 107.

147. Kamau Brathwaite, *Roots* (Ann Arbor: Michigan University Press, 1993), 231.

148. Robinson, *Black Marxism*, 143–44. For scholarship on Nanny, see Karla Gottlieb, *The Mother of Us All: A History of Queen Nanny, Leader of the Windward Jamaican Maroons* (Trenton: Lushena Books, 2000), 23–42; Kenneth M. Bilby, *True-Born Maroon* (Tallahassee: University Press of Florida, 2005), 72–80, 110–12; Werner Zips, *Nanny's Asafo Warriors: The Jamaican Maroons African Experience* (Kingston: Ian Randle Publishers, 2011); and Jennifer L. Morgan, *Reckoning with Slavery: Gender, Kinship, and Capitalism in the Early Black Atlantic* (Durham: Duke University Press, 2021), 228–37.

149. Neil Roberts, *Freedom as Marronage* (Chicago: University of Chicago Press, 2015), 12; 165–69. I am also thinking about Wedderburn elaborating a "line of flight," which Gilles Deleuze and Félix Guattari discuss in *A Thousand Plateaus* (Minneapolis: University of Minnesota Press, 1987), 55, 202–5. For work that takes "line of flight" to Indigenous contexts, see also Leanne Betasamosake Simpson, *As We Have Always Done: Indigenous Freedom through Radical Resistance* (Minneapolis: University of Minnesota Press, 2017), 17–18.

150. Wedderburn, *The Axe Laid to the Root*, No. 1, 86.

151. Castellano, "Provision Grounds," 17.

152. Kamau Brathwaite, "Caribbean Culture: Two Paradigms," in *Missile and Capsule*, ed. Jürgen Martini (Bremen, Germany: Universität Bremen, 1983), 9–54; 25.

153. As Hazel Carby observes, a 1761 law imposed "a limit of £2,000 on the amount that free people of colour could inherit," while "a law of 1775 severely restricted women's inheritance rights" (295). These laws became somewhat less stringent in 1813 when free people of color successfully petitioned "for the removal of limits on inheritance" (297). See Hazel Carby, *Imperial Intimacies: A Tale of Two Islands* (New York: Verso, 2019), 294–98. On women as property holders and enslavers, see also Christine Walker, *Jamaica Ladies: Female Slaveholders and the Creation of Britain's Atlantic Empire* (Chapel Hill: University of North Carolina Press, 2020).

154. Mavis Campbell, *Maroons of Jamaica, 2655–1795: A History of Resistance, Collaboration, and Betrayal* (Granby, MA: Bergin and Garvey, 1988), 6–7.

155. Roberts, *Freedom as Marronage*, 181.

156. Richard Waswo, "The History that Literature Makes," *New Literary History* 19, no. 3 (Fall 1988): 541–64; 541.

157. Édouard Glissant, *Caribbean Discourse: Selected Essays*, trans. Michael J. Dash (Charlottesville: University of Virginia Press, 1999), 64. For a reading of the Haitian Revolution as an expression of marronage, see also Paget Henry, *Caliban's Reason: Introducing Afro-Caribbean Philosophy* (New York: Routledge, 2000), 1–18.

158. Wedderburn, *The Axe Laid to the Root*, No. 1, 86.

159. Wedderburn, *The Axe Laid to the Root*, No. 4, 98.

160. See the account in *Blackwood's Edinburgh Magazine* from January 1839, 404.

161. Scott, *Conscripts of Modernity*, 12. See also Robinson, *Black Marxism*, 275–78.

162. Scott, *Conscripts of Modernity*, 185.

163. Fred Moten, *The Universal Machine* (Durham: Duke University Press, 2018), 193; 190.

164. Scott, *Conscripts of Modernity*, 182.

165. Ariella Aïsha Azoulay, *Potential History: Unlearning Imperialism* (New York: Verso, 2019), 10.

166. Benjamin, "Theses on the Philosophy of History," 263. In calling Wedderburn's prophetic posture a form of messianism, I am drawing a distinction between messianic and eschatological time, what Giorgio Agamben in *The Time That Remains: A Commentary on the Letter of Romans*, trans. Patricia Dailey (Stanford: Stanford University Press, 2005) calls "not the end of time, but *the time of the end*" (62). Agamben also notes that "Messianic time is the time that time takes to come to an end. . . . It is the time we need to make time end: the time that is left us" (64).

167. Paul K. Saint-Amour, *Tense Future: Modernism, Total War, Encyclopedic Form* (Oxford: Oxford University Press, 2015), 23, emphasis original.

168. Wedderburn, *The Axe Laid to the Root*, No. 6, 109.

169. Wedderburn, *The Axe Laid to the Root*, No. 6, 109.

170. Deborah Thomas, *Political Life in the Wake of the Plantation: Sovereignty, Witnessing, Repair* (Durham: Duke University Press, 2019), 126.

171. Wedderburn, *The Axe Laid to the Root*, No. 6, 110.

172. For a nineteenth-century account of the Second Maroon War, see R.C. Dallas, *The History of the Maroons, from their Origin to the Establishment of their Chief Tribe at Sierra Leone*, 2 vols. (London: T.N. Longman and O. Rees, 1803). For critical histories, see Carey Robinson, *The Fighting Maroons of Jamaica* (Kingston: William Collins and Sangster, 1969), 73–154, and *The Iron Horn: The Defeat of the British by the Jamaican Maroons* (Kingston: LMH Publishing Company, 1969, 2007), 120–271; Campbell, *The Maroons*, 209–49; and Michael Craton, *Testing the Chains: Resistance to Slavery in the British West Indies* (Ithaca: Cornell University Press, 2009), 211–23.

173. For the Maroons and Nova Scotia, see Mavis Campbell, *Back to Africa: George Ross and the Maroons* (Trenton: Africa World Press, 1993), i–xii; and John Grant, *The Maroons in Nova Scotia* (Halifax: Formac, 2002).

174. For a history of the radical press and its repression in Britain, see McCalman, *Radical Underworld*, 152–77.

175. Frances Botkin and Paul Youngquist, "Anarchival Research and the Jamaican Maroons," Conference Presentation, 11th Annual International Charles Town Maroon Conference and Festival, (June 21, 2019).

176. Benjamin, "Theses on the Philosophy of History," 263.

177. Maurice Blanchot, "Prophetic Speech," in *The Book to Come*, trans. Charlotte Mandell (Stanford: Stanford University Press, 2003), 79–85; 81.

178. Campt, *Listening to Images*, 17, emphasis original.

179. Michelle M. Wright, *The Physics of Blackness: Beyond the Middle Passage Epistemology* (Minneapolis: University of Minnesota, 2015), 4, emphasis original.

180. As Arturo Escobar reminds us, if another world is possible, then "another possible is possible." See *Pluriversal Politics: The Real and the Possible* (Durham: Duke University Press, 2020), ix.

181. Ryan Hanley, "A Radical Change of Heart: Robert Wedderburn's Last Word on Slavery," *Slavery and Abolition* 37, no. 2 (Summer 2016), 423–45. See also Hanley, *Beyond Slavery and Abolition*, 236–39.

182. Wedderburn opens *The Axe Laid to Root* with a call for nonviolent resistance: "Follow not the example of St. Domingo, let not your jubilee, which will take place, be stained with the blood of your oppressors" (81). On Wedderburn and the general strike, see also Joseph Albernaz, "Abolition, Ultraradicalism, and the Generation of the General Strike," *Critical Times* 5, no. 3 (December 2022): 538–69.

Coda

1. On the "great acceleration," see J.R. McNeill and Peter Engelke, *The Great Acceleration: An Environmental History of the Anthropocene since 1945* (Cambridge: Harvard University Press, 2014), 1–6. On the "golden spike," see Elizabeth DeLoughrey, *Allegories of the Anthropocene* (Durham: Duke University Press, 2019), 24–26.

2. William Blake, "Book the Second," in *Milton, a Poem in Two Books, The Complete Poetry and Prose of William Blake*, ed. David Erdman (Berkeley: University of California Press, 2008), 97. See also Peter Linebaugh, *Red Round Globe Hot Burning* (Berkeley: University of California Press, 2021).

3. On 1610 as a "golden spike," see Mark A. Maslin and Simon L. Lewis, *The Human Planet: How We Created the Anthropocene* (New Haven: Yale University Press, 2018), 13. On dating the Anthropocene's origins, see also Heather Davis and Zoe Todd, "On the Importance of a Date, Or, Decolonizing the Anthropocene," *ACME: An International Journal for Critical Geographies* 16, no. 4 (Winter 2017): 761–80; and Arun Saldanha, "A Date with Destiny: Racial Capitalism and the Beginnings of the Anthropocene," *Environment and Planning D: Society and Space* 38, no. 4 (September 2019): 12–34.

4. Dana Luciano, "The Inhuman Anthropocene," *Avidly* (March 22, 2015).

5. Jennifer L. Morgan, *Reckoning with Slavery: Gender, Kinship, and Capitalism in the Early Black Atlantic* (Durham: Duke University Press, 2021), 11–23. See also Ariella Aïsha Azoulay, *Potential History: Unlearning Imperialism* (New York: Verso 2019), 122–24.

6. Kathryn Yusoff, *A Billion Black Anthropocenes or None* (Minneapolis: University of Minnesota Press, 2018), 23–24; Sylvia Wynter, "Unsettling the Coloniality of Being/

Power/Truth/Freedom: Towards the Human, After Man, Its Overrepresentation—An Argument," *CR: The New Centennial Review* 3, no. 3 (Fall 2003): 257–337; 260; and Fred Moten, *Stolen Life* (Durham: Duke University Press, 2018), 153.

7. Benedict Anderson, *Imagined Communities: Reflections on the Origin and Spread of Nationalism*, Revised ed. (New York: Verso, 2016), 167–90—see especially the discussion on 173–80.

8. See Saidiya Hartman, *Lose Your Mother: A Journey Along the Atlantic Slave Route* (New York: Farrer, Straus and Giroux, 2007), 6; and Fred Moten, *Black and Blur* (Durham: Duke University Press, 2017), xii.

9. Dionne Brand, *A Map to the Door of No Return* (New York: Vintage, 2002), 42.

10. Mary Prince, *The History of Mary Prince, a West Indian Slave, Related by Herself*, ed. Moira Ferguson (Ann Arbor: University of Michigan Press, 1997), 64.

11. Angelique V. Nixon, "Poem and Tale as Double Helix in Joy Harjo's *A Map to the Next World*," *Studies in American Indian Literatures* 18, no. 1 (Spring 2006): 1–21; 2.

12. Joy Harjo, "A Map to the Next World," in *A Map to the Next World: Poems and Tales* (New York: W. W. Norton, 2001), 19–21; 21.

13. Azoulay, *Potential History*, 10.

14. Harjo, "Map to the Next World," 19.

15. Harjo, "Map to the Next World," 19.

16. Samson Occom, "Letter to Benjamin Lathrop" (1778), in *The Collected Writings of Samson Occom, Mohegan*, ed. Joanna Brooks (Oxford: Oxford University Press, 2006), 115–16; 116.

17. Harjo, "Map to the Next World," 19.

18. Robert Wedderburn, *The Axe Laid to the Root* (1817), in *The Horrors of Slavery and Other Writings*, ed. Iain McCalman (Princeton: Princeton University Press, 1991), No. 1, 81–88; 87.

19. Harjo, "Map to the Next World," 19.

20. Linda Hogan, "Map," in *Dark Sweet: New and Selected Poems* (Minneapolis: Coffee House Press, 2014), 160–61.

Index

Page numbers in italics refer to figures.

Abenaki people, 108

African diaspora, 68

African Institution, 129

Agamben, Giorgio, 8; *Remnants of Auschwitz*, 75; *The Time That Remains*, 202n166

Ahmed, Siraj, 145n4

Albernaz, Joseph, 113

Algonquian people, 17–18, 23–24, 29, 32–37, 40–44, 160n55; customs of the, 95, 161n81; dream interpretation of the, 167n176; emergence narratives of the, 41; relational cosmogony of the, 47

Aljoe, Nicole, 63

Allewaert, Monique, 69

American Revolution, 5, 38, 40, 96, 110, 144

Amy, Talkee, 114–17, 120, 127

Anderson, Benedict, 142

Anderson, Misty, 30, 59

Anthropocene, 83, 87, 102, 141–42, 181n30, 182n37

Antigua, 59, 63, 65

antislavery: activism of, 4, 52; discourses of, 68, 77

Apes, William and Candace, 85

Apess, William, 2–11, 14–15, 19, 78–108, 122; *A Eulogy on King Philip*, 82, 102–5, 108; *The Experiences of Five Christian Indians of the Pequot Tribe*, 90; *Indian Nullification of the Unconstitutional Laws of Massachusetts*, 82, 95–102; *An Indian's Looking-Glass for the White Man*, 82, 89–102; *A Son of the Forest*, 18, 78, 82–86, 89–90, 95–102, 106

Arendt, Hannah, 42, 93, 167n174

art: African American, 139; in *The New Union Club* (print), 130

Augustine, 66, 93

Aupaumut, Hendrick, 24

Azoulay, Ariella Aïsha, 4, 105, 136, 144

Banner, Rachel, 76

Baptist War in Jamaica, 140

Barad, Karen, 69

Barbados, 84, 140

Barker, Joanne, 5

Barrett, Lindon, 62, 92, 149n34

Barthes, Roland, 51

Basso, Keith, 95

Bell's Life in London (populist weekly), 113

Benjamin, Walter, 136–37; "Theses on the Philosophy of History," 113, 120

Bennett, Jane, 157n25

Bennett, Joshua, 9, 86

Bermuda, 53, 84

Best, Stephen, 20, 112

Betasamosake Simpson, Leanne, 8, 12, 81

Bible: *Genesis*, 21, 23–24, 41–42; *Jeremiah*, 56; *John*, 67; *Psalms*, 67

Biden, Joseph, 101

Black Hawk: *The Life of Black Hawk*, 97

Black people, 3–4, 6–9; brutality towards, 31; collective embodied and ecological knowledge of, 124, 133; cosmogonies of, 8, 71; cosmologies of, 71; experiences of, 11; performance traditions of, 119; revolutionary

Black people (cont.)
preaching of, 127–28; studies of, 9, 12, 15–16, 19; worldmaking of, 20. *See also* Indigenous peoples

Blackwood's, 62

Blake, William, 141

Blanchot, Maurice, 109, 139

Blaser, Mario, 8, 36, 154n94

Boisseron, Bénédicte, 9

bones, 157n25

Botkin, Fran, 138

Boudinot, Elias, 93; *A Star in the West*, 187n107

Bradford, William, 83

Bragdon, Kathleen, 104

Brand, Dionne, 72–74, 141; *A Map to the Door of No Return*, 143

Brathwaite, Kamau, 132–33

Brault, Pascale-Anne, 74

Britain, 110, 122; the radical press and its repression in, 202n174

British Empire, 129, 180n14

Brooks, Joanna, 33, 118

Brooks, Lisa, 34–35, 37, 79, 88, 101; *Our Beloved Kin*, 103–4

Brothers, Richard, 128–29; *A Revealed Knowledge of the Prophecies & Times*, 129

Brown, Vincent, 119; *The Reaper's Garden*, 197n76

Bruyneel, Kevin, 96–97

Bry, Théodore de, 12; *Balboa Throws Some [Indigenous People], Who [Were Perceived to Have] Committed Sodomy, to the Dogs to Be Torn Apart*, 13

Bussa's Rebellion, 140

Byrd, Jodi, 6, 25, 47, 107

Cadena, Marisol de la, 8, 36

Campbell, Elizabeth, 131–34, 140

Campbell, Mavis, 133

Campisi, Jack, 90

Campt, Tina, 130–31, 139

capitalism: Black reordering of, 10; plantation, 51; racial, 2, 6, 11, 15, 82, 122–24, 135, 142, 145n6, 149n34, 178n153

Carby, Hazel, 51, 201n153

care work, 114

Caribbean, 110; Black traditions in the, 112, 119

Carlson, David, 83

cartography: Black and Indigenous, 144; colonial, 142

Castellano, Katey, 132

Catholic iconography, 134

Cato Street Conspiracy, 127

Cave, Alfred: *The Pequot War*, 184n53

Celan, Paul, 106

Cervenak, Sarah Jane, 4–5

Cherokee people, 156n18

Chow, Jeremy, 13, 42

Christ, 66; reading queer representations of the gender of, 175n111; somatic feminizing of, 175n111; as wounded woman or mother, 67–68

Christianity, 24, 123; colonial, 29; and legal freedom, 128

Christophe, Henry, 130

Church, Benjamin, 104

Church, Thomas: *Entertaining Passages Relating to King Philip's War*, 104

Clarkson, Thomas: *The History of the Rise, Progress, and Accomplishment of the Abolition of the African Slave-Trade*, 54

climate change, 95, 101, 140–42; colonialism and, 141; Indigenous dispossession and, 102

Cobb, Amanda, 47

Colden, Cadwallader, 38

Collection of Hymns (1754), 58

colonialism, 3–14, 22–24, 85, 89, 94, 102; apocalyptic unfolding of, 43; brutality of, 105; churches as culpable for, 118; and climate change, 141; expansion of, 24, 32, 37; and Indigenous decline, 182n32; legal codes of, 33; mandates for, 126; settler, 82, 107; teleologies of racialized extraction

colonialism (cont.)
of, 142; transatlantic insurgencies against, 110–11; violence of, 9, 13–14, 22, 91–92, 104, 108, 115, 119, 142. *See also* imperialism
colonial modernity, 15, 31, 112
Colville, Andrew, 113, 116–17
commoning: colonial and early American literature and, 146n14; Indigenous, 101, 124; Maroon traditions of, 124; transatlantic solidarities, 139
Connecticut, 27
Connecticut River Valley, 37
Constitution, 97
conversion, 118, 197n70
Coulthard, Glen, 36
Cronon, William, 183n47
Cruikshank, George: *The New Union Club*, 129–31, 130
Crutzen, Paul, 181n30

d'Anghiera, Pietro Martire, 12, 14
Darrell, Robert, 49
Dartmouth College, 27
Daut, Marlene, 116, 136
Davidson, William "Black," 127
Dawes Act (1887), 101
Dayan, Colin, 5, 46
Declaration of Independence (American), 97
Declaration of Independence (Haitian), 111
Defamation Act (1708), 155n10
Defoe, Daniel: *Robinson Crusoe*, 124–25
DeJohn Anderson, Virginia, 84
DeLanda, Samuel, 157n25
Delaney, Martin: *Blake*, 194n25
Delucia, Christine, 103–4
de Man, Paul, 120
Demerara Revolt, 140
democracy, American, 98
Derrida, Jacques, 8; *The Beast & the Sovereign II*, 106–7; "This Is Not an Oral Footnote," 76

devotional literature, 30
Diggers, 110
Dillon, Elizabeth Maddock, 79, 124
Dinshaw, Carolyn, 66
Douglass, Frederick, 98, 111
dreaming, 21–48; Mohegan interpretation of, 44
Dungy, Camille, 72

ecocriticism, 14
ecologies: edge, 80–81; missionary, 73
education, 61; Indigenous, 27
Edwards, George, 127
Edwards, Jonathan, 29; "Personal Narrative," 30
embodiment, 18
English Civil War, 110
Enlightenment: conception of the individual in the, 156n16; myths of the, 122; philosophies of liberal humanism of the, 4
epistemologies: Enlightenment, 9, 44; settler, 149n34
Equiano, Olaudah: *Interesting Narrative*, 198n90
Estes, Nick, 99
Esteva, Gustavo, 117

Fanon, Frantz, 87, 90, 94, 185n75
Fanonne Jeffers, Honorée, 70
Favret, Mary, 27, 129
Fay, Jennifer, 87
Federici, Silvia, 124
Fenimore Cooper, James: *The Last of the Mohicans*, 180n22
Ferreira da Silva, Denise, 180n19
Fielder, Brigitte, 12
Fish, Phineas, 96, 98
Fitch, James, 26, 28
Fitzgerald, Stephanie, 45
Foner, Eric, 192n2
Foucault, Michel, 8, 15
Fowler, David, 35
Fowler, Mary, 33
Freeman, Elizabeth, 28

French Revolution, 110
Fuentes, Marisa, 9, 65

gender, 12–13; theories of, 32
George, Sally, 84, 88–89
Georgia v. Cherokee (1831), 91
Gerbner, Katherine, 60
Gibbs, Jenna, 130
Gikandi, Simon, 76
Gilroy, Paul, 70
Glave, Dianne, 14
Glick, Jeremy Matthew, 110
Glissant, Édouard, 17, 51, 133
Gold, Harriet, 93
Gordon, Avery, 54, 92
Grandjean, Katherine, 83
Great Awakening, 29
Great Migration of 1630 (Puritan), 83
Greer, Allan, 3, 84
Grimes, William, 92
Gumbs, Alexis Pauline, 52
Guyana, 140

Hairston, Andrea: *Redwood and Wildfire*, 91
Haitian Revolution, 4–5, 18, 109–40, 194n16; as expression of marronage, 202n157
Halévy, Elie, 117
Hallett, Benjamin, 98
Hanley, Ryan, 114, 130, 140
Haraway, Donna, 44, 89
Harjo, Joy, 102, 107, 141; *A Map to the Next World*, 143–44
Harney, Stefano, 117
Harris, Cheryl, 5
Hartley, Daniel, 102
Hartman, Saidiya, 9, 50, 52–53, 73, 112, 121, 136, 143
Haschemi Yekani, Elahe, 12
Haudenosaunee people, 79, 88, 108; commoning of the, 101; customs of the, 95
Heidegger, Martin, 8
Hejnol, Andreas, 188n120

Hernandez, Jessica, 14
hierarchy: animacy, 100; racial, 90, 92, 95
Hillhouse, William, 86
historiography: colonial, 104; decolonial, 105; settler, 106
Hobbes, Thomas, 47
Hogan, Linda, 37, 43, 78; "Maps," 144
Holland, Sharon, 6, 31
Hopkinson, Nalo, 49, 53
Hopkins Street Chapel, 110, 127, 199n98
Horne, Gerald, 37
Hume, David, 55
Hunt, Nadine, 114
Hurston, Zora Neale, 74
Hutton, J. E., 172n61

imperialism, 8, 11; global, 90; nineteenth-century, 126; unlearning, 144. *See also* colonialism
Indian Removal Act (1830), 5, 43
Indigenous peoples, 3–9, 21–24, 42, 83; archives of, 183n47; brutality towards, 31, 142; Caribbean, 125; cosmogonies of, 89, 100, 119; cosmologies of, 8, 24; descent of, 187n107; economic development of, 80; epistemologies of, 105; era of removal of, 91; experiences of, 11, 29, 81; histories of nineteenth-century, 90; itinerancy of, 28; land inhabitance of, 100; performance traditions of, 119; polities of, 106; population decline of, 182n32; presence in historical archives of, 105; representations in eighteenth-century anglophone literatures of, 147n26; settler teleologies of the vanishing of, 87–88; traditions of commoning of, 101, 124; women of the, 87; worldmaking of, 20, 25. *See also* Black peoples
Indigenous studies, 9, 12, 15–19, 25
Iton, Richard, 94

Jackson, Andrew, 91, 99
Jackson, Zakiyyah Iman, 9

Jacobins, 126; Black, 135
Jamaica, 109–40
James, C.L.R.: *The Black Jacobins*, 135
Jarvis, Ereck, 170n22
Jennings, Francis: *The Invasion of America*, 184n53
Jewett, David, 29
Johnson, Jessica Marie, 114
Johnson, Joseph, 38–39
Johnson, William, 27
Judaism, 128
Justice, Daniel Heath, 22–23

Kant, Immanuel: *Perpetual Peace*, 2
Kaufman, Gershen, 61
Kazanjian, David, 132
Kelley, Robin D. G., 116
King Philip's War, 26, 102–5, 108
Klee, Paul: *Angelus Novus* (painting), 120
knowledge: Black and Indigenous, 72; Indigenous botanic, 14, 31; Indigenous traditional, 32–34, 44; Maroon botanic, 132; Mohegan aquatic, 36; relational, 32
Kohn, Eduardo, 100, 122, 168n186
Kotzebue, August von: *The Stranger*, 134
Kucich, John, 91

LaFleur, Greta, 13, 32–33
language: Abenaki, 103; Algonquian, 35, 104; Indigenous, 144; Pequot, 89; settler, 23; vernacular, 114
law: English, 10; universal, 2
Law, John, 7–8
lebensläufe: *The Memoirs of Salone Cuthbert*, 73; *The Narrative of Archibald Monteith, a Jamaican Slave*, 73
Lepore, Jill: *The Name of War*, 103
Lethabo King, Tiffany, 6, 50, 72
Levellers, 110
Levi, Primo, 75
Lewis, Simon, 141
Lightfoot, Natasha, 60
Linebaugh, Peter, 114
Linnaeus, Carolus, 32

Litany of Wounds of the Husband (1744), 66
Locke, John, 1, 11, 38, 47, 77; Protestant ontology of consumption of, 42; *Second Treatise of Government*, 1–2, 41–42, 122–23
London, 110, 139
Lopenzina, Drew, 40, 80
Lorde, Audre, 16
L'Ouverture, Toussaint, 135
love: as anticolonial exercise, 94; and settler regulations of intimacy, 92
Lowe, Lisa, 12, 19, 112
Lowenhaupt Tsing, Anna, 70, 88
Luddites, 110
Lyons, Scott, 39

Macaulay, Zachary, 129
MacPherson, James, 137–38
Macqueen, James, 62–63
Mallipeddi, Ramesh, 57
Manifest Destiny, 81
Manitou (spiritual power), 36
Manshel, Hannah, 96
Maroons, 4, 111, 115, 132–33, 138–39
Marshall, Chief Justice John, 91
Mashantucket Pequot people, 82, 85–86, 89–90, 100
Mashpee people, 96–102; economic development of the, 99; lands of the, 96, 100; sovereignty of the, 97. *See also* Wampanoag Mashpee people
Maslin, Mark, 141
Mason, John, 85–86
Mather, Increase: *A Brief History of the Warr with the Indians in New-England*, 104
Maynard, Robyn, 8, 81
Mbembe, Achille, 120
McCalman, Iain, 126, 193n12
McKittrick, Katherine, 9, 71, 120
Menon, Madhavi, 16
Methodism, 60, 117–18
Middle Passage, 51, 73, 75, 114, 119, 143. *See also* slave trade
Mignolo, Walter, 8

Miles, Tiya, 6, 156n18
Miller, Derrick, 66
Million, Dian, 82, 157n21
Miranda, Deborah, 12, 48, 94
Mohawk people, 39
Mohegan people: beliefs of the, 46;
    green corn festival of the, 35, 44;
    kinship reckoning of the, 34; lands of
    the, 27, 30–31, 35, 39; leaders of the,
    26; rituals of the, 26, 44–45
Montaukett people, 14–15, 33, 44;
    marital customs of the, 34; medicinal
    practices of the, 24, 32
Montejo, Esteban, 176n123
Moravianism, 52; blood and wounds
    theology of, 72; church of, 65;
    missionaries of, 59–62; penitential
    practices of, 68; "sexual license" of,
    175n99. See also Zinzendorf, Nicolaus
    Ludwig von (count)
Moreton-Robinson, Aileen, 5, 93–94
Morgan, Jennifer L., 56, 113
Morgensen, Scott Lauria, 17
Morrison, Toni, 179n170
Moten, Fred, 111, 117, 135, 142–43,
    149n34
Muñoz, José Esteban, 43, 117
Muscogee people, 107; cosmology of
    the, 143

Naas, Michael, 74
Napoleonic wars, 126
Narragansett people, 103
nationalism, American, 92
Neimanis, Astrida, 36
Nelson, Dana, 95
Nelson, Melissa K., 14, 32
Nersessian, Anahid, 123
newspaper, 131
Niantic people, 39
Nichols, Robert, 81, 100
Nipmuck people, 103
Nixon, Angelique, 143
Nixon, Rob, 57, 83
Nullification Crisis (1832–33), 86

Núñez de Balboa, Vasco, 12, 46
Nwankwo, Ifeoma, 60, 111

Obeah, 114–16; criminalization in
    Jamaica of, 114
O'Brien, Jean M., 31, 99
Occom, Samson, 2–11, 14–48, 122, 144,
    156n18; "Account of the Montauk
    Indians," 32, 34; "Herbs & Roots," 25,
    32–33; "O Happy Souls How Fast You
    Go" (hymn), 35; Sermon on the
    Execution of Moses Paul, 17, 21–24, 31,
    47–48, 93, 101; "A Short Narrative of
    My Life," 25–31
O'Connell, Barry, 79
Oldham, John, 84
Oliver, Kelly, 107
Oneida people, 24, 38–39

Paine, Thomas: The Rights of Man, 131,
    199n96
Palmer, John, 134
Parker, Arthur C., 79
Parliament, 126–27
Patterson, Orlando, 11, 56, 120
Paul, 120
Paul, Moses, 21–22, 47–48
Payne, Joseph, 114–15
Peabody and Essex Museum, 44
Peiser, Megan, 14
Pequot War, 84–85, 91, 184n53
Peterloo Massacre (1819), 126
Philip, M. NourbeSe, 74
Pinto, Samantha, 55
Plane, Ann Marie, 34
plantation economy, 51, 91, 133;
    enslavement in the, 136. See also
    slavery
Pocumtuck people, 103
politics: liberal democratic, 95; and
    political ontology, 154n94; queer and
    ecological, 158n33; refusal of sociality
    and, 195n64
Popol Vuh, 8
popular sovereignty, 122

Povinelli, Elizabeth, 23, 33, 71
Pratt, Richard, 88
Prince, Mary, 2–11, 14–15, 19, 122, 143; *The History of Mary Prince*, 4–5, 17, 49–77, 140
Pringle, Margaret, 171n43
Pringle, Thomas, 51, 55–56, 62–65, 74–76
prosopopoeia, 120, 126, 133, 138
providentialism, 47, 71; British, 68–71; colonial, 70
Puritans, 104, 184n53
Pyle, Kai, 12

Quashie, Kevin, 10
Quechua people, 100
queer ecology, 158n33; and water, 166n154
queer studies, 25

race: early American views of, 159n40; Western ideologies of, 6
Rediker, Marcus, 114
Richardson, Alan, 115
Richardson, Robbie, 6, 25
Rifkin, Mark, 29, 80, 93
Roach, Joseph, 119
Roberts, Neil, 133
Roberts, Strother, 99, 164n119, 180n20, 184n53
Robinson, Cedric, 2, 72, 124
Roppolo Wieser, Kimberly, 39
Rousseau, Jean-Jacques: "Essay on the Origin of Languages," 54, 75; *Second Discourse on Inequality*, 1; theories of property of, 145n2
Rowney, Matthew, 50
Royal Gazette, 173n73
Ruffin, Kimberley, 14

Saint-Amour, Paul K., 137
Salisbury, Neal: *Manitou and Providence*, 184n53
salt, 49–77
Sandler, Matt, 192n2

satire: British, 130; political, 129
Savageau, Cheryl, 37
Scarry, Elaine, 66
Schmitt, Carl, 47, 166n157
Schwartz, Ana, 15
Scott, David, 20, 135–36
Second Maroon War (1795–96), 138
Sensbach, John, 73
Serres, Michel: *Malfeasance*, 123
Sexton, Jared, 19, 113
sexuality, 12–13; history of settler colonialism and, 152n64; queer, 176n123; regime of, 31; theories of, 32
Shakespeare, William: *The Tempest*, 149n34
shame, 61
Sharma, Nandita, 100
Sharpe, Christina, 10, 51, 69, 73, 112
Simpson, Audra, 19, 81
Sinanan, Kerry, 55
slavery, 10, 51–54, 67, 143; Black freedom seekers and, 133; Black women's dissent to, 112, 116; brutality and terror of, 115; Caribbean, 74, 110; ecocritical discourses and, 71; expansion of, 186n99; generational scope of, 118; New World, 62; plantation, 19; resistance to, 11, 115; saltwater, 59; transatlantic insurgencies against, 109–10. *See also* plantation economy; slave trade
slave trade, 74. *See also* Middle Passage
Sleeper-Smith, Susan, 183n47
Smallwood, Stephanie E., 59
Smith, Adam: *Theory of Moral Sentiments*, 53–55
Smith, William, 129
Snorton, C. Riley, 12
Society for Propagating the Gospel (Boston), 27
Society of Spencean Philanthropists, 126, 131
Somerset v. Stewart (1772), 173n75
sovereignty, 7, 126; Indigenous, 43, 47

Spanish conquistadors, 8
Speitz, Michele, 50, 68
Spence, Thomas, 110, 123–26, 199n96;
    The End of Oppression, 122; *Important
    Trials* (pamphlet), 131; *Pigs' Meat*
    (periodical), 122, 131; *The Reign of
    Felicity*, 124; *The Rights of Man*, 122; *A
    Supplement to the History of Robinson
    Crusoe*, 124–25
Spillers, Hortense, 67, 149n34, 194n26
spirituality, African diasporic, 118
St. Domingue, 109
Stengers, Isabelle, 42, 121
Stoermer, Eugene, 181n30
Strickland, Susannah, 51, 74–75
subjectivity: colonial, 42; colonial
    Christian, 93
Sullivan, John, 39
sympathy: British discourses of, 50, 57;
    and imagination, 54

Tacky's Rebellion, 114
Tait, Sue, 58
Takahata, Kimberly, 160n68
Tallbear, Kim, 100
Tantaquidgeon, Gladys, 26, 35, 44
Tantaquidgeon, Lucy Occom, 5, 44–45
Tantaquidgeon Zobel, Melissa, 44
theology: anti-resurrection, 136;
    Christian, 135, 155n12; decolonial in-
    carnational, 93; white supremacist, 92
Thomas, Deborah, 137
Thomas, Sue, 73
Thompson, E. P., 117
time: Black and Indigenous structures of
    space and, 3, 25; eschatological,
    202n166; imperial affects across space
    and, 94; messianic, 139, 202n166;
    multidimensional orientation to, 144
Tinsley, Omise'eke Natasha, 68
Todd, Zoe, 8
Tomacham, Joshua and Sarah, 28
Trouillot, Michel-Rolph, 52, 111
Trump, Donald, 101
Tucker, William Howard, 99

Tuhiwai Smith, Linda, 80
Turner, Cass, 8
Tuscarora people, 39

Uncas, Ben, 27

violence: colonial, 9, 13–14, 22, 91–92,
    104, 108, 115, 119, 142; critiques of,
    137; imperial, 105, 124, 139; legal and
    extralegal, 93; physical, 54; plantation,
    57–58; racial, 9, 29, 70, 90, 98, 142;
    settler, 42; sexual, 54, 62–64, 67–68,
    116; slow, 57, 83

Wabanaki people, 103
Walcott, Derek, 143
Walkiewicz, Kathryn, 6
Wall Kimmerer, Robin, 14, 100
Walsh, Catherine, 8
Wampanoag Mashpee people, 82, 103,
    108. *See also* Mashpee people
Warner, Michael, 161n74
War of 1812, 5, 88–90, 108
Warrior, Robert, 27, 102
Waswo, Richard, 133
Weaver, Jace, 6, 94
Wedderburn, James, 110
Wedderburn, Robert, 2–11, 14–19,
    109–40, 194n21, 195n64; *An Address
    to the Right Honorable Lord Brougham*,
    140; *The Axe Laid to the Root* (periodi-
    cal), 1, 10, 18, 109–12, 115–16,
    120–24, 129–40, 144, 194n25,
    195n29, 203n182; *A Forlorn Hope*
    (periodical), 110, 131; *The Horrors of
    Slavery*, 110, 112–17, 120–21, 140;
    Truth Self-Supported, 110, 112,
    117–21, 136
Wheatley Peters, Phillis: "On Being
    Bought from Africa to America," 70,
    187n109; "On Imagination," 42
Wheelock, Eleazar, 22, 27
Whitefield, George, 45–47
Whyte, Kyle Powys, 83
Wigginton, Caroline, 43

Wilberforce, William, 55, 129
Wilderson, Frank B., 121, 151n53
Williams, Roger, 80–81
Williams, William, 86
Winthrop, John, 83, 85, 157n25
Wisecup, Kelly, 22
Wolfe, Patrick, 182n34
women: Black, 67, 115–16; enslaved
    African, 114–15; Indigenous, 87
Wood, John Adams, 52
Wood, Marcus, 130
Wood, William, 38

Worrall, David, 126, 193n12; *Radical Culture*, 199n96
Wright, Cynthia, 100
Wynter, Sylvia, 3–4, 67

Youngquist, Paul, 138
Yusoff, Kathryn, 50, 82, 142

Zinzendorf, Nicolaus Ludwig von
    (count), 66, 177n131. *See also* Moravianism
Zong massacre, 74–75

Printed in the USA
CPSIA information can be obtained
at www.ICGtesting.com
LVHW040938100124
768567LV00006B/31